PRODUCTIVITY AND PROSPERITY

A Historical Sociology of Productivist Thought

This book is a genealogy of the *idea* of productivity, from early economic theory and the development of statistical measures of productivity to the uptake of productivity as an objective for government economic policy. It examines how the productivity concept was used and defined in three historical contexts: in the development of the National Accounts in the Dominion Bureau of Statistics (known today as Statistics Canada), in the short-lived and little-known National Productivity Council (1960–3), and in the establishment and evolution of the Atlantic Canada Opportunities Agency (1986–present).

Drawing these cases together with sociological and political theory, Karen R. Foster argues that there is a productivist ideational regime guiding government policy in Canada and elsewhere that is based on several cultural assumptions, the foremost being that more productivity, regardless of its impact on employment or environment, is good in and of itself. Also dominant and closely related is the stubborn assumption that economic productivity fully or partly determines standards of living and prosperity. Systematically questioning and critiquing these two most fundamental assumptions, *Productivity and Prosperity* destabilizes the myth that economic growth has made us happier and richer and is indeed essential for our quality of life.

KAREN R. FOSTER is Canada Research Chair in Sustainable Rural Futures for Atlantic Canada and an assistant professor in the Department of Sociology and Social Anthropology at Dalhousie University.

KAREN R. FOSTER

Productivity and Prosperity

A Historical Sociology of Productivist Thought

UNIVERSITY OF TORONTO PRESS
Toronto Buffalo London

ISBN 978-1-4875-0078-8 (cloth)   ISBN 978-1-4875-2057-1 (paper)

Printed on acid-free, 100% post-consumer recycled paper with
vegetable-based inks.

Library and Archives Canada Cataloguing in Publication

Foster, Karen R., 1983–, author
Productivity and prosperity : a historical sociology of productivist
thought / Karen R. Foster.

Includes bibliographical references and index.
ISBN 978-1-4875-0078-8 (cloth). – ISBN 978-1-4875-2057-1 (paper)

1. Industrial productivity – Canada – Case studies. 2. Industrial
productivity – Government policy – Canada – Case studies.
3. Canada – Economic policy – Case studies. I. Title.

HC120.I52F68 2016   338'.060971   C2016-902137-8

This book has been published with the help of a grant from the Federation
for the Humanities and Social Sciences, through the Awards to Scholarly
Publications Program, using funds provided by the Social Sciences and
Humanities Research Council of Canada.

University of Toronto Press acknowledges the financial assistance to its
publishing program of the Canada Council for the Arts and the Ontario
Arts Council, an agency of the Government of Ontario.

Contents

Acknowledgments

After writing a book of nearly 100,000 words, *this* is where I get writer's block. Not knowing who to thank first, I will start where most people end: with family. To my partner, Brian: thank you for your unwavering support, encouragement and reassurance, and for bragging about me, and the book, to anyone who'll listen. It is always mortifying, and I like it. Thank you to my sweet girl, Alice, for coming into our lives in the middle of this project and changing them forever. You're the one I wanted to see every time I closed my computer and stopped writing for the day. Thank you to my parents and parents-in-law, especially Grammie and Nana, for doing the unpaid labour of caring for Alice so I could do this.

I thank my mentor, Andrea Doucet, for continuing to advise and inspire me long after her PhD supervisor duties ended. Thank you to Albert Mills and the rest of the Saint Mary's University Management Department for hosting the postdoctoral research that culminated in this book. I could not have pulled this off without the support of a Banting Postdoctoral Fellowship from the Social Sciences and Humanities Research Council of Canada (complete with a four-month maternity leave, during which time my productivity was not monitored or tracked). Nor could I have written anything without the vast resources of Library and Archives Canada – particularly the ACOA fonds, to which the family of the late Alistair B. Graham granted me access. I'm thankful for the feedback and cheerleading from my new colleagues in Sociology and Social Anthropology at Dalhousie University, where I put the finishing touches on the manuscript. I must also acknowledge the value of the Halifax Public Library, not necessarily as a resource for information, but as a bright and busy space where I could write in peace but in public – my favourite setting for drafting and editing. Finally, thank you to Douglas Hildebrand at University of Toronto Press, and the three generous readers whose thoughtful critiques and encouraging praise actually made revisions *fun*.

PRODUCTIVITY AND PROSPERITY

A Historical Sociology of Productivist Thought

Introduction

This book is not a study of Canadian productivity per se. It does not try to account for any declines or increases in productivity, nor does it seek to explain productivity "gaps." While it does explore the documented trends in Canadian economic productivity and competitiveness, it is not the objective here to boost either of them.

Instead, the point is to ask *what we are talking about when we talk about productivity* – what does the word mean, what are its connotations, how does it change over time and context, and who is involved in deciding how to define and measure it? To ask these questions is to make the familiar strange; it means subjecting a taken-for-granted concept to the kind of inquisition normally reserved for brand-new ideas.

It does not mean that the "documented trends" in productivity over time – the actual statistical ups and downs and correlations – are entirely untouched here. Occasionally, what the statistics have purported to tell us is important for the narrative that unfolds in the chapters that follow. I will point to numbers and mention "productivity gains" from one year to the next, or "productivity gaps" between regions or countries. The reader may wonder if productivity is being treated as a "real" thing or a construct. My pre-emptive answer to them is that it is both.[1] Dealing with and drawing on productivity statistics is unavoidable. So many important policy decisions have been made on the basis of those kinds of statistics. And there is no denying that shifts in productivity performance, measured statistically, no matter how "real" or "accurate" they are, correspond to shifts in how people relate to and feel about work, income, well-being, and the distribution of wealth.

But the statistics, and the assumptions that underlie and follow from the statistics, are familiar to us. Making the familiar strange, as is the goal here, involves the additional step of asking: How does the idea of productivity relate or respond to political-economic (i.e., economic, political, social, cultural, and technological) changes? How does its measurement as an economic indicator affect the lives of ordinary Canadians, and via what mechanisms? When and where have definitions and measures been contested? How do everyday understandings of productivity relate to the technical, economic understandings of it? How does our *thought* about productivity affect our *practices*, as people, communities, governments, workers, politicians, economists, bankers, and employers?

There is a critical assumption operating behind these questions: that economic policies, and the economic theories often used to justify them, do not simply spring up naturally and singularly from some objective, indisputable economic reality. Nor is economic policy necessarily dictated from some place of great and immovable power, in service of elite interests. Rather, the ways in which we imagine, define, and attempt to control "the economy" (and even the ways in which we claim to let it control itself) are always and everywhere a matter of some economic rhetoric or discourse winning out over others. Importantly, the discursive and political battle over economic governance proceeds, most of the time, at a glacier's pace; even in revolutionary times, it is possible to see a basic continuity behind every seeming rupture. Yet the conflict of ideas is visible too, especially in those moments when an established economic theory or policy approach gives way, gradually or quickly, partly or completely, to an apparently "new" economic concept, theory, or policy approach. It is also potentially visible whenever policies are proposed or made, in the public, political, and academic debates and battles over how best to deal with localized economic issues.

In 1986, sociologists Fred Block and Gene Burns illustrated one such localized debate with their history of the statistical measurement of economic productivity in the United States.[2] Their project looked specifically at the "sophisticated" measures of *aggregate* productivity developed in the 1930s and used, more or less, to this day. These modern indicators are the same ones that spur the quarterly lament of Canada's chief economists over "Canada's lagging productivity" and the perennial targeting of Atlantic Canada as the country's productivity laggard. The indicators take measures of productivity from every specific, single industry and then aggregate them into one unified, singular indicator that ostensibly captures the productivity of the whole national economy. The news-consuming public rarely encounters the actual figures, nor the calculations made; they simply receive the report: either productivity is up, it's unchanged, or it's down.

Block and Burns's work unsettled these widely accepted measures of aggregate productivity in the United States by piecing together the human, institutional, cultural, political, and ideological factors involved in their development. They showed how these seemingly "scientific" concepts "operate as intellectual resources in political conflicts." Specifically, they traced the historical emergence and development of productivity, as a generic concept backed up by a sophisticated statistical indicator, in US political discourse around labour and remuneration. As they wrote,

> the invention of sophisticated measures of productivity was a part of the legitimation of a new system of collective bargaining that enhanced the position of trade unions. This was institutionalized through the rise of productivity bargaining that linked wage gains to trends in aggregate productivity. However, the choice of a particular indicator of trends in productivity created the potential for a reversal as the most visible measures of productivity showed a dramatic slowdown of growth in the 1970s. This *apparent* slowing created the grounds for a major conservative counterattack on trade unions and the growth of civilian state spending. Conservatives were in the enviable position where they did not have to develop new concepts or measures; all they had to do was point to the well established and well respected indicator to "prove" the existence of a productivity crisis.[3]

In this instance, there was no real shift in the definition or measurement of productivity – no debate over how to measure or conceptualize it, no attempts to debunk it or to draw attention to its limitations. In order to gain traction with their vision of a "trickle-down" economy that distributes prosperity and hardship fairly, without intervention, all that US conservatives needed was for productivity to slow, according to measures already "established" and "well respected." And this illustrates something important about the critical perspective on economic concepts taken up in this book. The working assumption is that there are not necessarily "good" concepts and "bad" ones; there are just different potential uses of them, which may be good or bad depending on whose interests one has in mind. As Serge Latouche, whose work will appear many times throughout this book, understands well, "the opposite of a perverse idea does not necessarily give rise to a virtuous idea."[4] This is also what Michel Foucault was on to when he wrote:

> My point is not that everything is bad, but that everything is dangerous, which is not exactly the same as bad. If everything is dangerous, then we always have something to do. So my position leads not to apathy but to hyper- and pessimistic activism.[5]

The current project adopts this position too; it is driven not by some hope that we will liberate ourselves from false or detrimental conceptual devices and feel our way towards emancipatory, true ones, but by a commitment to vigilance. Thus, productivity is not seen here as an inherently *bad* way of making sense of economic production, nor an inherently *good* one. Rather, like all economic concepts, productivity is simply *dangerous*.

Block and Burns's work supports this orientation towards social critique, in that it shows how easily nearly the *exact same* conceptualization of productivity can go to work for very different interests. There are doubtless many other instances of productivity's multifaceted potential. In such cases, the difference between one use and another hinges on the answer to political questions – these, for example: What is to be *done* with the knowledge of national productivity? Who, if anyone, should benefit when productivity rises? Who should suffer when it falls? What should the consequences be, if there are any, when productivity levels fluctuate? Are we measuring it out of curiosity, or do we wish to use those measurements to guide us towards the best ways to manipulate productivity levels, to tie human fates, individually or collectively, to productivity's movements? How can a person or an institution increase or improve productivity?

Granted, there are also different conceptualizations of productivity, and key junctures where the concept's very definition and measurement are contested, over and above any questions of actions and consequences. In December 2012, for example, Canadian economists Erwin Diewert and Emily Yu released a paper that claimed to show that Canada's national statistics agency, Statistics Canada, had underestimated the country's multi-factor productivity growth for decades.[6] A rebuttal from the agency was almost immediate, listing the reasons for the discrepancy between official estimates and those computed by Diewert and Yu.[7] This example is more fully explored in chapter 2, but for now, suffice it to say that while productivity itself is well-established in Canadian economic discourse, it is by no means cemented there. As Block and Burns so convincingly showed in their analysis of a narrow slice of US economic history, economic "discoveries" do happen, and when they do, they can enable dramatic shifts in policy, in all levels of discourse, and in the way working people imagine their relationships to their families, their communities, the nation, and the whole world.

Methods and Key Terms

Theory and method are intertwined in this discussion and in the book. Throughout, I have drawn insights from two places: the "historical sociology of concept formation" approach developed in Block's later work and further refined by his colleague Margaret Somers, and the broad field of governmentality studies.[8]

Historical Sociology of Concept Formation

Margaret Somers's historical sociology of concept formation "demands that we question and problematize as *historical* objects much of what has long been taken to have been *discovered* in science."[9] As should be clear by this point, productivity is precisely the kind of object, conventionally understood as a scientific discovery, that can be studied historically and problematized. Doing a history of productivity – a genealogy, really – is more a matter of making some philosophical or ontological commitments than it is a "method" in the conventional sense of the term. It is about finding "the conditions of possibility" for the productivity concept as well as the networks of ideas and larger discourses that have "framed and constrained" productivity over time.[10]

I lean especially hard on one concept from Somers's work: the "ideational regime." An ideational regime is "comprised of those public narratives and assumptions that have become widely taken for granted in the political culture; it sets the parameters for what counts as worthwhile argument in social and political debates."[11] For Somers, ideational regimes can be dominant – that is, taken for granted and thus inherently difficult to "undermine, dislodge, and replace."[12] In part, the fixity of dominant ideational regimes is strengthened by their capacity to "embed" other ideas, events, institutions, and issues, a feature Somers calls "ideational embeddedness."[13] These concepts of ideational regimes and embedding are crucial to this project because they draw attention to the constraining power of ideas and the role this power plays in – or, perhaps more appropriately, *against* – social and political economic change.

Some readers will rightly wonder how the concept of an ideational regime compares to such apparently similar concepts as common sense, discourse, and ideology. Common sense can, like ideational regimes, be dominant and difficult to move. But unlike common sense, ideational regimes derive their stability by appealing to particular forms of authority. In the post-Enlightenment world, these forms of authority are connected to expertise and science and even to certain kinds of exceptional experience (e.g., in "the business world"). This does not mean that ideational regimes can ignore the matter of their "fit" with common sense and ordinary people's experiences; rather, the project of appealing to common sense often – and increasingly with a literate public – depends on simultaneously appealing to science and expertise. The notion of an ideational regime also bears some resemblance to Foucault's "discursive formation," but the latter was posed as a way of encapsulating disciplinary "groups of statements" – for example, *"medicine, economics,* or *grammar"* – rather than the groups of statements or discourses that constitute ideational regimes.[14] In contrast to the "dispersion" and heterogeneity of discursive formations, ideational regimes display (or at least foreground) unity, coherence, and, like ideology, a "directionality" that works (not necessarily due to the intentions of actors) to serve certain interests and deny others.[15] Further reflections on the differences and similarities between ideational regimes and ideologies appear below, under the heading "Productivism and Prosperity."

In any case, the concepts of *the ideational regime* and *embeddedness* are highly applicable to the study of productivity carried out here, as are additional concepts from another field of scholarship similar to that of Somers's work: governmentality studies. Governmentality scholars' concepts of *techniques, tactics,* and *strategies* of government help elucidate the ways in which ideational regimes become applied (as "practical" and "technical" actions) in government programs, interventions, and policies.

Governmentality

It was Michel Foucault who coined the term governmentality, over the course of a dozen lectures he gave between 1970 and 1984. He used it interchangeably with the term "governmental rationality," by which he meant "a way or system of thinking about the nature or the practice of government (who can govern; what governing is; what or who is governed), capable of making some form of that activity thinkable and practicable both to its practitioners and to those upon whom it was practiced."[16] He used the term to offer a new "perspective on political power."[17] But it was through the expansion of a whole field of studies of governmentality that the concept came into its own as a sort of "analytical toolbox" or a "diagnostic tool"[18] well-suited to "connect[ing] questions of government, politics and administration to the space of bodies, lives, selves and persons."[19]

By "government," governmentality scholars typically mean not only the state, its various apparatuses, and the capital-P Politics of parties, senates, parliaments, and elections, but also the governance that goes on in workplaces, in malls, schools, and playgrounds, and in public spaces, as well as in people's private lives. Even when it does focus on the state, governmentality emphasizes the *spread* of the state and its techniques and practices of government, far beyond the institutions, actors, and processes we readily recognize as part of *The* Government. The insights of a governmentality perspective arguably apply best to modern interventions that are meant to "improve" or preserve the welfare of a population and that often refer to a utopian vision, in contrast to other exercises of power that are objectively coercive, disciplinary, or punitive.[20] Governmentality draws our attention towards those efforts to "educat[e] desires and configur[e] habits, aspirations and beliefs" in pursuit of "better ways of doing things, better ways of living" – efforts that represent the "technical" expression of particular thoughts or ways of thinking.[21] Accordingly, governmentality studies homes in on how *thought* shapes conduct and the government thereof. As Mitchell Dean puts it,

> sociologists have sought to analyse the collective nature of thought by examining its social, political and economic conditions. Studies of governmentality, however, are more concerned with how thought operates within our organized ways of doing things, our regimes of practices, and with its ambitions and effects. Moreover, where historians of ideas and social thinkers have concentrated on the theoretical and abstract dimensions of thought, the analytics of government is more concerned with thought *as it is embedded within programmes for the direction and reform of conduct*. The analysis of government is concerned with thought *as it becomes linked to and is embedded in technical means for the shaping and reshaping of conduct and in practices and institutions.*[22]

There is obvious overlap here between the commitments entailed in governmentality studies and those of the historical sociology of concept formation. That is, both are committed to finding the "conditions" for particular ways of thinking and practices, and to the "embeddedness" of same. The two share at least one other epistemological commitment: both emphasize the importance of history and the past, particularly when it comes to the historicity of ideas, concepts, and knowledge(s) and the "regimes" of techniques, practices, and subjectivities under-pinned by these. Both subject what is "taken for granted" to historical analysis in order to reveal the contingency of seemingly natural, "self-evident" or inevitable ideas.[23] And both reach for the approach they call "genealogy" in order to do this.[24]

Genealogy

Genealogy is a mode of "doing history" popularized by Foucault in 1975 in *Discipline and Punish* and has been steadily employed ever since in historical sociological studies.[25] Its objective is to undertake "histories of the present" that neither hold the present up as an unprecedented, unhinged singularity nor depict it as an inevitable or natural outcome of the past. As Foucault put it, the present is always *both* "a time like any other" and "a time which is never quite like any other."[26] Genealogy is not a method for isolating and identifying the singular origins of events and things, but rather for *describing* the "excessiveness" of causal relations.[27] As William Walters explains, a genealogical approach entails insisting that every concept, term, regime, or object "must be allowed to become a site of historical emergence in its own right" and that "nothing is fixed or given in advance."[28] This approach has led to ground-breaking insights about the emergence of "the economy" as a "fixed space"[29] – "a quasi-naturalistic, semi-autonomous reality, composed of laws, tendencies or processes that we must at least respect when we attempt to guide our societies." It follows that a genealogical approach could do the same for concepts attached to "the economy," including productivity.[30] Indeed, that is what this book is supposed to do.

Like the historical sociology of concept formation and governmental-ity studies, genealogy is not a strict formula or a set of steps; it is more like an *orientation* towards history, or a way of thinking and representa-tion. It means putting concepts, terms, regimes, and objects in historical perspective, only without suggesting that they have some essential form that has changed or corrupted over time. Instead, genealogy "shift[s] from the study of objects to the *practices that produce those objects* as their effects."[31] It means thinking about "the emergence and transformation of practices as 'events'"[32] and, for Somers and me, seeking to understand those events (and thus the practices) as part of a larger narrative.[33]

Productivism and Productivity

In an argument that will build over the course of the genealogy and case studies in this book, I will make the case that *productivism* is the dominant ideational regime from which productivity has gotten its meaning, especially since the interwar era of the 1920s and 1930s. Many before me have described productivism as a "system," a hegemonic idea, or an ideology.[34] I do not take issue with those prior classifications. I have merely found that productivism does what an ideational regime does: it embeds most other ideas, it is taken for granted, and it delimits "what counts as worthwhile argument in social and political debates."[35] Choosing to see productivism as an ideational regime instead of, for example, an ideology, a form of symbolic violence, or an effect of hegemony, signals a reluctance to assume, at the outset, that productivism comes from some "deep social interests" or is held up by false consciousness on the part of those who do not detect and resist it every day.[36]

This does not mean that ideational regimes do not privilege some interests and deny others; it does not mean that they are detached from domination and subordination, or that they do not mystify social relations. They can and do exhibit these qualities and connections. As an analytical framework, the concept of ideational regimes makes the foregoing issues of interests, consciousness, domination, subordination, and mystification empirical matters. It raises the questions rather than assuming the answers. How has the productivist ideational regime worked, in different times and places, to advantage some interests and disadvantage others? When, how, and why have the people behind these various interests accepted, resisted, or rejected productivism? What other ideas and discourses have come into contact with the productivist ideational regime, and have they been complementary or contradictory, absorbed or expunged, legitimated or dismissed? These questions will be posed and considered throughout the main three chapters of this book, and studied intensely in the concluding chapter.

The notion of an ideational regime draws attention, overall, to the *relationality* of ideas and concepts over and above that of actors and institutions.

The latter play a part in the narrative in this book, but they do not drive it in the way they drive other kinds of history. The ideational regime is perhaps no better a framework than ideology or discourse formations, but it corresponds better with my findings and interpretations thereof. The "productivist ideational regime" presented here is comprised of several cultural assumptions, the foremost being that more productivity (regardless of its impact on employment or the environment) is good in and of itself. The second is the related and stubborn assumption that economic productivity fully or partly determines standards of living and prosperity. The main contribution of this book, I believe, is to challenge productivism by critiquing and questioning these two most fundamental assumptions: to ask where they come from, to historicize them, and to show how they have been studied, tested, articulated, contested, or supported at various points in (*mostly* Canadian and North American) history. The third assumption, on which the second ultimately depends, is that a singular "National Economy" exists that circumscribes and contains the social – an assumption that I argue only coheres and compels because we collect statistics at the national level. Finally, productivism supports and is in turn supported by a persuasive metanarrative, based on a constricted view of history, that connects economic growth to progress and to increased average incomes, happiness, and freedom.[37] In short, this is a myth that draws selectively from human history to suggest that economic growth has made us happier and richer and is indeed essential for our quality of life – inclusive of the "goods" we derive from the welfare state *and* from the market.

Relating these tenets of the productivist ideational regime to the notion of governmentality, I propose that we can think of any governmentality as a specific manifestation of an ideational regime. The latter, which is composed of ideas and not practices or techniques, is "made practical and technical" in a governmentality – translated into policies, interventions, programs and approaches that aim to reform social, political, and economic life to bring it more in line with the kind of world idealized by the dominant ideational regime.

The reader should bear in mind that the productivist ideational regime is a historical development. All of the tenets listed above – the three assumptions and the overarching metanarrative – existed in some form or another well before they cohered into anything that could be called a regime. This book highlights examples of productivist thought, and iterations of the productivity concept, from as far back as the late 1700s. But for various reasons that will be explained in due course, the productivist ideational regime does not come together as a dominant, almost all-encompassing way of thinking until some time around the 1940s, when the idea of the National Economy became a statistically representable "reality." In other words, while one can point to elements of productivism in the nineteenth century, it has been impossible to speak of a productivist ideational regime until quite recent history.

Each of the chapters that follow has something to say about the productivist ideational regime and especially about its impacts on governmentality and the way we think about productivity. The first chapter is a brief and general exegesis of the productivity concept in the nascent nineteenth-century field of economics, and its adoption and development in government research and policy bureaux in the United States and Canada in the first half of the twentieth century. Following that, I pursue the productivity concept in three analytically distinct but overlapping cases in Canadian political economic history.

Case Studies of the Productivity Concept in Canada

Except when the focus is on universal health care or bitumen extraction, Canada is not often held up as an exemplar in economic theory or the history of economic thought. Geographically, Canada is huge, but it has a comparatively small population. It was later and slower to industrialize than its main trading partners. Although it is among the wealthiest nations in the world, it has mostly been seen as peripheral in the so-called "global economy" since the latter opened up. Canadian economists and political leaders, and the journalists who convey their ideas to the public, have long compared Canada to the economic powerhouses of the United States and, more recently, China, with regard to productivity, exports, "business environment," entrepreneurialism, manufacturing, and innovation, and found it wanting. Economists and economic historians have puzzled over the country's struggle to shift away from its early emphasis on "staples" – as "hewers of wood and drawers of water," in Harold Innis's infamous terms – and they continue to argue over the proper government of trade, production, resource extraction, and taxation in the ten provinces and three territories, each of which has its own natural endowments, social structure, and political-economic history. I focus on Canada because I live in Canada, but the country offers more to this study than convenience. Its near-constant anxiety about productivity has meant that the concept is often and self-consciously at the forefront of Canadian governmentality.

The three case studies introduced below offer different vantage points on the emergence and development of the productivity concept, and the productivist ideational regime, in this ordinary and extraordinary country.

Productivity Research in the Dominion Bureau of Statistics

The first case explored here examines the founding of the Dominion Bureau of Statistics (DBS), and especially its development of national economic/industrial statistics. Tracing the productivity concept alongside the construction of the National Accounts – the body of data that gives us quarterly productivity estimates, as well as measures such as GDP and GNP – this case illustrates the early motivations for developing aggregate, national productivity indicators and reveals the nascent productivist ideational regime within which such indicators were interpreted, legitimated, and elevated to such a central place in Canada's program of official statistics. Of particular importance is the convergence – visible in the history of the DBS – of three discursive developments: (1) the *idea* of "the national economy," a concept whose history is first explored in chapter 1; (2) the expansion and centralization of statistics-gathering in Canada; and (3) the widespread belief that "a rising tide lifts all boats": the notion that rising aggregate productivity would translate into prosperity for all.

The National Productivity Council

The second case study is the short but intriguing life of a Canadian political apparatus, the National Productivity Council (NPC), from 1960 to 1963. The council emerged during a time of heightened anxiety about productivity – anxiety that would continue to grow in the 1970s and 1980s. That anxiety found its clearest expression in neoliberal economic thought, but its principal residence is productivism, and (as will be discussed further) productivism transcends the more precise ideological divisions between neoliberalism and its alternatives. The controversy building in the 1960s touched the ground where workers and bosses most publicly clashed: in the sphere of "labour–management relations." The NPC, like similar bodies the world over, spearheaded a series of labour–management seminars that brought together government, business leaders, and union representatives to talk about productivity and how the three parties could work together to improve it. What went on in these seminars – the different and sometimes competing definitions of productivity, the attempts to pin the productivity "crisis" on various groups and problems, and the increasing public relations role of the NPC – tells us just how contentious the productivity concept can be, how it relates to the organization of production in Canada and other capitalist nations, and what the stakes are in efforts to define, measure, and manipulate it. Yet it also points to the hegemony of productivism as an ideational regime, in that labour, capital, and government alike could not seem to think outside the parameters of productivism even as they squared off about working conditions, national productivity, and profits.

Choosing Productivity in the Atlantic Canada Opportunities Agency

The third case study in this book examines the establishment and evolving mandate of the Atlantic Canada Opportunities Agency (ACOA). The focus zooms in to Atlantic Canada because nowhere else in the country have concerns about "lagging" productivity been so consistently prominent in economic development and governance discussions as in the four easternmost provinces of New Brunswick, Prince Edward Island, Nova Scotia, and Newfoundland and Labrador. The ACOA case study shows what the productivity concept does to policy and everyday life at the regional level (bearing in mind that the regional level is itself a social construct with debatable significance). In ACOA, productivity meets up with two of the most relevant concepts in its conceptual network today, both of which are powerful tropes in the metanarrative of economic growth and progress: *competitiveness* and *opportunity*. I argue that the interactions among productivity, opportunity, and competitiveness, embedded in the still-dominant productivist ideational regime, are a defining feature of twenty-first-century Canadian governmentality and indeed of Canadian (and perhaps global) life.

Critiquing Productivity

Before turning to the first case, I provide a genealogy of productivity that reaches beyond the Canadian and Atlantic Canadian contexts, to the emergence of the productivity indicator in economic thought – first as an abstract, eighteenth- and nineteenth-century notion of the ratio of outputs to inputs in production, and later as a statistical calculation that became increasingly complex and far-reaching over the twentieth century. Drawing on the governmentality perspective, I show how the productivity concept has factored into questions of international (economic) governance, how its discovery and development related to the discovery and development of The Economy, and, importantly, how its existence is tightly interwoven with concerns over industrial strife and other perceived threats to the capitalist economic and social order, (inter)national economic competitiveness, and national unity – themes that will be explored from different angles in the three case studies.

A note about scope is in order here. I refer to this work as a genealogy, a story, and a narrative to emphasize its selectiveness and its construction, in which my *choices* – this event, not that one; starting here, not there – as a historical sociologist have been decisive. The scope of the story, which begins in the mid-1700s and ends around the turn of this century, and which unfolds mainly in Canada, the United States, and Britain, is not arbitrary; it reflects the flows of ideas that I was able to trace through the English-language historical and contemporary record of academic economic thought and government discourse. I have no doubt that the discourses described and analysed here can be found in French, Mandarin, Spanish, Russian, Hindi, or any other language in which ideas about economy and policy are communicated. But I would wager that in other places in the world – places where it is normal to take a midday nap, for example, and where aspirations to global economic superpower status are not so high – productivism has been "checked" by other discourses to a greater extent than it has been in the United States, Britain, and Canada.

There are also untold provincial and regional stories within Canada, and undoubtedly there is a very different history of productivity in Quebec, where the division of responsibility between market, state, and society has always been a little bit different from the rest of the country. The case studies that were *not* done are orders of magnitude more vast than the three actually chosen. The choice to cover the DBS, the NPC, and ACOA was primarily a matter of the availability of historical records and the apparent connections between these apparatuses and contemporary debates about productivity in Canada and beyond.

I am certain, too, that from the 1700s to the present, the idea of productivity and the notion that more of it is a good thing would be found outside the modern industrial capitalist contexts in which it is explored here – in the home, on the small farm, in schools, and on the plantation. A genealogy that began from any of these other worlds would be a welcome and important companion to the work presented here, as well as a major contribution to historical sociology, the history of economics, and governmentality studies. I regret that I had to start and stop where I did – for now.

The reader looking for a definition or explanation of productivity will not find it here, for the point of this book is to situate the concept historically. It is not my aim to throw back the curtains and reveal productivity's true meaning; what I want to show, when the curtains part, is that although productivity means different things at different times and in different places – and the current prevailing understanding of it is no more fixed than any previous iterations – there are certain persistent assumptions that have structured thought about productivity over roughly the last century, which point to its *embeddedness* in a productivist ideational regime. At the same time, as the case studies and genealogy that follow will attest, the meaning of productivity has often eluded those who throw it about loudly and publicly to bolster their political agendas, those bureaucrats assigned periodically to study or increase productivity, and the poor secretaries who struggle to keep minutes at their rambling meetings.

There is, however, a critique of productivity in this book. It is a critique of the versions of the productivity concept at work in contemporary debates and discussions around economic growth, social justice, and wealth redistribution – debates that erupt over "corporate welfare" and "cultures of dependency," "getting government out of business" and "competing in the global economy." These are persuasive discourses that implore us to care about competitiveness, efficiency, and job creation. The idea of productivity therein deserves critical attention because, like many other economic concepts, it often serves as a Trojan horse, disguising powerful normative assumptions about how the economy *ought* to work so that they look like the empirical truth of how it *actually* works, and wielding these assumptions as weapons in a battle to define and thus control the socially constructed field we call "the economy."

In our time (which stretches a long way back), the prevailing assumption is that increased economic productivity – producing more objects for consumption at the lowest cost per unit – will translate naturally into a higher standard of living for those who live within the territorial boundaries of the economy doing the producing. It is also assumed that increasing productivity is how we "grow," how we "compete" economically with other jurisdictions, how we "maintain our competitiveness"

and thus preserve our living standards – our prosperity. This alignment of assumptions, beliefs, and concepts, embedded in the ideational regime of productivism, has fostered a way of thinking that
looks increasingly suspicious to a growing number of analysts, some of
whom are quite conservative and orthodox, but others of whom subscribe to the doctrine of "de-growth" – a project whose "goal is to build
a society in which we can live better lives whilst working less and consuming less."[38]

I share with these de-growth advocates the contention that productivism, and the assumptions about productivity, prosperity, and economic growth therein, are faulty. Their inadequacies have been shown
time and time again at every scale, often by the very empirical data used
to support them. Simply put, many of the biggest economic problems
of our time – rising unemployment, stagnant job creation, slowdowns
in consumer spending, and the runaway polarization of wealth – are
at least partly the results of *increased* productivity. We are, in a sense,
productivity-ing ourselves out of work and, indeed, out of a planet.
The idea that we can continue to create enough jobs (or almost enough)
for everyone who wishes to work for pay, at rates of remuneration
and hours adequate to provide the necessities of life, and perhaps
enough discretionary income to keep up consumer demand, while also
whittling the costs of production down to the lowest levels possible,
all without completely destroying the earth, is a fantastic one that is certain to fail. This is a value statement, but I came to it through the careful
empirical research presented here. I now agree with Serge Latouche,
Ivan Illich, and a growing legion of others that in order to maintain a
decent standard of living for their citizens – perhaps a bit lower than
that to which they are now accustomed – nation-states will have to *slow*
productivity growth, emphasize quality over quantity, and even think
of jobs as resources that should be limited and distributed more evenly
among those in the labour force.

Others have made these kinds of arguments before.[39] The historical
record exhumed for this book shows that many people, sometimes the
most unlikely people – political leaders, technocrats, bureaucrats, economists, from the "apocalyptic" predictions of Ricardo and Marx to the
similarly apocalyptic predictions of environmentalist economists – have
pointed to flaws in the assumptions underpinning the productivity concept, only to have their voices drowned out by the majority that cannot
or will not take their criticisms seriously. Their marginalization speaks
to the power of productivism in making certain ideas unutterable.

Perhaps, as Thomas Piketty has recently argued, the apocalypse is not nigh. But even he proposes that unless something changes, the future of work, wealth, and well-being is not pretty.[40]

Yet it is precisely because the productivity concept has a history that its future is an open question – that there might be an opportunity to challenge it. The fact that we can dig beneath it to see where it is embedded means that it may be possible to re-embed it "in a different logic," or to re-embed somewhere else the notion of prosperity that seems, as yet, inseparable from it.[41] That is why this book is partly a history of the concept's development in economic theory and policy. We begin, in chapter 1, with a look at the metanarrative from which I argue the productivity concept gets whatever meaning and rationality it has at any given moment: the story of the "discovery" of The Economy.

Chapter One

The Discovery of Productivity

The Discovery of the Economy

Although the economy today is a place of much uncertainty, speculation, and chaos, most of us are confident that, at the very least, it *exists*. Most would also agree that while the economy overlaps with and is tightly connected to politics, households, and cultures, it is at least *analytically* separable from these other realms of reality. Thus, we can work with concepts such as the "world economy," the "national economy," and the "local economy"; we know, in a general way, what "economists" do; and we have a practical sense of what it means when we are told that "the economy" is booming, strong, struggling, weak, recessed, depressed, or recovering. In any case, most of us speak of the economy so naturally, and we so take it for granted, that it is difficult to believe that we have only been doing so for a short time. The history of the idea of the economy is crucial for understanding the related history of the idea of productivity and the assumptions that support it.

According to anthropologist Tim Mitchell, our contemporary understanding of the economy "dates only from the mid-twentieth century."[1] At first, this assertion seems to contradict some very obvious evidence. After all, Adam Smith, known by many as the "father of modern economics," was writing in the late 1700s.[2] There were economics journals in circulation as early as 1886, by which time there was already a burgeoning field of economic theory, comprised mostly of contributions from Austria, France, Britain, and the United States.

However, calling it a "field" may imply an inordinate level of cohesion to what was, by all accounts, several relatively small, dispersed, and insular bodies of economic thought – most of them not yet going by the name "economics" – comprised of thinkers not yet calling themselves "economists." Most, from Adam Smith to Karl Marx, professed instead to study "political economy." The distinct academic discipline and method called "economics," and the professionals known as "economists," would not emerge until the 1870s.[3]

In the British colonies that would become the Dominion of Canada in 1867, economics and political economy were marginal bodies of thought. According to economist Crauford D.W. Goodwin, even the distinction between them barely mattered in the late 1800s. Both were viewed not as scientific or academic fields but as normative or political stances on free trade synonymous with "a policy of laissez faire." And both were dismissed, especially by protectionists, as "'simple nonsense.'"[4]

Thinking of economy and political economy in this manner is perplexing for the contemporary mind. The economy appears to us today as a space and a set of processes, not a theory or a political position; economics, to us, is the study of that space and those processes. Political economy is that too, but with attention to the ways in which politics, culture, power, class relations, and other factors – all treated as "exogenous" by simple economics – affect the economy. Yet there was a time when political economy, simultaneously a method and a theory, was the only means of analysing and describing the exchange of goods, services, and currency beyond the household. It took centuries after the birth of what can be called economic thought, and the concerted, deliberate efforts of economic thinkers, for simple "economics" to emerge and be hived off from political economy as the latter's ostensibly apolitical, scientific cousin.

As Mitchell convincingly shows, the specific idea of *The* Economy as a singular, "fixed space" containing *all* "relations of production, distribution and consumption of goods and services within a given country or region" and excluding "the state" and "the household" – in other words, the notion of The Economy we take for granted today – was not yet a part of economic thought. Before the 1930s, among the political leaders, economists, industrial engineers, and industrial psychologists who will appear in this book's central narrative, "economy" referred to an abstract notion of the "prudent" or even "efficient" use of resources (which is distinct from the *productive* use of resources).[5] As Mitchell explains,

> both in academic discourse and in popular expression ("the Egyptian economy," "the economy is a mess"), this meaning of the term emerged during the years around the Second World War. Adam Smith, dubiously claimed as

the father of modern economics, never once refers in *The Wealth of Nations* to a structure or whole of this sort. When he uses the term "economy," the word carries the older meaning of frugality or the prudent use of resources.[6]

Mitchell finds one of the earliest appearances of our contemporary understanding of The Economy in John Maynard Keynes's *General Theory of Employment, Interest, and Money*, published much later, in 1936. Not coincidentally, this work is widely considered to be the "origin of what came to be called macroeconomics."[7] Its publication coincided with another critical development in the history of economics: "the birth of econometrics, or the attempt to create a mathematical representation of the entire economic process as a self-contained and dynamic mechanism" (although it is important to note that Keynes was "critical" of this development).[8]

Given its emphasis on the "entire economic process," econometrics was especially important in giving The Economy a precise and scientifically knowable form. Its role in advancing this totalizing conception is illustrative of a critical point about the "discovery" of The Economy, as well as the subsequent evolution of the Economy concept in economic, social, and political thought. Econometrics is tightly linked to two other developments: first, the development and advancement of statistics – the foundational method in econometrics – and second, the emergence of another seemingly durable spatio-political construct – The Nation.

Looking at the advancement of statistics, it may be tempting to view the birth and growth of econometrics as an apolitical sign of progress in the field of economics, as many of its proponents did. But the turn towards statistics was a political and ideological move, as it was simultaneously "a break with the tradition of political economy from Smith to Ricardo to Marx."[9] Where the latter tradition concerned itself with the slippery and seemingly unquantifiable factors of human relationships, political struggle, class conflict, power, inequality, values, and morality, the new mathematical economists would begin to bracket off these exigencies in order to study economic patterns, develop theories, and discover laws dispassionately, objectively, scientifically. They borrowed terminology from physics and "developed mechanical metaphors" for economic activity, creating, in a sense, a closed system of signs – a "conceptual network," in Somers's terms – and forming "the economy ... as a new discursive object."[10]

This language was in limited circulation as early as the turn of the century, burgeoning by the 1930s, and hegemonic by the 1950s. It laid the crucial foundations for productivism – the ideational regime I identify over the course of this book – a key feature of those foundations being "a reimagination of the nation-state."[11] Thus, the productivist ideational regime does not – cannot – pre-date the idea of a singular national economy. Some productivist tenets certainly did exist in the 1800s and early 1900s, as will be clear by the end of this chapter. But the regime of thought I will trace through the three government apparatuses in this work did not come together as such until The Economy and its statistical representation were elaborated in professional economics and adopted in Western, and specifically Canadian, governmentality.

Earlier economists had concerned themselves mainly with transactions between individuals and individual markets; this was their "abstraction," the location of their object of study, and it "had no geographical or political definition." The new and growing body of scientific and professional economists, by contrast, focused their attention on their own construct – the "economic system as a whole" – which mapped neatly onto the "geopolitical boundaries" of the nation-state.[12] As Mitchell describes it,

> the [economic] system was represented in terms of a series of aggregates (production, employment, investment and consumption) and synthetic averages (interest rate, price level, real wage, and so on), whose referent was the geographic space of the nation-state ... This idea of the national economy was not theorized ... but introduced as a commonsense construct providing the boundaries within which the new averages and aggregates could be measured.[13]

Among these new averages and aggregates were the National Accounts and the "national income," figures that have elsewhere been credited with "inventing" the economy and that still underlie the economic indicators published by Canada's national statistical agency on monthly and quarterly bases.[14] (The emergence and wide acceptance of aggregate measures taken at the level of the nation-state will be important in the genealogy of the productivity concept that unfolds over the next two chapters.) It is no coincidence that the same period – the early twentieth century – saw the establishment of the censuses in Canada, the United States, and Britain, as well as the birth of national statistical agencies in these same places.

Yet another related development was taking root during this period, slowly coming to life in the early 1900s, and becoming lodged in place between the 1930s and 1950s: the reimagination of economic growth. In late-nineteenth- and early-twentieth-century economics, "growth" was primarily a spatial or material development – something that happened as economic transactions between individuals expanded into new regions or began to involve new commodities. It was also imagined – as it was in Adam Smith's work – in terms of the "accumulation" of capital stock and increases in population. But as The Economy became fixed to The Nation, growth took on a novel meaning as "the internal *intensification of the totality of relations* defining the economy as an object."[15] Economic growth became, in other words, something that nations did. Subsequently or simultaneously, it became something they *should* do, as the intensification of economic relations within the National Economy came to be seen as essential to the wealth and prosperity of the nation. Granted, growth was good for Adam Smith, too. He argued that growth was *progress*, that stasis or decline were either "dull" or "melancholic." But he believed that economies could only grow for a finite period of time before having to settle at a "stationary state," no matter how boring this might be for their inhabitants. He believed, like many of his day, that population growth would exhaust the earth's natural resources and force economies to stop growing. But at some point, rather ironically, these concerns receded in economic theory, political economy, and politics itself. The closer the world moved towards the inevitable stasis predicted by Adam Smith (and others, to be discussed in the final chapter), the deeper it buried any concern about the limits of growth. Gradually, it accepted the crux of the productivist ideational regime: growth for growth's sake.

Situating productivism historically shows just how integral to it are the concepts of The Nation and The (National) Economy: although we now proclaim that we live and work in a "global" economy, productivism is a decidedly national sport. The obsession with growth is almost always an obsession with the growth of a particular nation (sometimes a region, although even then, often in service to a larger nation), which is seen to be in competition with other nations pursuing the same productivist goals. As the next chapter will show, the centrality of The Nation to productivism would only be further solidified by developments in statistical research.[16] At the same time as economic growth became the modus operandi of nations everywhere, Canada and other nation-states were creating the statistical agencies, censuses, and research departments to construct and measure aggregate indicators of economic change – growth being the change most desired, and gross domestic product (GDP) being the most obsessed-over measure – on which The Economy construct depends.[17] These institutions, embedded in the productivist ideational regime, would soon vault the productivity concept to the status of an economic fact and, with help from other spheres, a social good. Before we get to that point, we should step back again, to a time before The Economy existed, and trace the emergence and development of the productivity concept itself.

Productivity in Early Economic Thought

The basic notion of productivity as a ratio of outputs to inputs in a production process was around long before anyone was talking about The Economy as a "fixed space." It was certainly in circulation well before the emergence of nation-states, which circumscribe our contemporary economies (although the latter are increasingly pressing outward, threatening the ontological security of national boundaries). It pre-dates the establishment of annual censuses of manufacturing and population in North America and Britain and the National Accounts in Canada.

But the earliest utterances of productivity bear little resemblance to the concepts we employ today in everyday parlance, economic theory, quarterly statistics, and business performance indicators. To complicate matters further, there is no unambiguous straight line connecting our contemporary notion of productivity to a single origin. Rather, there have been numerous developments, some even simultaneous, spread out across geography and society, that I will argue have laid the conditions of possibility for the way(s) we understand and operationalize productivity today, as well as the reasons *why* we do so at all.

The narrative on which my argument rests begins with the central but rudimentary idea of productivity in the political economy of the late 1700s, and traces the concept's evolution and contestation over the next few centuries. Over this period, there were significant shifts or transformations – some just short of ruptures – in the productivity concept and economic thought more broadly. Two of them are particularly important for the ways in which the productivity concept has shaped economic relations, economic policy, and ordinary people's lives in the distant and recent past.

The first is a shift from abstract, theoretical conceptions of productivity towards its precise empirical, statistical measurement. This shift follows the broader movement of economics mentioned earlier in this

chapter, away from abstract theorizing and towards mathematical formulae and principles. As will be shown, this shift happened gradually,
with mathematical formulae coming into use and debate before the
data to actually test them were available on a large scale. The second shift
foregrounded in the narrative presented here is away from early, firm-
level productivity statistics for single businesses and single products
towards *aggregate* measures portending to capture the productivity of
many different businesses in entire industries and, later, all of the different industries in entire nations.

These two changes in thinking about productivity come together to
form a politically charged, historically and culturally contingent history
of a contemporary concept whose form and utility are anything but
natural or inevitable. But there are also recurring themes in productivity's story; instead of "developments" or "transformations," they
emerge as repetitive inflammations, the same arguments over and over
in different settings, the same ideas trotted out by different interests for
different audiences. Often they take the form of assumptions that have
simply stood the test of time, either because they work for powerful
interests, or because they *seem* to work for everyone's interests (or, not
coincidentally, for both reasons). I consider there to be three analytically
separable themes of this kind.

The first theme is the persistent connection drawn between productivity and prosperity – that is, the idea that rising productivity (at the level
of the worker, firm, industry, and/or nation) translates naturally into rising prosperity (for capitalist, business owner, worker, and dependants
alike) – despite compelling evidence, at key moments and over time, to
the contrary. The notion of prosperity, in turn, is occasionally forwarded
as a component of national or regional economic "competitiveness" or,
conversely, as a consequence of competition. This is the most important theme, to my mind, for the critique that will build in this book. It is
also one of the main structural supports for the productivist ideational
regime, and the clearest example of how productivism limits our thinking about productivity.

Then there are the ongoing efforts to determine once and for all *who* or
what does the actual producing in economic production: Is it capitalists
and their investments, or workers and their labour? This theme presents
itself early in Ricardo's engagements with the value of commodities,
Marx's critique of capitalism, and turn-of-the-century efforts to define
capital as a productive factor (i.e., as a component of production that has
measurable productivity) on par with labour; it also appears later, in the

sweeping obsession with efficiency and labour productivity exemplified in F.W. Taylor's *Principles of Scientific Management*. There is much at stake in these recurring debates – for whomever or whatever is defined as an agent of production, or as the most important agent of production, can lay claim to any surplus value (i.e., profit) created in the production process. But as history shows, they can also be blamed and penalized if productivity slows or profit dries up. The tensions around productive factors and surplus value illustrate the dominance of productivism, in that after the interwar era, labour, capitalists, and governments, although they were ideologically opposed in some ways, were actually all in agreement that growth was *good*.

The final ongoing theme is the mutual reinforcement of scientific or mathematical economics on the one hand – its counting, measuring, and census-taking functions – and nation-building on the other, the latter inclusive of the strengthening conception of "The Nation" as a territorialized, bounded entity that encompasses and in some cases erases local, parochial divisions. The symbiosis between statistics and the nation-state, as I began to argue in the introduction, is characteristic of the metanarrative of The Economy, and critical to the assumptions entailed in productivism. Its implications for how productivity is understood, and how it comes to *matter*, are far-reaching.

Productivity before the Twentieth Century

It makes sense to start the story of productivity with one of modern economics' founding fathers: Adam Smith, who, as the reader might recall, was writing before anyone was talking about The Economy. In his 1776 *An Inquiry into the Nature and Causes of the Wealth of Nations*, Smith divided labour into "productive" and "unproductive" types. Productive labour, for him, produced a tangible and more or less durable object, while unproductive labour's value was consumed in production. The primary example Smith used for the latter was servants' work. Cleaning, answering doors, and getting a master dressed, he argued, produced nothing "tangible" of value – nothing that could be exchanged for something else. Importantly, the category also included the work done by lawyers, bankers, and capitalists, "who deducted their incomes from the sum of values created by others, that is, who consumed without producing."[18]

Smith's examination of the "productive powers of labour" is where we find a notion resembling what we would today call "productivity."

The former, for Smith, referred simply to how much stuff a worker, or workers, could produce, and he argued that the "greatest improvement" in that quantity came from the "division of labour." Using the hypothetical example of pin-manufacturing, he illustrated how the separation of production into numerous discrete tasks, each carried out by a different worker, could increase the number of pins produced in a single day, far above the number a solitary worker could produce on his own in the same time if he were responsible for every step of production.[19] He acknowledged that the introduction of labour-saving technologies – "proper machinery" – also helped boost "the productive power of labour," but in his view this was not as important in his analysis as division and specialization.

This basic understanding of productivity as a function of the division of labour prevailed for more than one hundred years. Productivity itself was only of minimal concern over this period, but it did appear in some interesting and disturbing places. John Stuart Mill, in his 1848 *Principles of Political Economy*, would reflect on Smith's pin-making example and discuss how increased "efficiency" in production – whether thanks to improvements in the labour itself (by repetition and mastery) or to the aid of "machines" – might affect wages, cost of living, and profits. He also ruminated on the relative efficiency of slave versus free labour.[20] As historians David Roediger and Elizabeth Esch have documented, Mill was not alone in contemplating these differences. Plantation owners in the antebellum South wrote to and for one another about the productivity of "white" versus "negro" slaves. More broadly, "capitalists" in "the industrial North" and "the agrarian South ... debate[d] not only the relative merits of slavery and free labour but also the productivity of 'black' versus 'white' workers."[21]

Mill never used the *word* productivity, nor did many of these capitalists and managers. But they did consider the impact of certain management strategies (sometimes brutal and threatening displays of authority) on how much each slave or worker produced. Plantation owners and managers even performed rudimentary calculations of productivity, dividing the costs of materials, housing, and food, as well as labour time, by the volume of harvests or the area covered in a day's work. As will be discussed further along in this narrative, the histories of slavery, "race management," and industrial productivity are deeply intertwined.

As the productivity concept subtly structured daily life on the plantation, it remained peripheral in professional economic thought. But during this period, a crucial change was taking place – a condition of possibility for the productivity concept and the space it has occupied in social and economic thought ever since. "Capitalism," the system not yet widely or exclusively known by that name, had been "maturing" thanks to the intensification of "a peculiar form of market pressure, which first appeared in early modern agrarian England along with the growth of wage labor." Howard Brick, summarizing Ellen Meiksins Wood's argument in *The Origin of Capitalism* (2002), explains:

> The expansion of a propertyless working class forced laborers to purchase goods for their own sustenance; thus, not only did commodity exchange become the unavoidable center of material existence but there also emerged a market for cheaply produced food, shelter, and manufactured articles. Such a market reinforced the distinctive role of *production* in capitalism, for in contrast to traditional commerce, where profit stemmed from "buying cheap and selling dear," profit under capitalism rests in production as such, namely, in the ability to produce articles for sale more cheaply than competitors.[22]

This role for production – an expression of productivism – is not unique to capitalism; socialism can work like this too. But in a capitalist economy, the "market system" described above induces a "compulsive" and "competitive pressure to innovate and maximize profit"; it creates "swings of boom and bust" and, "by making the owners (as well as workers) into objects of uncontrolled forces, qualifies or disguises the social, economic, and political power they hold."[23] This development, tied to the rise of wage labour, the growth of commodity markets, and the increasing importance of production itself, is a historically critical, if not inherently necessary, precedent for the obsession with productivity that would take hold over the next century and a half.

But near the turn of the twentieth century, as it rose to new prominence, the productivity concept was still limited mainly to two bodies of theory. First, the Austrian School of economics began working with the theory of the "productivity of capital" to explain how money appeared to beget more money, beginning with Carl Menger's *Principles of Economics* (1871) and carrying through with a second generation of Austrian economists, including Ernst Böhm-Bawerk.[24] Productivity was taken for granted as a concept and used as an assumption in other, bigger theories. Second, when Karl Marx, over nearly the same period, took up the "labour theory of value" in the work of Smith, Ricardo, and other classical (political) economists, he outlined the likely effects of *increased* labour productivity, and the "surplus production" it enabled, on economic relations and wealth (more on that below). The Austrian marginalists in turn attempted to theorize capital as a productive entity, and in some instances to measure its specific productivity. Their work was in many respects a response to Marx, who in *Grundrisse* and *Capital* had argued that any productivity attributed to capital was actually labour productivity that had been appropriated by capital rather than a quality of capital on its own.[25] By the 1890s, the ideas of both Marx and the Austrian School would resurface with new significance in the work of American marginalists.

Marginalism, the Labour Theory of Value, and the Productivity Concept

The publication of Menger's *Principles*, besides drawing attention to the productivity of capital, is commonly referenced as one of the significant turns in the "marginal revolution" in economics. The emergence of marginalism as a dominant mode of economic thought in Europe and North America, with its engagement with Classical predecessors and its contemporary, Marx, is an important plot line in this story of the productivity concept. There is far more to the exchange between Marx and the Austrian school than can be covered here – more connections to be made between conceptions of productivity and these competing strands of economic thought – so what follows should be read as a basic narrative that might help make sense of the productivity concept in different contexts.

Along with Menger, British economist W.S. Jevons and French economist Leon Walras are widely considered to be the "discoverers" of marginal utility, although some have suggested that at least nine economists "struck on" the law simultaneously and were ignorant of one another's work.[26] One such case was John Rae, an immigrant to Upper Canada from Scotland, whose 1834 treatise *Statement of some New Principles on the Subject of Political Economy* was found to contain "a marginal theory of capital" when it was "rediscovered" during the marginal revolution near the end of the century. Indeed, other marginalists, including Irving Fisher in 1897, credited Rae with laying "the foundations" for their own work.[27] Rae's *Statement* was received primarily as a critique of Adam Smith and free trade – indeed, its subtitle is "Exposing the Fallacies of the System of Free Trade" – which would be useful in the battle between free traders and protectionists in Canada at the turn of the twentieth century. But many have since emphasized its importance as a "progenitor" of marginalist thought, and even, as will be discussed later, the "economics of competitiveness."[28]

The terms "marginal" and "marginalism" derive specifically from a set of principles and theories of value that emerged in the late 1800s as a response or challenge to the labour theory of value. That theory, again commonly attributed to Karl Marx but appearing in the work of Smith, Ricardo, and other classical (i.e., political) economists, held that the value of a commodity was a reflection of the labour-time *necessary* to produce it, and for a time this dominant explanation seemed to hold true.[29] As the necessary labour-time for a given commodity decreased, thanks to machinery or a more efficient division of labour, the price of that commodity had generally dropped.

But in the growing industrial economies of late-1800s Europe and North America, it became obvious that prices were fluctuating almost independently of the labour expended in production. The task became, as Stephen Gudeman put it more recently, figuring out "which tail wags the dog": Were wages simply whatever was left over after capital took its share? Or did capital only get what was left over after wages were paid out? Or was the distribution of surplus value a product of a constant struggle between workers and capitalists?[30] Whatever the case may have been, for the new professional economists of this period, the labour theory of value appeared to lack the capacity to *scientifically explain* the changes in prices and wages that were plainly evident to them and to ordinary people. If the average amount of labour expended during the production of a commodity was the sole determinant of its value, why did prices and wages go up or down with no change in labour productivity?

Yet the problem with the labour theory of value was not only that it did not stand up to empirical evidence. In making labour the source of all value, it also failed to justify profits going anywhere but back to the worker in wages. At the time, however, profits were obviously going elsewhere on a grand scale. The labour theory thus failed to *legitimate* the emergence of a "modern class society" and the existing social order. (It was, therefore, a source of great ideological support for socialism.[31]) The developing school of marginalism, with its principles of marginal utility and, later, marginal productivity, offered a "scientific" explanation for price fluctuations and, not coincidentally, an ideological justification for dividing profits between labour *and* capital.[32] It is no wonder it proved so influential.

The marginalists' theories rejected the premise that the labour necessary for the production of a good explained its price on the market. They argued instead that values were set outside the production process by consumer demand, with the value of an object determined by how useful it was to those who acquired it. But the marginalists also concluded that the *simple* utility of a good was equally incapable of accounting for its market price. As historian James Livingston summarizes it,

> the crux of the argument based on marginalist principles was that commodities had more or less value not because they cost more or less in human labor – this is what the classical political economy had supposed – but because consumers found more or less utility in them. [But] since less demand naturally followed from increased consumption of the same commodity, its utility would fall as its supply increased; the final or marginal unit demanded would therefore determine the utility – the value – of the entire supply.[33]

The principle of marginal utility shifted the locus of value from the production side (labour) to the consumption or demand side; its "discovery" was thus a pivotal moment in the birth of modern American "demand-side" economics, which looked to consumer demand as the trigger of economic growth.[34] On its own, this marginalist principle did not necessarily say anything about wages, about what happened to the money derived from consumers, or about whether profits, especially as they increased, should be distributed between labour and capital. But it *did* offer the language and logic for such an argument to be made, and that argument has shaped the productivity concept and directed its uses since. In the first half of the nineteenth century, as Goodwin has shown, marginalist economics had a home in Canada, filtered through the burgeoning economics periodicals and entering the country in the suitcases of immigrants to the New World's northern reaches.[35]

The American economist John Bates Clark first applied the marginalist principle to the production side in his 1877 work, *The Philosophy of Wealth*. There and in related articles, he was concerned not with explaining the value of consumer goods, as his predecessors had been, but with determining who or what was responsible for the value created during production and to whom should go whatever profits accrued from the sale of the product on the market. The question of how market price related to utility or demand was set aside, and replaced with the question of how wages related to the commodities produced and sold. In response, Clark posited a theory of "specific productivity" to explain wage rates – "specific" can be considered here as synonymous with "marginal" – arguing that the "final productivity of labour ... fixes its pay."[36]

But Clark's ultimate goal was not to decipher the mystery of wages; rather, it was to theorize *capital's* role in production and, relatedly, to justify capital's claim to a portion of profits – a goal he shared with many other economists of his time. As Livingston has shown, Clark admonished attempts to repudiate the "mental" labour of capitalists as somehow less productive or valuable than the physical labour of workers.[37] In *Philosophy of Wealth*, this position was something he simply staked out as a "moral high ground," predicting a future in which capital and labour were equal partners in production and thus not at odds politically. In 1899's *The Distribution of Wealth*, however, he laid out the "dispassionate or 'scientific'" argument he and his contemporaries had circled around for a decade. In his "law of wages," he wove the principle of marginal utility into a larger argument about the productivity of capital, proposing specifically that "the addition of capital to any given mix of productive inputs would increase the output of labor."[38] This shifted the focus from marginal utility towards marginal *productivity* by theorizing both labour *and* capital as "productive factors" whose productivity per unit (and the value they created) diminished as their supply increased. His theory, and the mathematical calculations it supported, ostensibly enabled economists to determine how a gain in output triggered by an injection of capital "was, or ought to be, divided between capital and labor."[39] As Brett Christophers argues in *Banking across Boundaries*, Clark and the other marginalists effectively "dispense[d] with hard-and-fast distinctions between productive and unproductive economic processes and labors" found in Smith's work, thus changing the focus of economic theory and laying a particular groundwork for the National Accounts that will be discussed in chapter 3.[40]

Through this work, Clark became involved in a burgeoning debate about productivity. Whether they were interested, like Clark, in the productivity of capital, or the productivity of labour, or something else, many economists of the period (most of them still going by the title of "political economist") were converging on the sticky question of just *who* or *what* produces profit in capitalist production. In other words, what parts of the production process are actually *productive* of value, how do their levels of *productivity* compare to one another, and how, then, does the economy grow?[41] In pursuing these lines of inquiry, they were slowly piecing together the assumptions necessary for a productivist ideational regime. They were not, however, working on a consensus.

Rae, although he was talking into the wind, proposed that the productivity of capital depended on the knowledge to do something with it – what might be called innovation; the value of capital, in turn, was not determined by the amount of it, but rather by its capacity to produce. In Rae's formulation, the *desire* to accumulate more and more capital was "subject to the law of diminishing returns," but the "inventive faculty" overcame that law.[42] The Austrian Böhm-Bawerk, whose ideas would later be said to have been presaged by Rae's, emphasized the unique productivity of capital, setting it apart from the other two "pillars" of production – labour and materials. He was criticized for this by American economist and American Economics Association (AEA) treasurer Frederick B. Hawley, who was adamant that capital was no more or less important than labour and materials, and therefore not "unique," in the production process.[43] Others, including the eminent American political economist Francis Amasa Walker (the AEA's founding president and superintendent of two US censuses), weighed in to remind – in line with the older marginalists – that value was not created in production, but rather in consumption; in other words, value was a demand-side creation, not something inherent in supply.[44] Others, including Hawley again, entered the fray to propose that value was produced not by supply or demand, but in the assumption of risk.[45]

Thus, numerous influential works and theories were published during this period, but as Livingston points out, it was largely thanks to Clark's *Distribution* that "capital could hereafter appear as a factor of production."[46] Indeed capital has continued to claim this status everywhere, and in this sense, Clark's perspective won out.[47] The most important aspect of his perspective for the present work was that "far from being a parasite on productive labor, [capital was] the condition of labor's productivity and the linchpin of what we would now call total factor productivity."[48] Situating the productivity concept historically shows, then, that it grew up in a time of larger political economic struggle to define the "factors of production" and, in this case, "describe the conditions under which capital could be defined as ... a legitimate claimant to a share of national income."[49] This struggle has been composed of many smaller battles and forks in the road along the way.

The emergence of marginalist principles was a fork in the road for another reason, one that will be clearer by the final chapter of this book. Marginalist thought highlighted a "paradox" of economic growth – economic growth still understood in mainly spatial terms. Jevons, one of the economists credited with spurring the marginal turn, developed a theory, later called the "Jevons Paradox," that explained how increases in the efficiency of energy use led not to a decrease in the use of that energy, as was commonly assumed, but to an increase. The prevailing wisdom had been that if industry learned how to use a resource more efficiently, it would need less of it to produce the same (or greater) amounts of goods or services. In his 1865 book, *The Coal Question*, Jevons showed that efficiencies in coal use had actually led to increased use of it because production kept expanding. He said the same of labour: as human workers became more efficient, employment shot up. Jevons was likely correct, but only because economic activity, along with capital, profits, and consumer demand, kept expanding. This revelation caused Jevons much anxiety. He believed, rightly, that the coal would one day run out. And he worried that the British Empire would grow too big, too fast (in population *and* industry), to a size and a level of global influence that could never be maintained on scarce resources. To his readers, he posed an uncomfortable question: "Are we wise in allowing the commerce of this country to rise beyond the point at which we can long maintain it?"[50]

But just at the point when Jevons was treading close to the question of the ecological limits of economic growth, the historical narrative under construction here dovetailed with another storyline in the history of economic thought: the rise of mathematical economics. In this other narrative strand, what was monumental about the "discovery" of marginal utility was not the problem that it solved, nor the reliability of its formulae, but rather the fact that it provided a basis on which its adherents could defend "the methodological advantages of abstracting from historical and institutional considerations in the interest of obtaining perfectly general results from [a] minimum number of assumptions."[51] The marginal revolution – again, perhaps more of a gradual, inconsistent, and incoherent movement than a revolution – entailed the shift from an inchoate field of study concerned with social, moral, historical, and philosophical questions about labour, production, distribution, and consumption, towards a more consolidated and professionalized *discipline* that focused on economics as a set of general laws and principles that could (and should) be studied and mastered in isolation from the "exogenous" factors of society and population, morality, history, and philosophy.[52]

Marginal utility specifically appeared as a legitimate example of the kind of economic *principle* that the new breed of economist was supposed to concern himself with discovering, testing, and formulating so that it could be used to explain and predict economic processes. Such principles needed dispassionate, standardized methods, and as will be shown below, mathematical economics appeared to offer exactly this. Although it would be several years between the "discovery" of marginal utility and the spread of mathematical economics beyond a handful of adherents, and several more until the birth of econometrics, by the last quarter of the nineteenth century the seeds for their respective flourishing were being sown. Both mathematical economics and econometrics have shaped indelibly the productivity concept in use today.

The Rise of Mathematical Economics

Writing in 1898, American economist Irving Fisher remarked that "a decided change [had] taken place in the modes of conceiving and treating economic problems. For good or for ill the mathematical method has finally taken root, and is flourishing with a vigor of which both its friends and enemies little dreamed."[53]

Fisher, who would become president of the AEA in 1918 and found the American Econometric Society in 1931, was astonished at how quickly the field of "mathematical economists" had grown from a few people in the 1830s to "some thirty active enthusiasts and a much larger number of followers and sympathizers" by the end of the nineteenth century. Reflecting on this sea change, which he traced first to the 1838 publication (in France) of August Cournot's *Principes Mathematiques*, and then to English economist Alfred Marshall's *Principles of Economics* (1890), he observed that "opponents of the new method no longer venture to ignore or ridicule it, but, in academic circles at least, seek to acquaint themselves with its history and present aims as matters of necessary and professional information."[54] Not coincidentally, it was just a few years earlier, in 1885, that Richard T. Ely had founded the AEA. The professionalization of the discipline was being bolstered by its claims to scientific authority.

Yet a look at the foremost economics publication of this period – *Quarterly Journal of Economics* – suggests that the actual *use* of statistical manipulations in orthodox economics was rare until the mid-1900s. However, what are arguably Cournot's math-inspired *ideas* appear with frequency quite early, around the turn of the twentieth century. It has even been suggested that the theory of marginal utility originated with Cournot's *Principes*; the handful of economic minds credited with the "discovery" of marginalism are, in this interpretation, said to have "rediscovered" it along with Cournot's contemporaries in the Austrian School, all of them having been mostly "ignorant" of his work before its publication in English.[55] In any case, *Principes* was an early adopter of a new mathematical approach to economics. It concludes with two chapters on what Cournot calls "the social income," where he appears to grapple with a primitive idea of what we might today call "gross domestic" or "gross national product": "the sum of commodities 'for consumption.'"[56] These and other math-based ideas are readily visible, and appear as central concerns in the field, in *Quarterly Journal of Economics* around the turn of the century. And they travelled to Canada with J.B. Cheriman, a professor at University College in Toronto, who wrote "what was perhaps the first recognition in the English-speaking world of Cournot's great work" in *Canadian Journal of Industry, Science, and Art* in 1857.[57] In my view, the invention and spread of mathematical economics is among the conditions of possibility for the concept of productivity we have today.

Mathematical Economics and Productivity

The relationship between mathematical economics and the productivity concept is dynamic, always unfolding; it is a matter of historical development rather than a single discrete event. The slow and incremental pace of mathematics' spread into economics meant that the productivity concept was shaped early on by a subtle shift in the way economists wrote about money, markets, prices, and wages before it was actually treated or analysed as a numerical datum. This stage in the history of the productivity concept is well illustrated in the *Quarterly Journal* debate, wherein many participants offered only hypothetical formulae to explain the production of value, and the conversation stayed at the near-philosophical level of economic theory. Economics was *inching* towards the empiricist, statistics-based mode of argument we associate with it today; in the meantime, math was mainly proposed or played with and equations were populated with hypothetical numbers and imaginary data.

That the various positions were staked out around divergent logics (as opposed to divergent empirical evidence) can be attributed to the fact that the data to actually test the formulae were simply not available. Plant- or firm-level numbers may have existed for specific outfits, but there was nothing so all-encompassing as industry or national statistics.

This limitation notwithstanding, the growing popularity of mathematical economics legitimated a new way of thinking about productivity, that is, in terms of levels and ratios. It also allowed political questions to be abstracted into scientific, ostensibly value-neutral ones. Economists could now talk about who deserved a share of profits without appearing to engage the moral dimension of deservingness. Yet one does not have to study their positions very closely to see its moral ends – indeed, the moral work that the productivity concept can do, even (perhaps especially) when it is broached as an objectively knowable and measurable aspect of productive enterprise.

All participants in these debates seemed to believe that if they could find the locus of productivity in any venture, they would find where the "surplus value" or profit should go.[58] Some also considered the impacts of increasing productivity and especially the introduction of labour-saving technology on employment, foreshadowing the concern with "technological unemployment" that would move to the forefront of national economic policy in industrializing nations in decades to come.[59] All of this boiled down to the question of *how the costs and benefits of industrial production ought to be distributed among those involved in the process* – an inescapably moral question, despite the many concerted efforts to present it as an empirical one. At a time when the spectre of socialism loomed large in Canada, the United States, and Europe, everyone who offered a theory of productivity, whether they acknowledged it or not, was making an appeal for a certain political-economic order.

Thus, in this instance, as in every instance where productivity becomes a topic of debate or a target of policy, the moral–political impetus and implications are just beneath the surface. At the beginning of the twentieth century, marginalist principles, and particularly Clark's argument that capital counted as a productive factor, were gaining acceptance within the growing and professionalizing discipline of economics. Accordingly, mainstream economists and their understanding of productivity came to occupy a particular space in the wider public debate over socialism, capitalism, labour relations, and, as will be explored further in chapter 3, "economic planning." With the seemingly inarguable tenets of mathematical economics bolstering their expertise and proving their disinterestedness, their position was all the more influential. Each of the case studies in this book highlights, in its own way, how the productivity concept, like the discipline and practice of economics, exerts power in moral matters such as the distribution of wealth by laying claim to objectivity and hard science.[60]

To summarize the narrative thus far, three things are especially interesting to observe about conceptions of productivity in this period before the twentieth century. First, it is apparent that productivity was a significant part of economic discourse, but beyond the general acceptance that greater division of labour yielded greater productivity, there was little interest in methods to improve or increase it. While the general business objective of producing more with less was certainly in circulation, the primary concern of economists was simply theorizing and in some cases formulating *how* the inputs in capitalist production could come together and produce something more than their individual values combined.

Second, within these theories of surplus value the productivity concept emerged and became tangled up in an ideological battle over who or what produced value, and thus was entitled to surpluses, in the production process. This second theme would flare up whenever the productivity concept was discussed. By the first decade of the 1900s, it was widely accepted (except in staunch socialist circles) that capital is a productive factor, essential to economic growth and thus deserving of a chunk of the profits of enterprise. But it was also accepted that labour relations and productivity impact each other, especially when conflict arises over the distribution of profits or the introduction of labour-saving machinery. Accordingly, few treatises on productivity neglected the "labour problem," even if that problem was increasingly cordoned off as one of the "exogenous" factors best left to sociologists and psychologists. In any case, no matter how one believed the proceeds of productive enterprise ought to be divided, most agreed that increasing those proceeds was a worthy objective – which placed economic growth at the centre of even the most radical vision for social and political economic organization.[61]

Third, partly because of the novelty of mathematical economics, and partly because of a dearth of available data, few efforts were made to quantify productivity – to express or analyse it in numerical, mathematical, or statistical form. This disinclination towards numbers, as mentioned, was not limited to discussions of productivity. Although the American Statistical Society (thankfully later renamed the American Statistical Association) was in operation by 1839, the nascent field of economics was just broadly coming around to statistics and math in the mid-1800s. Yet the *desire* to put productivity and other economic processes into mathematical terms was there, as was the effort to hive scientific economics off from political economy. In this we see the third theme stated at the outset of this chapter – the mutual reinforcement of mathematical economics and nation-building – beginning to take shape. Once nation-states began to prioritize the collection and standardization of agricultural and manufacturing data, the possibility of measuring productivity statistically became a feasible reality. As should be clear by the end of this book, the development of increasingly refined statistical techniques and the widespread collection of data on which to use them were crucial in deterring anyone from questioning productivity as a government priority *or* linking the productivity concept with questions of fairness in redistribution.

National Productivity and Prosperity

When it came to measuring productivity, the marginalists were concerned only with "the marginal productivity of the nth worker hired," so they had no use for a concept like "average productivity."[62] It was a contribution from France around the turn of the twentieth century that brought statistical economics to bear on questions of explicitly *national* proportions and, albeit crudely, on the comparison of aggregate productivity levels in different countries. After producing a similar three-volume economic study in France, French economist and geographer Pierre Émile Levasseur was dispatched to the United States to perform a "study of the American workman in his environment." That he was sent to do so is a strong indication that national comparisons of industrial production were high on the priority list of the French government and likely others.

In his resulting two-volume work, *L'Ouvrier Americain* (1898), Levasseur concerned himself with many of the same kinds of questions as the other turn-of-the-century economists had introduced thus far: the production of value, the determination of wage rates and prices, and the "labor problem."[63] "Productivity" entered the picture in the context of these discussions as well as in a more focused analysis of productivity differences between France and the United States. Levasseur was especially interested in the "peculiar efficiency" of the American "workman" and its effect, alongside consumer demand and improvements to machinery, on profits as well as wages (which he found to be exceptionally high in America).[64]

Throughout his analysis, productivity is considered alongside another term that has now become commonplace in economic policy discussions: competitiveness. The frame of reference is different from that of contemporary economists, who are mainly concerned with the competitiveness of economic jurisdictions (countries, regions) vis-à-vis one another. Instead, Levasseur focused on competition *between* labour and capital, which he argued would determine how products and surpluses were distributed among workers and employers. He also posited that competition *within* the labour pool, especially between immigrants and American-born workers, would drive down wages.[65]

His basic lines of inquiry foreshadowed the discursive connections between productivity, prosperity, and competitiveness that would take root and quickly become a fixture of economic policy discussions over the next century.[66] Levasseur considered prosperity in terms of both the profit accrued to an enterprise and the "standard of living" of employees and their dependents. He made an assumption that most if not all of his contemporaries would have agreed with: that increases in productivity trigger increases in prosperity for the average "workman." While he noted that the latter depended on how surpluses were distributed, he asserted nonetheless that the basic relationship was fairly incontrovertible: more productivity meant more prosperity. Crucially, like many of his time and countless others to follow, Levasseur would casually apply this assumption to entire nations and their inhabitants just as easily as to individual businesses and their employees. It is worth noting that just over a century earlier, such a connection between productivity and prosperity would have been more difficult to make – not only because the productivity concept itself was at that time undertheorized, but also because rapid industrialization in late-eighteenth-century Britain – and specifically the "boom in trade" from the 1760s and 1770s – had plunged more people into miserable poverty and pauperism than it had lifted into prosperity. As Karl Polanyi put it, people during this period were awakened to "the incomprehensible fact that poverty seemed to go with plenty."[67] Yet by the time Levasseur landed in North America, all of that was apparently wiped from memory, or perhaps invalidated by American exceptionalism.

The national scale of Levasseur's analysis and his assumptions about prosperity are interesting on their own – the former as an innovation at the time, and the latter as a reflection of dominant understandings of the economic order. But also pertinent for the purposes of this book is Levasseur's attempt at an actual aggregate measure of productivity, among the first ever to encompass the entire nation's manufacturing sector. To offer this "bird's-eye view," Levasseur relied on federal census statistics and industrial censuses in particular.[68] He even went so far as to avoid the "duplication" of counting raw materials twice (once in raw form, and again in whatever products they were eventually used to make), as other pseudo-economists had done.[69] To be sure, the reliability of his numbers was far from what economists and statisticians would expect today.

One of his contemporaries cautioned that Levasseur had come "face to face with one of the most perplexing statistical problems": "The rise of new industries, the exploitation of new sources of power, the adoption of new processes of production, the reorganization of industry and the instability of values are variables tending to vitiate comparative statistical estimates of material resources, past and present."[70] This particular critic, one J. Cummings, admitted that Levasseur considered L'Ouvrier to be a work of "historical, statistical, and narrative description" rather than one of "theory" or a "treatise in economic science." But Cummings also maintained that the subject of economic production and productivity demanded a scientific approach and that Levasseur's "unrefined mass of data" did not quite meet scientific standards.[71] Nevertheless, the veracity of the figures aside, and even if they were not the first, Levasseur's calculations marked a crucial step in the development of national economic statistics. They furthered the notion of a unified economy whose boundaries overlapped with the "imagined" territorial boundaries of the nation, and whose gross, aggregate production – and productivity – was meaningful and measurable.[72] Moreover, they reinforced the idea that it was necessary to keep track of these large figures in order to govern the economy and the nation properly and efficiently.

Thus, L'Ouvrier Americain touches on each of the two ruptures and each of the three themes that opened this chapter. It marks one further step towards seeing productivity as something statistically measurable and meaningful in aggregate form; it draws the concepts of prosperity and competitiveness into a powerful conceptual network with productivity; it draws the eye to the productivity of labour – the "workman" – and away from other inputs like capital and technology; and it works, through the tabulation and classification of numerical data, within the framework of the nation.

Nation-Building, Statistics, and Productivity

L'Ouvrier was but one notable manifestation of a wider shift in the way governments related to their citizens. As historical sociologist Bruce Curtis has shown in his research on Royal Commissions in Canada, prior to the nineteenth century, the numerical data drawn on or gathered by the Dominion government were limited to "inventory-making": simple counts and categorizations of people, places, and things, a mode of statistics exemplified by early censuses and church registers. But Curtis shows that leading up to and after Confederation – that is, in the country's transition from a collection of colonies to a nation-state – its engagement with numbers changed: "from the second decade of the 1800s, and with increasing frequency thereafter, the epistemological move from inventory-making to statistical abstraction and the proposition that such abstraction yielded irrefutable facts that should guide policy were well in evidence."[73]

Indeed, by the time Levasseur arrived in America to undertake his study, there were already censuses of industry being carried out, albeit in a rather unscientific fashion. In Canada in 1879, the Dominion government passed an act calling for national censuses of population and agriculture every ten years and for one in the prairie provinces every five years. By 1905 it had established a permanent Census and Statistics office in the Department of Agriculture, and passed another act calling for that office to be staffed continuously.[74] Across the Atlantic, by 1907, Britain had conducted its first census measuring economic production, and in 1909 the United States released its own industrial census, which enabled statisticians, including McGill University's A.W. Flux, to make crude comparisons between the two countries.[75] After the first decade of the twentieth century, the collection and analysis of statistics of all kinds intensified rapidly in North America, Europe, and Britain, with most of the national statistical bodies therein racing to keep pace with one another for the sake of international cooperation and competition.

The idea of both cooperation and competition around statistics might seem contradictory, but these modes of relations were two sides of the same coin: national statistical or census bureaux were working in the service of governments that wanted economic growth and the ability to track it in comparison to other countries. They wanted to compete economically and to know how they were faring in the competition. But accurate comparison required standardization – agreement on what and how to measure – and hence these government bodies cooperated with one another to develop international standards and classification systems that have survived to this day.

As others have argued about internationalism in other contexts, such acts of dealing with other countries *as nations in a world composed of nations* (as opposed to empires, for example) had the effect of constructing *an* international – an image of the world as one community – but in the process they also shored up and emphasized national boundaries.[76] Recalling the opening focus of this chapter – the construction of the economy as a "fixed space" whose boundaries conformed to the territorial boundaries of the nation – we can see how intertwined are the three narratives of nation-building, the "discovery" of The Economy, and the expansion of (inter) national statistics. In creating a system of measurement to describe, compare, and forecast the future of national economies, the fledgling statistics bureaux were an integral part of building the territorialized nation-states, the "international community," and the spatially "fixed" economies we know today.[77]

More narrowly, developments in these three narratives also set the parameters for a particular understanding of, and interest in, productivity. Chapter 3 delves into the establishment and evolution of centralized statistics in Canada in the Dominion Bureau of Statistics, using this as a case study of the relationships between statistics, the state, and the evolving productivity concept, and thus the topic will be explored no further here. Suffice it to say that the rapid expansion of state statistical agencies and bureaux, their efforts at international standardization, and the construction of The Economy were crucial, interrelated events in both the process of nation-building at the turn of the century and the pursuit of aggregate productivity indicators, both of which have marked the productivity concept indelibly.

The narratives unfolding thus far represent just the beginning of the story of productivity – indeed, there are other historical and ideational developments that have shaped the concept as much as or more than marginalist economic theory. My reading of events suggests, nonetheless, that these developments are part of the same productivist ideational regime – that the marginalists' language and view of economics makes possible, or at least legitimates, the operationalization of the productivity concept in two other prominent places: the highly influential "scientific management" of Frederick Winslow Taylor, and the human relations school of management. These are the main characters in chapter 2, to which we turn next.

Chapter Two

Managing and Measuring Productivity

Productivity and Industrialization

In the late 1800s the world that marginalist and Marxist theories alike sought to describe and comprehend was changing rapidly. The Industrial Revolution was well under way in North America, Europe, and Great Britain, although the Canadian experience of industrialization was different. As historian Doug Owram put it, the country's "rural and agrarian state" made it "an observer on the fringes of the industrial giants."[1] But it was still fundamentally shaped by industrialization, as firms, factories, and corporations – the latter a brand new development – grew larger, reaching for "market control," becoming "national in scope," squeezing out or buying up competing firms, and making it difficult for small ones to get off the ground.[2]

A Royal Commission on the Relations of Labor and Capital in Canada began in 1886 to investigate earnings, hours, and other working conditions in the new and rapidly growing industrial workplaces and to assess how best to "[improve workers'] material, social, intellectual and moral prosperity, and [develop] the productive industries of the Dominion so as to advance and improve the trade and commerce of Canada."[3] At the same time, debates raged over the right of corporations to merge (in the language of the day, "combine") and the role of the government, especially through tariffs, in preventing monopolies and ensuring true competition.[4] As Owram's work shows, a reform movement, comprised of intellectuals and clergy, began to rise up in response to industrialization's social ills, just as it did in other industrialized nations. Clearly, industrialization mattered both to Canadian politics and to its economic thought. Indeed, the agrarian base of the

Canadian economy during this period did not so much diminish the importance of industry as add an interesting instability to class politics and pluralize political-economic ideologies in the country.[5]

Industrialization nudged the productivity concept in new directions everywhere. For economic theorists the main stage for reflecting on innovation and productivity shifted from measurement and theories of value, and crude considerations of the comparative productivity of different races, to the labour *process* itself, as it unfolded on the production line. Neither economic theory nor the racialist understandings of productivity went away, but the concept became more tightly intertwined with that of efficiency, and more readily associated with technological progress and industrial relations.

In other words, there was a change in who was doing most of the talking about productivity, and why, and to what audience. Once it became taken for granted as a feature of industrial production and a concern for workers, managers, and capitalists – not to mention governments – the productivity concept moved from the halls of the university and the pages of economics and trade journals into the realm of everyday parlance. Several things transpired to make this happen. First, the very impetus behind the "modern multiunit business enterprise" – the corporation – was now to *increase productivity* through "administrative coordination."[6] Second, it quickly became clear that old ways of managing employees were not easily scaled up to fit these new, larger workplaces; from the employer's perspective, *proper* management was all the more crucial in bigger firms because they had higher overhead costs. If capitalists and employers wanted to make increasingly high profits, they needed to produce goods as efficiently as possible.[7] Granted, making production efficient was not an entirely new concern. As Roediger and Esch remind us, these new, management-focused industrial models in the United States descended from earlier plantation models of production, and operated on many of the same assumptions about race and productivity.[8]

But perhaps more important than the rise of corporations, and changes in management strategies to adjust to these new organizational forms, was that in the last decades of the nineteenth century, economic growth slowed – no longer did it promise to be boundless. Certainly, the late 1800s in Canada and the United States saw rapid and sustained economic expansion. But compared to the initial spike and spread of economic activity during most of the 1800s, especially after the protectionist National Policy "created a spurt of industrialization in

central Canada and the Maritimes during the 1880s," near the turn of
the century it appeared as if economic expansion was losing momentum.[9] And it was. "Manufacturing growth was unusually slow" in
Canada in the 1890s, and per annum growth rates in the United States
shrank between 1870 and 1899.[10] More importantly, capitalists of the
period were crying out about falling prices, erroneously connecting
them to falling profits.[11] There were a variety of reasons given for the
slowdown, from "patterns of investment, production and employment
peculiar to the post (Civil) war era," to a more widespread failure of
consumption to keep up with increased production in the right sectors.[12]
Whatever the cause, the problem of "economic 'retardation'" seemed to
demand new ways of organizing production and distributing the gains
among workers and employers.[13] It would no longer be enough for businesses to just squeeze out competing firms or create more demand for
products.

Meanwhile, the threat of labour unrest from increasingly powerful
unions meant it would not be easy to simply slash workers' wages in an
effort to cut costs. When relatively "cheap" immigrant labour dropped
during the First World War, employers could no longer "drive" their
employees to work hard without getting some kickback; as at least one
economist argued, non-immigrant workers, more skilled and less desperate, would not submit to such brute force.[14] A different approach
was needed. But it couldn't be the divide-and-conquer strategy of pit-
ting workers of different origins against one another, because the war
had effectively turned off the unending flow of potential labourers
from other countries (just as laws restricting immigration would do,
again, in 1924).[15]

According to James Livingston, a near-consensus emerged that
the "solution" to "economic 'retardation'" hinged on owners and
employers taking "*control* of the supply side" and "accelerat[ing]
the pace of mechanization at the point of production, because that
meant abolishing the high labor costs associated with craft skill."[16]
But workers and their union representatives caught on early to the
potentially devastating and displacing effects of mechanization, so
even this apparent solution needed to be implemented subtly and
carefully in order to circumvent resistance from a well-organized
workforce. Governments, including Canada's, thus became nearly
obsessed with how to ensure "harmonious relations" between workers
and employers, as anything else appeared to threaten economic
growth, national wealth, and productivity.

Scientific Management and Productivity

Enter Frederick Winslow Taylor. His life and work unfolded in America, and from there, his ideas spread, first-hand and through like minds, throughout North America and Europe. The son of wealthy Pennsylvania Quakers, Taylor had worked his way up from labourer to chief engineer at the Midvale Steele Company in the 1880s. There he developed the now famous system at the heart of his 1911 *Principles of Scientific Management*. For Taylor, "wastes of human effort" were "greater than [the] waste of material things," which had already "stirred" the United States "deeply."[17] Although then-president Theodore Roosevelt had named productivity – going by the name of "national efficiency" – as a chief concern, Taylor saw no concerted governmental effort to bring it about.[18]

For him, the problem was that employers were placing too much emphasis on finding the "right" worker – the "better, more competent ... ready-made ... man" – when their goal should be "systematically cooperating to train and to make this competent man" through "systematic management ... resting on clearly defined laws, rules, and principles."[19] In emphasizing the design of systems and workflows over and above the management of individual, often racial characteristics, Taylor shifted the focus of discussion from the worker's inherent, racially determined productivity potential towards the components – time and motion – of the labour process itself. As will be shown below, his ideas and the wider movement they represented would shape the way the world thought about productivity and its relationship to prosperity for over a century; they would come to be embedded by the productivist ideational regime.

Taylor's timing was propitious. Momentum had been building for decades; he had been working on *Scientific Management* for thirty years, and he was not alone in applying a scientific method to the problem of industrial productivity.[20] By the time his book was finally published, it was the Progressive Era in America, and in many spheres of life, science was king and *reform* was its kingdom. Social scientists were suddenly at the forefront of efforts to solve "the poverty problem," gathering data through community surveys and "join[ing] research with reform."[21] Meanwhile, the US government was increasingly drawing on "experts" from the social sciences to assist in its foreign diplomacy, particularly around conflict (such as in the Venezuela Boundary Dispute of 1895 and, later on, in the peace talks following the First World War).[22] Expertise from the new "scientific" economists was transforming the economy generally; the profession was growing into an international community built on marginalist principles, one that also championed, in its darker moments, "eugenic approaches to social and economic reform."[23]

All of these various realms of expertise had a common problem: the industrialized world seemed a more chaotic place than the pre-industrial world, and the goal of governments, business owners, and various other authorities was to organize it. But, as other historians have shown, these were *liberal* governments and reformers whose very identities had been forged in opposition to authoritarianism, and as such they were wary of appearing to exercise anything other than the will of the people.[24] Thus, any organizing had to abide by principles that no one could argue with, and the scientific rationality offered by Taylor and others appeared to offer these "objective" and "rational" qualities. Granted, liberal reformers were not the only ones reaching for scientific methods to rationalize and improve economic production. As Roediger and Esch have shown, pro-slavery businessmen were making crude attempts at quantifying the productivity of workers and developing management strategies on the basis of "ethnological" knowledge about racial differences in, for example, levels of submission to authority.[25] Still, the connection between liberalism and science – especially social science – is well supported in the historiography of this period.[26]

Even more pertinent for Taylor's work than the government's use of scientific experts in economics and diplomacy was the more diffuse "efficiency movement" that was sweeping through everything from government to library cataloguing systems, from dressmaking and cooking to housecleaning.[27] Although Taylor is sometimes credited with beginning this obsession – referred to variously as the "productivity movement," the "management movement," the "efficiency craze," and, in Janice Gross Stein's more recent work, the "cult of efficiency" – it was well under way by the time *Scientific Management* was published.[28]

While the "principal object" of Taylor's management approach was maximizing *prosperity* for both employer and employee, he argued that "prospering" for employees was as much about achieving "maximum efficiency" as it was about wages. Here again is the nascent productivist assumption that recurs across time and place in reflections on the industrial economy: that increasing productivity means, *ipso facto*, increasing prosperity for worker and employer alike.

Unfortunately for the employees at the Midvale Steel Company, most of Taylor's energies were devoted to maximizing efficiency – extracting the most productive work out of each working hour – and not to designing the mechanisms through which employee wages would increase along with their output. For him, increased wages were just a logical consequence of increased efficiency, and he trusted that the world was a logical place in which

> the greatest prosperity can exist only when [the] individual has reached his highest state of efficiency; that is, when he is turning out his largest daily output. The truth of this fact is also perfectly clear in the case of two men working together. To illustrate: if you and your workman have become so skilful that you and he together are making two pairs of shoes in a day, while your competitor and his workman are making only one pair, it is clear that after selling your two pairs of shoes you can pay your workman much higher wages than your competitor who produces only one pair of shoes is able to pay his man, and that there will still be enough money left over for you to have a larger profit than your competitor.[29]

The word "can" – in "can pay your workman" – is key. Taylor did not dwell on what would actually motivate an employer to pay more than a competitor; he merely assumed that it would be wise to do so in order to retain the employee one had just trained. He also banked on a reasonable employee with a justified sense of entitlement: as "the true interests of the two [employer and employee] are one and the same ... prosperity for the employer cannot exist through a long term of years unless it is accompanied by prosperity for the employee, and *vice versa.*"[30] Thus, he explained, "workmen will not submit to ... more rigid standardization and will not work extra hard, unless they receive extra pay for doing it."[31]

Accordingly, a pillar of scientific management was its system of pay incentives, which were to be tied to productivity through target-setting and close monitoring, and paid out in the form of either daily bonuses or "differential piece rates" that increased with output. However, Taylor maintained that such bonuses and wage increases had to be capped at the scientifically determined level of 60 per cent of starting wages, even if there was more than a 60 per cent increase in output.[32] He defended this figure on two fronts: first, he argued that his experiments proved that if workers "receive much more than a 60 per cent increase in wages, any of them will work irregularly and tend to become more or less shiftless, extravagant, and dissipated ... in other words ... it does not do for most men to get rich too fast."[33] Second, in a nod to demand-side economics, he argued that at least some of the fruits of increased efficiency should be given to the consumer through lower prices, thereby offering "the greatest gain" of increased efficiency to "the third great party": "the whole people – the consumer."[34]

Taylor's understanding of incentives was grounded in some common assumptions about the connection between productivity and the interests of employers and employees. Although he did not take up the theories or concepts of John Bates Clark and his interlocutors, Taylor was still playing on the same discursive field – in Somers's terminology, the same "conceptual network" that would soon be implanted in the productivist ideational regime.[35] The guiding assumption in Taylor's time was that capitalists, workers, and consumers should, or naturally would, benefit from increasing productivity, in the form of higher profits, higher wages, and lower prices, respectively. However, largely *because* of Taylor's ideas, the world that had inspired them was changing. Another party was entering the production process, taking a position somewhere between the employer and the worker: the manager.

Scientific Management and Managerialism

Roediger and Esch are not the only historians who see Taylorism as far more than the pursuit of standardized and scientific production. James Livingston's history of corporations in America embeds the "scientific method" within a larger narrative about the rise of "managerialism" – that is, the reorganization of relations between workers and employers, and ultimately workers' loss of control over the labour process itself. In this broader context, Taylor's method was not just "compulsive clockwork"; it was "the original manifesto of the managerial revolution."[36]

The managerial revolution was philosopher James Burnham's term for the invention and rise of a new "managerial class" between employers and capitalists. So positioned, managers were not like labourers because they did not actually produce things, but they were also not like capitalists because they did not own the means of production. However, they did *control* the means of production, and for Burnham, this placed them among the "ruling elite" along with capitalists and business owners. Burnham traced the managerial revolution to some time around the First World War, but there is convincing evidence – for example, compiled in Chandler's 1977 *The Visible Hand* – that it was well under way before then.[37]

One early indication of managerial thinking was the emergence, around the turn of the century, of administrative "best practices" literature in trade journals that had previously focused on "techno-logical and commercial" content. During this period, as sociologist Leland Jenks has shown, "value judgments characterizing particular procedures as 'good' or 'scientific' rapidly appeared. So did the notion of 'standards,' a term carried over from technical practice with a new range of meanings. The very language in which systems were described increasingly carried the overtones of quasi-professional sanction."[38]

Taylor would have read these journals, and thus he was not the first to put pen to paper about "scientific" approaches to management and administration. But he was among the first to take part in a conversation about management *per se*.[39] Jenks, writing in 1960, argued that this shift in trade literature was part of an emerging "consensus" "that business management should be the object of deliberate inquiry and that stand-ards are ascertainable by which management practice may be judged."[40] Managers, engineers, administrators, and even labourers were awak-ened to the possibility of, and the need for, "self-scrutiny." In other words, Taylor's experiments had come about during a period of new-found "self-consciousness" on the part of managers who, like Taylor, were largely engineers by trade at that time. They were self-conscious not in the sense that they were anxious about their existence and role, but in the sense that they were *reflexive* about what they were doing and how they could do it best.[41] Soon, they went so far as to refer to their approach as a "gospel," presenting it to the world as "an approach to vexing problems of labor relations, a weapon of international competi-tion, [and] a remedy for the sins of waste. It was the way of science, the purposeful promotion of the processes of social evolution."[42]

By the middle of the twentieth century they would find themselves part of a new profession that specialized in management as a distinct set of normalized practices – a profession widely regarded as guarantors of productivity and efficiency in industry and as a first line of defence against socialism. Engineers were suddenly serving as advisers in the highest levels of government, bringing with them an intriguing combi-nation of interests and beliefs, about management, scientific expertise, efficiency, and productivity.[43]

Taylor might be one of the best remembered industrial engineers from the early days of that burgeoning profession, but another industrial fig-ure was competing for attention at the same time. By the time *Principles* was published in 1911, Henry Ford's motor company had been crank-ing out Model T cars for almost three years. The "moving assembly line" for which Ford is famous was not in operation until 1913, but in these first few years of the Ford Motor Company the administrative and managerial groundwork for that technology was being laid. Ford "devised ... administrative systems that tied sales to production; and ensured that materials and labour were allocated 'just in time.'" He hired more than a thousand clerks to manage this up-to-the-minute information, and he integrated "white collar" managers, armed with gauges and pencils and clipboards to monitor productivity, into the production process on the shop floor. He even relied on a "Sociological Department" to assess, based on productivity and morality, which employees should receive the company's signature five dollars a day.[44]

Yet Ford and his top managers were adamant that they "owed nothing to Taylorism"; none were "'acquainted with [his] theories'" at all. The Ford assembly line, by most accounts, had been inspired by the system used for slaughtering, eviscerating, and packaging pigs in the Chicago stockyards. So Ford and his management team need not have studied Taylor's theories to be part of the same "experimental search for efficiency [that] was the *lingua franca* of all American engineers."[45] The scientific refinement and standardization of the physical aspects of automobile production – right down to the assignment of shorter men to tasks on the car's undercarriage – and the mental, data-driven managerial tasks were all examples of what Jenks calls "deliberate thinking about management," driven by an interest in understanding and maximizing "the specific productivity of labour."[46] Experimenting with comparative measures of costs and efficiency across firms, Taylor, Ford, and countless engineers presaged the more complex statistical measures of productivity that were yet to emerge.[47] But the links between the productivity concept, managerialism, and scientific management run far deeper than that. The explanation that follows now will seem like a digression at first, but it will lead back to productivity. Here we go.

James Livingston's work highlights how the establishment of management as a legitimate and valued component in industrial production depended on an additional factor: the separation of craft knowledge from craft skill. Not coincidentally, this separation was one of scientific management's most important achievements. The first step in finding the most efficient (i.e., productive) workflows, after all, was to appropriate extant knowledge and try to streamline it – to take it out of the messy, ad hoc "oral tradition" of craftsmen, standardize it, and consolidate it in the training manuals of a new stratum of managers. (Taylor's contemporaries and followers did not explicitly seek to extinguish unions; however, given that craft knowledge was one of labour's most valuable bargaining chips, this discursive split between knowledge and skill was a huge threat to organized labour.[48]) This is what Livingston means when he calls Taylorism "more than ... compulsive clockwork." The method is about capturing power.[49] Only by stripping workers of their seemingly irreplaceable *skill* could employers and managers wrest control of the labour process from them.

Doing so was partly a matter of mechanization, as is well-documented in such tracts as Braverman's *Labour and Monopoly Capital*, but it was also about severing the apprentice and craft traditions and installing managers to control the introduction and training of new workers with the employer's interests in mind. Most importantly for my purposes, *nearly all of this reorganization was done in the name of productivity and "sold" to everyone outside the ruling elite as a means of increasing prosperity*. It would gain adherents over the first half of the twentieth century because it fit so well within the dominant productivist ideational regime; by mid-century, it aligned with *common sense*. As the case studies in this book show, the link between productivity and prosperity was and still is a public relations campaign as much as a scientific truth.

Productivity and the Personal Relation

By 1914, three years after the publication of *Scientific Management*, Taylor's model would be tested in conditions far more complex than those of the workplaces in his experiments. That year marked the beginning of the First World War and the rise of American and Canadian hysteria over socialist and communist "threats" from abroad. It was also, not coincidentally, a bumper year for labour unrest in the United States, a pivotal moment in the managerial revolution, and a formative period for the productivity concept.

A year earlier, on 23 September 1913, coal workers at the Colorado Fuel and Iron Company (CF&I) had launched what would become a bloody two-year strike that would lead to a collaboration between an American business baron and a future Canadian prime minister. The coal workers' union wanted recognition, and it wanted to free its workers from control by the company town and store. It also wanted the removal of the armed "Camp Guards" that the company had hired immediately after the union began recruiting in 1913. John D. Rockefeller, then the owner of CF&I, would have had plenty of other business owners to commiserate with about his employees' insubordination. The unrest at his company was at the front end of a wider, worldwide movement for an eight-hour workday, during a period when the first challenge most unions faced was getting recognized as legitimate representative bodies by employers who refused to hear or negotiate with them.

But the Colorado Coal Strike was a brutal fulcrum point, punctuated by several bloody skirmishes, the worst of which took place on 20 April 1914 in what came to be known as the Ludlow Massacre. Camp Guards opened fire on a miners' celebration, and the miners retaliated. The guards fled but returned with the Colorado National Guard, raining bullets on the encampment of striking miners and their families and finally setting the camp ablaze. As many as twenty-five men, women, and children burned or suffocated to death in their tents in this incident alone. More than seventy-five would be killed over the course of the strike.[50]

Critics of scientific management, labour-saving technology, and other purported means of increasing productivity had warned of the potentially dire consequences of speeding up and standardizing production. They fell into two camps: the emerging "behaviourists," foremost among them Hugo Munsterberg, worried that scientific management ignored the human and psychological aspects of work; the unionists objected to the method because it deepened exploitation and threatened craft skill. Neither camp normally predicted violence on the scale of the Colorado massacre; they merely cautioned, in Marxist fashion, that work that had once been solitary craft – a source of pride and personal satisfaction – became alienating and oppressive on the assembly line. Scariest for employers, critics argued that alienation would damage worker morale and lead to lower productivity – especially once workers started to kick back.

These warnings confronted employers with a conundrum. Scientific management and technological advance had promised them *greater* control over their workforces and production. But, as Braverman would argue in 1974, Taylor's method was "representative of management masquerading in the trappings of science," doomed to fail because it set out to *manage* "a refractory work force in a setting of antagonistic social relations" without figuring out why such antagonism existed in the first place.[51] Yet the Colorado strike was not a response to scientific management *per se*; it appears to have been about much more than alienation. Histories of the preceding decade offer ample insight into the specific and extreme conditions that enabled such devastating events: miners who spoke out against the CF&I Company were "sent 'down the canyon' (blacklisted) or 'kangarooed' (beaten up)"[52]; the company was known to have interfered with workers' voting in elections; miners complained about being forced to shop at the company store; and working conditions in general were dangerous, but the company was almost never held accountable for worker deaths or injuries.[53]

As extreme as these events might have been, the animosity and unrest in Colorado is but one especially brutal thread in a larger, less (physically) violent narrative of industrialization and corporatization, one that entailed the steady separation of employers and employees, and of craft skill and craft knowledge. This narrative is also about the growing recognition that none of the parties to industry could afford to neglect the human element – the "personal relation" – if they wanted to improve and maintain productivity. No matter how much of the production process was carried out by machines or divided into smaller tasks among increasingly specialized employees, no matter how much "market share" a single firm could gobble up as it grew, no matter how expendable the average, "unskilled" worker might have seemed, business would grind to a halt if workers were not treated like human beings. Thus the human capacity to resist domination presented a threat to the whole developing productivist agenda. To keep producing more and more things, workers had to believe they would benefit and that they were an important and autonomous part of the production process. They had to want their employers' businesses to grow and rake in increasing profits.

Even Rockefeller, who still refused to recognize the Colorado union after the strike came to its murderous end, eventually acknowledged the need to improve employer–employee relations. But in a move of astonishing stubbornness, instead of acquiescing to the union, he turned to William Lyon Mackenzie King for an alternative in 1914. Mackenzie King, a politically ambitious industrial consultant who would become Canada's tenth prime minister in 1921, designed for Rockefeller an industrial representation plan (IRP). The plan involved a "company union" meant to improve industrial relations while avoiding actual worker-led unions. He touted his IRP as a way to "improve productivity (and control costs)" through a "cooperative" model without ceding to unions or resorting to the increasingly popular Fordist approach of higher wages.[54] The IRP became a model of "employer–employee relations ... for nearly two decades in the early part of the 20th century."

In a later study funded by the Rockefeller Foundation and published in 1918, Mackenzie King would argue that technological advances in industry had enhanced productivity but altered relations between labour and capital, leading each to misunderstand and fear the other. He believed that the interests of the two, although they *appeared* to be opposed, were actually the same. Labour and capital could and should therefore cooperate, and Mackenzie King felt they could do this best under the "guiding genius of management."[55] He contended that the way to increase productivity was not solely through technology or generalized speed-up. Rather, it was to install or expand a group of highly skilled people – people with "managerial ability" – between manual labourers and business owners.[56] As Livingston's analysis makes clear, in *both* Taylor and Mackenzie King's approaches, managers did more than monitor performance and waste; they served an important additional function in consolidating and standardizing craft knowledge. Especially in the context of the IRP, they were the ever-present human face mediating between capital and labour.[57] Management, conceived as this omniscient, omnipresent, and arbitrating middleman, was the core idea in Mackenzie King's "'human relations' brand of industrial psychology."[58]

The term "human relations" is more widely associated with Elton Mayo and the Hawthorne studies of the 1930s than with Mackenzie King. However, it was long before Mayo's studies – during Taylor's heyday, in fact – that academics, the new "industrial psychologists," and businessmen, including the political and business elite in Canada, began to realize that happy workers might just be more productive workers.[59] Thus, before introducing Mayo and Hawthorne, it is worth highlighting some of the ideas that foreshadowed both.

The First World War and the Interwar Years

The same year the Colorado coal workers launched their strike – 1913 – Hugo Munsterberg published *Psychology and Industrial Efficiency*, a book now widely regarded as a foundational text in industrial psychology and as a forebear of human relations studies. In it, Munsterberg praised Taylor for introducing "most valuable suggestions which the industrial world cannot afford to ignore" and called his method "revolutionary." But he argued that it was insufficient because it did not pay enough attention to the psychological make-up of the individual worker. In Munsterberg's vision, industrial psychological knowledge could inform everything from the selection of the right worker for the right job, to the right management strategies to elicit peak "productiveness" from those workers.[60] Elton Mayo would adapt this vision in the 1920s, in the industrial experiments normally credited with launching the human relations approach.

But the seeds of the human relations perspective are plainly evident in Rockefeller's Founder's Day Address from 1917, three years after the Ludlow Massacre and several years before Mayo began his experiments. In that speech, titled "The Personal Relation in Industry," Rockefeller remarked that "every human being responds more quickly to love and sympathy than to the exercise of authority and the display of distrust." Unfortunately, he surmised, business owners had come to "regard labor as their legitimate prey, from whom they are justified in getting all they can for as little as may be," and labour had come to feel "that it was justified in wresting everything possible from capital."[61]

This point was partly a nod to the capitalist class's mounting anxiety that labour unrest in the industrial West was a product of socialist desires – that it reflected a political-ideological battle over the social order as much as a fight over specific working conditions and wages. Although Rockefeller admitted that capitalists had to take some of the blame for recent strife, he did not accept that their role was inherently exploitative as the socialists and Marxists would have it. Rather, he contended that business owners had become too distant from their businesses, too invisible in the process. In contrast to the early days of industry, many of today's bosses did not actually *see* their employees, a situation that was "inevitable" but "deplorable" and that was causing a "great" and "ever widening" chasm between employer and employee. Rockefeller assured his audience that this gap was not a product of inherently opposing interests, but was a physical, emotional distance that could be shrunk with the right attitudes.

This was a popular interpretation of recent events. In Rockefeller's America and in Canada, employers and government officials, and some labour leaders, were peddling "industrial peace," "cooperation," and "harmony" as the way of the future. In 1918 a leading member of the Canadian Manufacturers' Association (CMA), John Willison, who was also leader of the newly formed pro-tariff group the Canadian Reconstruction Association (CRA), remarked on the sad state of affairs where the "workman goes in and out of these huge establishments, a stranger to the manager and ignorant, often, of the very names of the boards of directors." In "such conditions," he surmised, "the organization of labor is natural and necessary and occasional misunderstanding and conflict are inevitable." But this was not to endorse unions – those, employers recognized only in "extreme cases." Instead, Willison and his associations "advocated a basic change in employers' attitudes and policies" towards "a spirit of mutual good-will and cooperation."[62]

So, foreshadowing many of the political leaders and business people who appear later in history and in this book, Rockefeller in his Founder's Day Address urged cooperation; employers and employees needed to be assured that their interests were the same, as was their goal: greater productivity.[63] The productivity formula was simple: first came the establishment or restoration of "the personal relation" – regular, sympathetic contact between employers and employees – which would make workers happier and more content. Then, because happier employees were (apparently) more productive employees, productivity would rise. Finally, rising productivity would mean cheaper goods, and thus greater purchasing power for workers, and higher and more secure profits for employers.

The possibility that labourers might work so hard they put themselves out of work (i.e., that supply would outpace demand) was countered by the argument that goods would be infinitely *more* in demand the cheaper they got. This formula for productivity has appeared repeatedly in the relatively short life of the concept, in various forms, for various purposes, with small adjustments here and there, from early economic thought to today's.[64] This is not to say that it has gone unchallenged, as the final chapter will show. But in Rockefeller's moment, the formula served as a guiding assumption in the movement towards a more managerial form of industrial production.

The benefits of increased productivity and efficiency were touted by other prominent people in the public sphere, on both sides of the Canada–US border. For most of these interlocutors, effective *management* and "expert advice," although these were arguably part of the scientific management that had caused so much industrial strife, were the keys to increasing productivity and efficiency. O.D. Skelton, a Queen's University political economist turned public servant and, later, Mackenzie King's adviser, and C.D. Howe, a long-serving and highly influential Liberal cabinet minister, were among the prominent voices calling for more expert management in economic affairs and promoting "managerial skill" in Canadian business from the interwar era to the postwar period. Such skill, Howe once said, suffered from a worse "shortage" in his country than resources or money.[65]

And this rising interest in productivity was not confined to industry and business schools (which were then brand new); it cropped up as well in government, university social science departments, and even the household chores of ordinary people.[66] The United States and other liberal democratic governments, once ostensibly judged by their "honesty" and "goodness," began in the first decades of the twentieth century to emphasize their "efficiency" and "economy" instead. Administrative structures, staffed by "professionals" and hived off from elected officials, proliferated under the guiding assumption that "political neutrality guaranteed efficiency, and efficiency legitimized political neutrality."[67] Public policy was increasingly evaluated in the economic terms of inputs and outputs, the language of productivity squeezing out alternative discourses that defined value in qualitative, non-monetary terms.

Regarding universities, Marlene Shore writes that the "desire to create 'human efficiency'" spurred growth in the social sciences in Canada – specifically, it strengthened the disciplines of social work and sociology at McGill University. The director of that school's Department of Social Work in 1918, John Howard Toynbee Falk, "like many people of his generation ... believed that the only way in which [a] new society would come into being was through economic productivity and human efficiency." For Falk and his circle, those two factors depended on "increased production and the right relations between capital and labour." Just as Mackenzie King would argue in *Industry and Humanity*, Falk believed "that economic growth and a wider distribution of wealth and goods would mitigate the potential for class conflict."[68] This, of course, is the main support beam of productivism.

There was a dark side to Falk's belief – much like the dark side of many aspects of and arguments for economic growth. As Shore explains, "because Falk placed such faith in economic productivity, he could not help but see the impoverished, the handicapped, the sick, and the imprisoned as anything other than parasites. 'We are apt to overlook the fact,' he said, 'that every person in poverty, hospital or gaol is not only a consumer but also a non-producer,' and as such 'a direct loss to the nation.'"[69]

Falk thought that his discipline of social work could "facilitate economic productivity by restoring the maladjusted to productive states"; helping the impoverished was thus a matter of advancing "the material prosperity of the nation," not the moral duty spurring the Social Gospel and social reform movements.[70] The extent to which productivism underpins social science and social work, historically and today, is an empirical question worth pursuing further. But for what it is worth, Shore argues that elsewhere in the university the "impulses" of reform movements "were channelled into institutional and scientific pursuits." The halls of academia echoed with "a widespread conviction that ... productivity would ensure national and international stability" and that "industrial efficiency would solve all social ills."[71]

Those "social ills" included the social worker's objects – the poor, sick, and "idle" – but also "the labour problem" and the threat of socialism. As management historian Ellen S. O'Connor has documented, business schools such as the one established at Harvard in 1908 were funded by "CEOs seeking to find a way to resolve industrial conflict without jeopardizing their status as the central locus of organizational authority."[72] Capitalists looked for ways to take back some of the territory ceded to labour out of necessity during the war and, buying into a pervasive faith in scientific solutions to social problems, funnelled money into the young business schools to support their industrial research.

Productivity and the Human Relations "School"

Perhaps the best-known industrial research from this period revolved around Mayo's Hawthorne studies, based at the fledgling Harvard Business School. The studies were a series of experiments, conducted at an electrical factory in a Chicago suburb, that sought to test the impact of working conditions on labour productivity. Industrial production had expanded rapidly during the war, but it did not fully reverse when war ended and was now, according to Mayo, "staggering" to "support the burden of demand." He piqued to the fact that "no one had ever sufficiently considered the enormous demand upon industry that would be exercised by a war-machine organized upon so heroic a scale ... Nor had anyone considered the effect of the strenuous and sustained exertion imposed upon those who worked to provide supplies."[73] The "failure" in industry was not due, he said, to "ignorance of the mechanics of production," but rather "to ignorance of the human conditions of sustained production" and "the primary laws governing human efficiency."[74] It was this ignorance that Mayo sought to correct through his experiments.

A look at Mayo's writing suggests he was driven by something other than concern for people's well-being at work; he cared most about productivity (especially that of the factory worker), and "human conditions" were a means to a productivist end. He and his team, installed in the electrical factory, conducted interviews with employees and managers and watched what happened when small changes were made to the working environment and workflows. What they found – not surprisingly from our contemporary vantage point – was that working conditions, from the adequacy of overhead lighting and the division of labour to the frequency and quality of social interaction, had effects on employee productivity. Contrary to the orthodox, rational-choice economists of his day, Mayo interpreted his findings to mean that humans, especially workers, were irrational, emotion-driven "savages" and "primitives" struggling to adapt to industrial life and its order. He blamed this failure to adapt, along with the "industrial fatigue" brought on by the kind of monotonous work encouraged under Taylorism, for stagnant or falling industrial productivity and for the "reveries" of socialism, Bolshevism, and even Syndicalism.

Mayo argued that it was the manager's job to "calm the worker's irrational, agitation-prone mind." He demonstrated that workers who were not just calmed but praised, allowed to socialize, and offered regular breaks and small incentives for good work, were more *productive* as well as less susceptible to socialist coercion.[75] Critics would later hypothesize (and in some cases prove) that the mere presence and attention of industrial researchers had the effect of increasing worker output.[76] Still, the point remained that workers who were attended to, and who felt that their personal contributions to production were noticed, were more productive as well as more adaptable to the existing socio-economic order. A link had been made, seemingly once and for all, between industrial productivity and what we might loosely refer to as job satisfaction, providing an important empirical foundation for the developing human relations school.

Support for and interest in the human relations perspective was building during the interwar years, in different, mutually reinforcing quarters: the Hawthorne studies appealed to "business and academic elites" looking "for ways to address threats to the political and economic order," and they also helped legitimize business schools in universities.[77] Still, as others have pointed out, it was not until well after the Second World War that Mayo, the Hawthorne studies, and the human relations school were counted as "a significant contribution" or a "school of thought" in the field of management studies.[78] Until then, management textbooks had tended to emphasize scientific management as the defining feature of their discipline, sidelining the "human" and "personal" questions addressed by the human relations approach (and the New Deal more broadly).[79] Taylor's work, then, controlled the field when it came to defining productivity from the early 1900s through to the Second World War.

None of this should suggest, however, that human relations existed across some great temporal or ideational chasm from scientific management, as is often presented in surface histories of management. The two schools of thought had plenty in common, and there was significant overlap in their development. Taylor was never too concerned about his exemplary worker "Schmidt's" feelings, and he *did* liken human labourers to oxen, but he was not ignorant of the need for management to design and ensure a labour process or "task system" that at least *appeared* to be in the worker's "own best interests."[80] He understood that "the average workman must be able to measure what he has accomplished and clearly see his reward at the end of each day if he is to do his best," and he maintained that people needed "proper encouragement either in the form of personal attention ... or an actual reward."[81] He also underscored the benefits of "the most friendly relations ... between management and the employes [*sic*]."[82] Munsterberg's *Industrial Psychology*, far from being a great leap away from Taylor, was an attempt to inflect scientific management with psychological knowledge. That Mayo followed in Munsterberg's "behaviourist" footsteps suggests that human relations was built on foundations that included scientific management.

Indeed, many of Taylor's interlocutors in the engineering trade journals of the day were similarly insistent on the need for "sympathetic management" that instilled "self-respect" among workers; they believed that workers' homes and communities needed to be "healthy" in order for them to be productive.[83] They recognized that "standardization had consequences for the individuals involved," and they "worried about the survival of discretion and initiative" under scientific management.[84] In other words, Taylor and his ilk believed that the success of scientific management depended on recognition of the tenets of what would later be called human relations. No doubt it was these types of continuities that led Braverman, in his critique of the labour process under "monopoly capital," to urge a rereading of the presumed "progression" from Taylorism to human relations in management.[85]

In Braverman's view, the field of management was comprised on the one hand of those theories, practices, and professions concerned with "the fundamentals of the organization of the labor process and of control over it" – as Taylor had been – and on the other hand, those concerned with "the adjustment of the worker to the ongoing production process as that process was designed by the industrial engineer." The two sides were simultaneous and in many ways complementary. Historians drawing a single straight line from early to contemporary iterations of management were as misguided as those who sought a distinct rupture. The reality was messier than that. "The successors to Taylor are to be found in engineering and work design, and in top management," Braverman argued, whereas "the successors to Munsterberg and Mayo are to be found in personnel departments and schools of industrial psychology and sociology."[86]

To these I would add two more threads that connect scientific management with human relations, challenging the view that the latter represents a complete departure from or improvement upon the former. The first is productivism. Both believed that the point of effective management was to increase productivity, which was a good thing in and of itself *and* – especially in Taylor's case – would solve humanity's problems and eventually eliminate any strife between workers and employers. The second thread is one of the three themes that recur throughout the productivity concept's history. Specifically, both scientific management and human relations directed attention to labour productivity over and above the productivity (theorized, measured, or assumed) of any other factor of production (e.g., capital). This legacy has made management's primary objective the maximization of *labour* productivity – but it has also influenced and bolstered wider, pervasive discourses about work.

Specifically, my reading of events, from the adoption of Taylorist principles in industrial workplaces to the Hawthorne experiments, strongly suggests that the emphasis on worker productivity in both scientific management and human relations thinking has influenced the way productivity is framed in the minds of business owners, managers, governments, and ordinary people to this day. Moreover, the focus on labour productivity characteristic of the last century, combined with the influence of workers' unions and concerns about labour unrest in the period following the First World War, helped give rise to the field we now know as human resources. The latter is not to be confused with human relations; human resources is concerned with the proper management of labour *as a resource* – as a *supply* of workers who should be employed according to *demand* for their skills, in the most efficient and sensible manner, with the right people with the right training doing the right jobs. The objective of human resources, be it at the level of a single firm or an entire country (as is the case in the Canadian government department formerly known as Human Resources Development Canada), is to ensure that there are no labour or skills shortages, with the view that "effective human-resource development policies" – and not, for example, government interference in capital investments – "are basic to economic growth and productivity."[87]

In large part, the influence and spread of these labour-centric ideas stems from their simplicity – their proximity to the commonsense understandings of productivity in the *Wealth of Nations* and earlier economic thought. There are other ways to boost productivity and stoke an economy to grow – which many recognized in the early 1900s – but directing discussions of productivity towards how much product an individual worker can churn out in the course of an hour is just *easier* than comprehending how varying amounts and forms of capital, technology, materials, and labour power can combine to affect the total output of a business or industry. This is how ideational regimes work – they make the lives of certain ideas easy.

Once the productivity of capital had been established in economic theory, the question of how productive it was or how it could be made *more* productive was pushed aside, and all of the attention focused on the productivity of labour. The question that must follow this observation is *cui bono?* Who benefits? Whose interests are furthered when productivity is understood primarily as a quality of labour, and when efforts to manipulate productivity are directed at workers rather than capital investment? The answer is historically contingent, and the development of aggregate productivity statistics, starting in Taylor's time, illustrates this well.

Productivity and the National Economy

The productivity concept articulated by Mayo, Taylor, Rockefeller, and Mackenzie King is different in two major respects from earlier iterations in economic thought and theory. First, although the concept evolving in the early twentieth century did not subscribe explicitly to the labour theory of value, it was a concept attached almost exclusively to labour – the worker – in isolation from other factors of production. Second, productivity was considered alterable rather than fixed, with much of the talk about it arising out of an explicit desire to maximize it rather than to formulate it theoretically. But apart from these two distinctions, discussions of productivity from the 1900s to the 1930s, whether under the banner of human relations, scientific management,

or industrial psychology, focused on the same scale as before: the individual firm, factory, or shop floor. Comparative studies (e.g., firm x vs.
firm y) were in vogue, but apart from vague considerations of "national
efficiency," few devoted serious study to the measurement, assessment, or manipulation of productivity at the level of entire industries or
national economies. Productivity and productivism were ideas without
much empirical, quantitative content.

But while the industrial engineers and psychologists were busy
designing workflows and management practices to boost labour productivity, statisticians and economists in the university and government
were toiling to build – or at least urgently asking for – a statistics-
gathering apparatus to measure economic production at greater and
greater scales. In terms of the central narrative of this book, these institutions were working towards two of the shifts outlined in the introduction: the first away from abstract, theoretical, or commonsense notions
of productivity and towards its precise empirical measurement; and the
second from measuring the productivity of isolated processes and firms
to measuring the aggregate productivity of The Economy.

By the time of the industrial psychologists, demand for better statistics at greater scales had been mounting for a century. Archivist Meyer
Fishbein's history of the US Censuses of Manufactures reveals that as
early as 1809, political representatives, legislators, and academics in
the country were complaining that the manufacturing and industrial
statistics available to them were unreliable and incomplete. In 1818, US
Democratic-Republican representative Adam Seybert famously compiled all of the economic data scattered throughout all the Congressional Records to date into a single volume titled *Statistical Annals*, and
lamented in the introduction that the figures therein were likely full
of errors, inadequacies, and underestimations. He was also possibly
the first to go on record to suggest what is now common sense: that
censuses of manufacturing ought to use a standardized questionnaire
in all establishments in order to create comparable data.[88] But progress
was slow. By 1839, rudimentary attempts at aggregate measures were
beginning to emerge – and the notion of aggregate data was suggested
as a way of assuring confidentiality – but remarkably, there was still
no serious discussion of data collection methods. In fact it was not
until 1878 that the US Census Superintendent (then noted economist
Francis Amasa Walker) gave any thought to the qualifications of the
people collecting the data, asking that they be "specialists" rather than
laypeople.[89]

Walker was also one of the first in North America to envision "a comprehensive inventory of the Nation," although his first attempt at one cost so much time and money that he began to worry it would never be possible.[90] Still, he maintained that an improved census "cannot fail to be of great value to a rapidly growing nation ... a work worthy of the nation and the age."[91] Even the 1890 census, also taken on Walker's watch, was subject to scathing criticism by professors of statistics, then a relatively new discipline in American universities. But after 1890, things improved as census data "came under even more careful scrutiny by economists, statisticians, and sociologists." Also, thanks to better standardization, there was "less variance in their content from census to census."[92]

Canada would follow, a few steps behind, but the gap between the countries in terms of statistical activity would not narrow much until the twentieth century. It is worth noting that in the first few decades of the 1800s, the land we now call Canada was several dispersed, fledgling British colonies spread out over thousands of miles between more heavily populated port cities (e.g., Halifax). But by the time it turned its attention to measuring industry and population, it was evidently taking more cues from the United States than from its British rulers. Thus, even though much has been written about the influence of British institutions on Canadian government in general, the history of national statistics in the United States is more revealing of and important to their history in Canada.[93]

Nevertheless, European and British census-taking – or at least the institutionalization thereof – advanced faster than in North America. The people routinely credited with "inventing" state statistics in the eighteenth century came from Germany and Scotland. Francis Amasa Walker sought support from European statisticians, using their reviews of his work to boost his requests to Congress for more resources and attention to be directed to his office. Europe and Britain saw the birth of statistics-focused institutions, such as the Royal Statistical Society, several years before similar bodies were established across the Atlantic. From the archival records of statistical bureaux in Canada and the United States, it is clear that the leading statisticians in both countries hoped to "catch up" to developments overseas. In addition, they dwelled on the need for coordination moving forward, so that cross-country statistical comparisons could be made. Progress on this front, too, was slow. As will be shown in the Canadian context in the next chapter, it took decades for the statistical bureaux established at the turn of the twentieth century to grow into the centralized, hierarchical national bodies they are today, and just as long for these same bureaux to develop the capacity to routinely collect industrial and economic data in a comprehensive, standardized manner.

And so, in a 1924 article comparing labour costs and productivity ("product per man") in the United States and abroad, the Harvard economist F.W. Taussig bemoaned that data were *still* imperfect and hard to come by. The best he could do was use figures "collected from scattered sources" and from any "material that happened to come under my observation," and present them "in the hope that others who have made similar observations may be able to enlarge the collection and add to its significance."[94] Taussig wanted to see data collected in a manner better suited for analyses of productivity specifically; he pointed out that the "accountant's figures" available to him at the time were recorded in dollars rather than labour hours, the latter being more suitable, he said, for measuring productivity. He pushed ahead with the dollar figures and offered a few conclusions – that "the effectiveness of labor in the United States is greater than in any other country" in coal production, for example – but he did so timidly, and with the recurring caveats that cross-country comparisons were very complex, and the data available too rudimentary.[95]

By this time, other academics were also pointing to the difficulty of moving from theories of productivity and value (including John Bates Clark's) to actual measurement.[96] They complained that the few statistics available at the time, including the industry-specific labour productivity numbers released by the US Bureau of Labour Statistics in its Monthly Labour Review since 1915, were only of limited use to economists looking to do their own comparative analyses of productivity.[97]

In the late 1920s, the pressure to improve these and other productivity statistics was also mounting outside academic circles as the productivity concept moved to the heart of several high-profile debates over wages and working conditions. Early "equal pay for equal work" advocates were beginning to argue for gender parity in wages on the basis of labour productivity.[98] Economic and philosophical tracts on "the labour problem" burgeoned, and the labour movement (including the American Federation of Labor) launched what would be a long-standing campaign for wages to be linked to productivity gains.[99] Both the parties making these claims to surplus value and their detractors alike knew that the legitimacy of their positions depended on their empiricism and objectivity, which in turn depended on their access to reliable data.

Momentum around the collection of explicitly *national* productivity statistics was also slowly building during this period, as national governments sought control of economies and societies thrown into disorder by the First World War, in a global context that seemed newly complex and integrated. The confluence of these events and assumptions is a straightforward example of one of the three major themes introduced near the beginning of this chapter – the connection between nation-building and the expansion of official statistics. Governments had to perform a delicate dance; conditions appeared to demand more coordinated and informed planning, but calling it "planning" stirred some controversy because the word had strong socialist connotations.[100] Even so, it was clear in most quarters that the prewar economic order had been transformed, and that policy and legislative responses to the new situation had to be coordinated at the national or federal level. There was a widespread belief that such responses should be guided by statistics, and productivity statistics in particular – a conviction that speaks to the embedding power of the productivist ideational regime. But the limitations identified by Taussig and others had not yet been addressed, and the validity of extant productivity statistics was still frequently called into question; hence, demand continued to grow for better, centrally coordinated and standardized data.

In Australia, the need for reliable productivity statistics in particular came to the fore in an influential court case over a proposed reduction of the standard workweek from forty-eight hours to forty-four. Arguments for and against the reduction revolved around productivity, and both sides appealed to the productivist belief in the necessity of economic growth. Those opposed to the reduction worried that productivity would fall, or that individual workmen would have to work too hard to keep it from falling in a shortened workweek. Those in favour argued that employees with more leisure time would be more productive workers when they were on the clock (and better citizens when they were off). They felt it was up to employers to figure out how to use scientific management and better machinery to keep productivity high. Productivity statistics were submitted to the court to argue against the reduction, but the judges were concerned that they were inaccurate.[101] In the end, the workweek was reduced.

Apart from their utility for specific policy questions such as the standard workweek, productivity statistics were also in demand for the empirical flesh they could put on the bones of a discourse only just coming into wide use: that of "competitiveness" between countries and their economies. At first, academic discussions of international competitiveness revolved around the relative efficiency of *single* industries in different countries. The 1920s saw a spike in this type of study, with increasing numbers of scholarly articles and books employing the concept of "comparative advantage" – an idea that had been in limited circulation since at least *The Wealth of Nations* – to study the costs of production in the same industry in different locales.[102] Studies comparing the productivity of entire national economies were almost non-existent.

In part, this is because there simply was no notion of a singular, territorialized economy to provide the boundaries for what we now know as "aggregate" measures of productivity. The productivist ideational regime had not yet absorbed the concept of The Economy because the latter had not yet been "discovered." The dearth of explicitly national productivity statistics makes sense given Mitchell's observation that it took "at least two decades, from the mid-1930s to the mid-1950s, for the economy to come to be understood as a self-evident totality."[103] As is clear from even a cursory reading of popular North American media, the phrase "the economy," even during the Great Depression (a period we now describe confidently as a downturn in "the economy"), was rarely used. When it was, it referred more often to the practice of balancing savings and expenditures rather than to the territorialized "space" of the national economy.[104]

Indeed, the phrase "Canadian economy" does not appear anywhere in the 8 million English-language books digitized by Google Books until 1930, at which point it increases in frequency, rising most sharply around 1940, 1960, and 1980.[105] Accordingly, while there was some interest in "national efficiency" among economists, government technocrats, and politicos before 1930, they did not take *the* national economy as their referent. The "national" aspect was vague, more piecemeal, and certainly not informed by any statistical measurement of all inputs and outputs in all production nationwide.[106] Although many professional economists writing in academic journals at the turn of the century envisioned a day when such measurement might be possible, the tools and capacity to actually collect data at a higher level than the individual firm were still, even thirty years later, embryonic at best.

Still, by the 1930s, a change was under way in the academic and popular imagination of the economy. Economists began to develop statistical methods and concepts that would eventually "fix" the economy to the nation and legitimize the view that the two were overlapping and even synonymous. Late in the decade, the collection and use of statistical data by and for both business and government took off galloping, with a decided emphasis (discussed in later chapters) on data that were "complete," "comprehensive," and "standardized" – words that really meant "encompassing all economic activity inside the territorial borders of the nation."[107] This is not to say that no one spoke of provincial or regional economies. The case studies in this book all reveal that the National Economy was understood as a system comprised of smaller economies. But the latter were envisioned as *feeding into* or *drawing from* the National Economy, and the federal government and "regional elites" worked to coordinate economic activity and trade in such a way as to strengthen and benefit the national whole, sometimes against the interests of peripheral provinces.[108]

As the new statistical techniques were developed and spread, productivity was one of a host of concepts subjected to new empirical measurement and imagined on a national scale. Its improvement, and therefore its measurement, became a top priority for governments, their statisticians, and industry leaders. From the 1930s onward, the productivity concept became entrenched in political, economic, and everyday discourse and tied to the intertwined societal and economic goals of prosperity and competitiveness.

As chapter 4 will show, Canada was comparatively late to the game on a number of developments, but it was nevertheless part of an international, largely state-led productivity movement. Working groups on productivity were established inside national statistical agencies, and from the 1940s to the 1960s, "Productivity Councils" popped up in Britain, America, Canada, some European countries, and India.[109] Regional economic disparities in Canada and elsewhere were increasingly blamed on productivity "gaps," and increased productivity became one of the most exciting prospects for futurists everywhere who imagined a world without work. Such optimism, along with the governmental pursuit of *higher* productivity, *more* prosperity, and *better* standards of living, is a rather standard feature of governmentality – of interventions mounted in the interests of the people and towards the general betterment of society – and of a specifically *productivist governmentality*.

Thus, for most of the twentieth century, productivity was considered central to the major economic problems troubling the world, and to their solutions. It was forwarded as an essential foundation for the competitiveness of countries and the prosperity of their people. As the next section shows, it was also highly contested territory, both in the larger and ongoing battle between labour and capital over competing definitions of economic justice, and in the divergent assumptions and claims of Keynesian and (neo)classical economists following the Great Depression. But beneath these disagreements lay a consensus: the belief in the necessity of ever-increasing productivity, the central tenet of the productivist ideational regime.

Productivity, Keynes, and the Great Depression

Productivity's importance as an economic indicator and measure of economic health was constructed by the so-called "Keynesian Revolution" in economics and amplified by the experience of the Depression. Until the latter, the belief that capitalism was a self-regulating system was rarely challenged.[110] In his *General Theory of Employment, Interest, and Money*, published in 1936, British economist John Maynard Keynes showed that the system was vulnerable and imperfect – something that was by then plainly evident given the simultaneous collapse of markets in most corners of the world – and argued that it needed the stabilization of government policy and investment. He took aim at the dominant neoclassical model of economics, arguing that it was not the supply of goods that determined employment levels, but rather the *demand* for goods, and that in order for demand to be sufficient to keep people employed, wages had to be high enough to guarantee workers and their families some discretionary income. Simply put, consumption triggered production and not the other way around.

It should be clear by now that Keynes was still speaking the language of productivism, echoing the demand-side theories of some earlier marginalists. But his contributions still pushed economic thought and government policy in new directions. They overturned the assumptions of supply-side, orthodox economics at a time when the old ways of thinking seemed incapable of describing current events. They opened up the space for others to argue that productivity gains had to be matched by wage gains. In linking consumer spending and discretionary income to economic growth, the *General Theory* legitimated the idea that the national employment rate could be raised or stabilized by tying wages to productivity and, conversely, that unemployment would rise if wages did not keep pace with productivity gains. These arguments – and the desire to test them – were another source of pressure to take stock of national productivity.

But the concept of national productivity at the heart of such arguments pre-dated the tools to actually measure it. Economists both on and outside the new productivity councils, for example, immediately recognized the difficulty of establishing a standard "unit 1" or base unit of production that could then be tallied across industries to give a total for the entire nation. Industries had unique units of measurement to reflect their unique products, and standardizing those units would be a conceptual and logistical nightmare. In the United States, the National Income statistics already in use by the National Bureau of Economic Research were of little help, as they included not just the value of goods produced, but also things like the potential "net rental value of owned homes" and the *interest* on "consumption goods" – which were especially nonsensical as measures of labour productivity.[111]

Measurement problems multiplied when the aim was to compare across countries. The desire for comparison was there, in the academic journals explored earlier as well as in government departments, but the data were imperfect and were measured differently.[112] Thus, one of the first things the new productivity councils did was set about coordinating and standardizing data collection across countries – an effort that culminated, for example, in the establishment in 1937 of the International Standard Industrial Classification (ISIC) system still in use (albeit modified regularly) to this day.

Productivity "Transformed"

It was a working group in the United States that apparently took the decisive first steps, in the 1930s, towards establishing a measure of *aggregate* productivity – that is, a number that ostensibly represented the productivity of the entire economy, enabling the cross-country comparisons so many economists desired. Their story is important for contextualizing the Canadian ones that follow in the next three chapters, because their work set the discursive, methodological, and institutional parameters for Canada's "initial experiment with Keynesianism in 1938" and subsequent work on productivity statistics.[113] Indeed, although Keynes hailed from Cambridge, England, the history of statistics in the United States is indispensable to the project of documenting and interpreting the development of productivity statistics, and the uptake of Keynes's ideas, in Canada. As a committee of fifteen Canadian government representatives assessing the state of productivity research in the bureaucracy in 1949 readily admitted, "research in productivity historically has been centred in the United States, which has developed the most elaborate techniques, and the most integrated research program to be found anywhere."[114]

How much of this conclusion was based on a careful comparison of activity in all countries around the world, and how much was American exceptionalism, is a valid question for future research. In any case, we return to Block and Burns, introduced at the beginning of this book, and their history of the development of aggregate productivity indices in the United States.

The backdrop for this history was President Franklin D. Roosevelt's New Deal, and specifically the Works Progress Administration (WPA), a body that launched hundreds of make-work projects from the construction of bridges and roads to literary and theatre projects. One such project was the National Research Project on Reemployment Opportunities and Recent Changes in Industrial Techniques (hereafter NRP), established in 1935. Providing work for unemployed statisticians and economists, the NRP was tasked with developing statistical measures that could produce aggregate productivity data – that is, data that could be summed to provide a single indicator of the national economy's productivity.

The Canadian government, "encouraged by popular opinion, was [also] compelled to play a more active role in economic and social life" in the 1930s. In Don Nerbas's interpretation of events, the "capitalist crisis" of the Depression "led to a political crisis" in which "the old political economy" of the National Policy (protectionist tariffs, settlement of the West, and private ownership of railways) was undercut, "and Canada's historic links with Britain – both economic and cultural – dissipated under the strain of continental integration." Even "stiff resistance from the economic elite" in the country could not suppress the movement towards a more interventionist state, led by "intellectuals and politicians operating with newfound authority" in matters of economic management.[115] This new "government generation," as Doug Owram has labelled them, grew from 1900 to 1940 and especially under Mackenzie King's leadership in the 1920s and 1930s, and was comprised mainly of men educated in economics and the social sciences. Statistics, and the new National Accounts in particular, thus played a central role in securing and legitimating their influence.[116]

Beyond the general context of government expansion, Block and Burns argue that the NRP's establishment and mandate were made possible by the convergence of two prior developments: first, "the development of a systematic framework of national income accounting as a means to provide the government with the key data necessary to pursue an activist economic policy"; and second, the "underconsumptionist analysis of the causes of the Great Depression."[117] The underconsumptionist argument, a productivist one based largely on Keynes's theories, held that when productivity rose, as it did in the lead-up to the Depression, businesses had to either reinvest their increased profits in capital (expand operations, bring in new machinery, and hire more people) or hand the benefits on to worker-consumers in the form of cheaper goods and/or higher wages. If they saved all their profits, the whole system would collapse. Underconsumptionists believed that businesses' failure to reinvest or redistribute the profits from productivity gains had brought on the Depression and ensured "the continuing high rates of unemployment" thereafter.[118] Fittingly, some argued for cheaper products to remedy the situation, others for wage gains. Both faced the same limitation: they lacked solid empirical proof that productivity gains had actually outpaced capital investment, wages, and consumption. (Some even blamed the lack of statistics for the severity of the Depression itself – had the state been monitoring output, presumably it could have intervened.) The availability of national income statistics greased the wheels for the development of the productivity statistics the underconsumptionist camp needed, but there was yet more work to be done.

Fortunately for the underconsumptionist camp, the Roosevelt administration had everything to gain by supporting this work. After all, the New Deal's massive injection of government money was driven by the same logic: that economic growth (the ultimate goal) depended on the expansion of production and a healthy level of consumption, the latter being dependent on above-subsistence wages. In a sense, as Block and Burns put it, the NRP's mandate was essentially to justify its own existence.

And that it did. Its chief statistician, Harry Magdoff (notably, a Marxist), spearheaded the creation of complex weighting schemes and other "systematic methods for developing cross-industry measures of changes in hourly [labour] productivity."[119] One of the most important things the NRP economists did was base their analyses on physical output measures instead of dollar figures, the latter being the standard at the time. In so doing, they confronted a new problem – how to establish a standard common measure of physical output across diverse industries – but they avoided the more complicated problem of monetary deflation, which had plagued other contemporary measurement schemes.

After the NRP folded during a period of departmental reorganization in 1939, other economists took up its physical output–based approach. But within a decade, advances made in the calculation of National

Income would lure economists and statisticians back to using dollar values to measure output. As Block and Burns recount, a National Income Division was established within the Department of Commerce, "committing the government to the preparation of current estimates of national income and product." The regular publication of those estimates – the gross national product or GNP – from 1947 onward made it possible for anyone skilled in statistics to calculate productivity trends without worrying about deflation, and without "the arduous work of linking together physical output indexes from a wide variety of industries."[120] Thus, the NRP's lasting influence was not its particular methods, but rather its legitimation or validation of the *idea* of aggregate labour productivity.

To say that this idea had staying power is an understatement. Subsequent statistical work would establish the "total" or "multi-factor" productivity indicators that take capital and technology inputs into account alongside labour inputs, but as Block and Burns point out, such "measures have played less of a role in policy debates and public discussions than the simpler measures of labor productivity."[121] Total-factor or multi-factor productivity (TFP or MFP) is a measure of whatever change in productivity cannot be accounted for by changes in labour and/or capital inputs. In other words, it is a measure of a *residual*. Economists have generally interpreted the residual as a reflection of technological improvements, but admit that this is somewhat of a cop-out. As economists Jorgenson and Griliches joked in 1967, TFP amounts to "the Measure of Our Ignorance."[122] As a number, it is simply a calculation of the proportion of productivity growth that the model does not explain.

The technical differences between TFP, MFP, and labour productivity are significant, but not terribly important for the discursive and cultural analysis presented here. What matters – and it matters *a lot* – is what productivity stands for in public and political discourse, and in that regard, not much has changed since the NRP. Despite the availability of more complex measures, productivity is still associated first with how hard or efficiently we are working. In the case studies that follow in this book, the people and institutions concerned with measuring, understanding, or improving productivity are usually thinking primarily about labour productivity. Then as now, those who reference productivity or who worry publicly about productivity gaps and growth rates do not need to be specific about what kind of productivity they mean. Their audiences will fill in the gaps in the language that comes naturally to them, and that language is about *work*. Although experts and elites are often concerned about technology and capital investment, they bring it up with their publics using other terms: "R&D" (research and development), "innovation," and "job creation."

Moreover, the aggregate productivity indicators still used in international comparisons, forecasts, and quarterly updates are labour productivity measures. Statistics Canada, for example, releases quarterly figures for aggregate labour productivity, while estimates of TFP and MFP are released annually and tend to describe sectors separately. It is the frequency and breadth of labour productivity estimates compared to the others that no doubt accounts for their "common sense" quality. TFP and MFP are also far more complex, and more difficult to explain in terms of people's experiences, than labour productivity's notion of how efficiently workers are being used. Moreover, the former are subject to ongoing esoteric debate around accuracy and interpretation, whereas labour productivity is mostly left alone.[123]

In any case, once the NRP put the notion of aggregate labour productivity into the public mind, the National Income accounts made it easier and quicker to calculate. They also obviated the need for economists and statisticians to *think about* what they were measuring – a key factor, say Block and Burns, in productivity's elevation to the status of economic fact. Outside a handful of sceptics and critics (who included Magdoff and others connected to the NRP!), users of the productivity indicators based on the National Income data cared little where their numbers came from or how they were compiled. The "facticity" (or "truthiness," as Stephen Colbert might say) of such convenient, accessible measures was simply accepted.

Following some high-profile negotiations in the auto sector, "productivity bargaining" became a key component of labour relations. Analysts at the time had been calling for "a rational and objective basis for wage determination," and productivity appeared to offer just that, particularly when supported by underconsumptionist logic.[124] Subsequently, through this and later developments in the Kennedy administration that are beyond the scope of this book, "economists, government officials, managers and trade union leaders developed a common interest in acting as though [the BLS's quarterly productivity numbers] were more than what they were – one set of figures for measuring productivity trends among many."[125] Moreover, the ease with which they could now manipulate productivity numbers enabled them to proceed "without a second thought as to what [the indicator] actually measures."[126]

The NRP's former chief statistician, Harry Magdoff, would later lament the "transformation" of productivity "from what was once a clearly defined technical term into the present amorphous catch-all." Block and Burns tie its transformation to "society's need for indicators that are 'objective' and 'scientific'" – a need "so strong as to overwhelm arguments that such indicators have a fragile relationship with the underlying realities that they are supposed to measure."[127] Tracing the public use of aggregate productivity measures from new collective agreements in the 1940s and 1950s (which moved the indicator "from academic and government studies into the policy arena") to the "productivity crisis" of the 1970s, Block and Burns showed that the productivity concept took on a life of its own, with so many interests bound up in defending its "facticity" that "any questions about how the data were actually generated and what they might actually mean" were swiftly and routinely silenced.[128]

The effects of this newly animated productivity concept were felt far beyond Washington. Chapters 3 and 4 offer an in-depth examination of what was happening in Canada from the early 1900s to the postwar period, but a few points are worth mentioning now. The Second World War set many statistical projects in motion, particularly inside the Dominion Bureau of Statistics. Areas such as "manpower accounting" and cost-of-living statistics were elevated to high priority, expanded, and refined in response to an "unprecedented demand for statistics" and the "increased complexity of social and economic problems."[129] The power of productivism as an ideational regime meant that efforts to measure and thereby have some control over economic growth would be already justified and highly prioritized. Just like in the United States, the expansion of the welfare state (including a "New Deal" under Prime Minister R.B. Bennett that was largely ruled unconstitutional), the costs of war, the realignment of "government responsibility" for problems like unemployment and industrialization, and new demands from the United Nations and Canadian government agencies placed unprecedented pressure on the rapidly growing Bureau of Statistics. By 1949, one prominent official in the bureau would emphasize that the government needed "as much knowledge as possible" on productivity if it was to succeed in making the right policies and plans for postwar employment and economic production.[130]

Internationalizing Aggregate Productivity

By most accounts, aggregate productivity analysis in the NRP was several steps ahead of statistical research bodies in other countries from early on. Some movement towards the establishment of an International Sub-Committee on National Income Statistics had taken place within the League of Nations in 1939, but the war's outbreak prohibited any substantial international collaboration until 1945. Individual countries had continued working in relative isolation during the war, and thus several league members had released estimates of National Income – the basis for the dollar-value aggregate labour productivity estimates that would soon become the international standard – by the time the sub-committee reconvened in 1945. In December of that year, representatives from Canada, the United States, Australia, the Netherlands, the United Kingdom, Norway, Mexico, and Switzerland met in Princeton, New Jersey, to consider how to develop national accounting systems that would allow for greater comparability. Productivity *per se* was not on their agenda, but the "social accounting" system they envisioned, along with the path-breaking analytical innovations coming out of the NRP, laid the groundwork for measuring it in an internationally consistent, aggregate form.[131]

It is no coincidence that as the measurement and reporting of national productivity became a routine exercise in most of these countries from the late 1940s onward, the productivity performance of national economies moved to the centre of public discussions of economic strength and competitiveness. These were in some ways the continuation of discussions begun during the "efficiency craze," but with new features – the quarterly productivity figures, and the newly developed measures of GDP and GNP.[132] The goal of *improving* productivity also wormed its way into the mandates of international organizations and international relations programs. For example, around 1950 the International Labour Organization (ILO) began to debate making "productivity" a central focus of its assistance programs. David Morse, then the ILO's director-general, was "pushing" for a productivity focus but encountered resistance both within the ILO and from labour groups outside it. His critics "feared that focusing on productivity could distract the organization from its original mandate, which was to protect workers."[133]

Morse had also championed productivity in his previous job in the Truman administration as Assistant and Under Secretary of Labor. He was instrumental in rolling out the Marshall Plan to help rebuild European economies (and beat back Soviet communism) in 1948, in the wake of the Second World War. The plan was premised on the idea that productivity would be the linchpin of economic recovery in nations crippled by war, and on the belief (borne out by comparatively strong economic performance) that American industry was a model for increasing it. As part of the Marshall Plan, European delegates were invited to American plants to observe production. Footage of their visits shows them peering over factory workers' shoulders, studying the hulking machinery, and scribbling furiously in their notepads, believing that the key to increasing the productivity of firms in their countries was in the process before them. It thus appears that through its influence in the ILO and its stimulation of European economic reconstruction, the United States was leading the world towards a particular understanding of productivity, and particular formulae for measuring and increasing it.

Also on display for European visitors were the fruits of rising prosperity – convincing evidence of the connection between productivity and prosperity. By the 1950s, American workers and their families could afford to own modest houses with lawns in the new suburbs, cars to drive from home to work, and labour-saving appliances of all kinds. Americans and their political spokespeople attributed their excellent quality of life and economic growth to none other than high productivity and the capital investment, machinery, and skills that made it possible. Thanks in part to the productivity bargaining begun in the 1930s and 1940s, during the lifetime of the NRP, workers' wages had indeed followed productivity gains in the national economy. As a host of other factors strengthened the positive relationship between productivity and individual prosperity – strong, export-driven economic growth, weak economies elsewhere, steady business investment and expansion, and an entrenched gender division of labour – the challenge to "the power of big business" that had been so strong during the lead-up to the war dissipated. As Brick has argued, in the United States, liberals' "confidence in modest Keynesian measures, wariness of 'statism,' retreat before postwar conservatism ... embrace of cold war anti-communism, [and] fear of red-baiting" impelled them to drop much of their emphasis on the reform of "economic institutions" and to focus on "social needs." Thus, American and likely Canadian advocates were caught with their backs turned when wages, Western economic dominance, and the other favourable conditions began to deteriorate or stagnate, along with both productivity and labour's share of the national income.[134] Although they were amplified and curtailed in different ways, these trends unfolded on both sides of the Canada–US border from the mid-1960s through the 1980s. Their effects – encapsulated well by the concept of neoliberalism – continue to this day.

Productivity and Neoliberalism

Economist Jim Stanford, writing in 2014, summarized Canada's transition from a robust postwar economy of strong growth, rising living standards, and an increasing "social wage," through the low-growth, high-unemployment, high-interest "stagflation" of the 1980s, to the austerity agenda of the last few years. At the beginning of that narrative, average real wages and productivity gains (measured by the type of indicator first developed in the NRP) were strongly positively correlated, the former rising in step with the latter. But in the 1970s, during what was widely known as "the productivity crisis," the two began to part ways. By all accounts, they have continued to grow further apart to this day.[135] As Stanford explains:

> In the latter years of the postwar expansion, Canada progressed both economically and socially. Living standards were improving quickly for most – fuelled by rising real wages (which doubled in a generation) and a dramatic expansion of the social wage ... This expansionary postwar "golden age" eventually ran up against its own internal limits and contradictions. As in other advanced capitalist countries, the happy recipe of strong profits and business investment, rising living standards, and Keynesian welfare-state fine-tuning, began to disintegrate ... As workers were empowered by long-run employment and income security, their expectations [grew], sparking increasing conflict with the interests of capitalist employers in maintaining a compliant, disciplined, low-cost workforce. A confident working class won a larger and larger share of the economic pie: in Canada, the labour share of GDP grew steadily through the postwar era, peaking in the late 1970s. Even worse for employers, workers demanded changes in the workplace, and in society, that constrained the freedom and power of business. The expansion of an interventionist state meant rising taxes and stronger regulations. Internationally, national liberation movements curtailed capitalism's geographic scope. Most importantly, business investment – the underlying engine of the postwar expansion – slowed appreciably.[136]

In Stanford's reading of events, "elites (in both the financial and the real spheres of the economy)" – backed into a corner by intensifying state intervention, powerful unions, and the standards they set even for the non-unionized workforce – found "a multi-faceted, deliberate, global strategy by [which] to turn the whole ship around" in neoliberalism.

I cannot avoid a description of neoliberalism here, but I will keep it brief. According to David Harvey, one of its foremost critics, neoliberalism is "in the first instance a theory of political economic practices that proposes that human well-being can best be advanced by liberating individual entrepreneurial freedoms and skills within an institutional framework characterized by strong private property rights, free markets, and free trade." Accordingly, neoliberal states see it as their responsibility to "create and preserve an institutional framework appropriate to such practices" – which involves developing the mechanisms to protect private property, "guarantee ... the quality and integrity of money" through inflation-controlling monetary policy, and "create" markets where previously there had been only public goods and services. Anything beyond these measures is seen as "intervention," and interventionism is, supposedly, the antithesis of neoliberalism.

The reader wishing to understand more about this can consult Harvey's *Brief History of Neoliberalism*.[137] For now, two things matter. First, neoliberalism is just one brand of productivism. According to Serge Latouche, one of productivism's greatest critics, "all modern regimes have been productivist: republics, dictatorships, authoritarian systems, no matter whether they were liberal, socialist, populist, social-liberal, social-democratic, centrist, radical or communist. They all assumed that economic growth was the unquestionable cornerstone of their systems."[138] Thus, neoliberalism needs to be understood as an ideology that is embedded, today, *within* a productivist ideational regime. The second thing that matters, for my purposes, is that Canada's "transition" to neoliberal governance is the backdrop for developments from the postwar era to the present in how productivity is conceptualized, manipulated, and measured, as well as what those measurements have claimed to tell us about our economic performance. But neoliberalism also makes the productivist connection between productivity and prosperity – previously presumed to be natural or inevitable, and supported coincidentally by empirical evidence – increasingly untenable. Contrary to what its proponents imagine, neoliberal policy, particularly the "implementation of Canada–US free trade" in 1989, has not improved Canadian aggregate productivity, nor has it brought increased wealth to most Canadian workers. Instead, as Stanford shows, productivity and real incomes here grew rapidly after the war – faster than in the United States, in fact – but after we signed on to the FTA in 1989, the situation almost reversed. He explains:

> Macroeconomic stagnation, weak capital spending, a chronic lack of initiative and innovation on the part of most Canadian business, and more

recently the growing dominance of resource extraction (which normally experiences falling productivity over time, as more accessible reserves are depleted) have produced a sustained downturn in relative Canadian productivity through-out the neoliberal era. Incredibly, relative productivity in Canada is now lower (compared to the US) than it was in 1950. Canada's great "catch-up" has been completely undone.[139]

Other factors, within and outside Canada, have contributed to this decline. Records of parliamentary debate and public discussion from 1964 suggest a general anxiety about structural or technological unemployment – caused by the "substitution of capital [including labour-saving machinery] for [human] labor" – and a weak position in international markets. Persistent unemployment was being exacerbated by "overpriced Canadian commodities, the productive inefficiency of Canadian manufacturing, trading deficits, and balance of payments problems."[140] Other economies in Europe, in part aided by the Marshall Plan, began to recover and even outperform after relatively weak performance in the immediate postwar period. Later, the OPEC crisis of 1973 sowed havoc in Canada and the United States, and then the globalization of capital simultaneously intensified Canada's dependence on big, multinational businesses and made that dependence all the more tenuous.

Through the 1980s and 1990s it became clear that capital could now move in ways that it formerly could not, and despite widespread protests from civil society, attention turned to creating inviting "climates" for business and investment (which often meant reducing tariffs and taxes and other regulations) to entice them to stay put. Neoliberal economic theory supported these measures, which supposedly were tantamount to loosening the state's grip on economic matters *and* to growing the economy. But just as Stanford tells it, measures introduced in the name of driving up productivity and strengthening economic growth did the opposite. As one prominent Canadian economist recalled of free trade and other neoliberal policies: "Had you told me at the time where this revolution would have gone, I would have called you insane. But it happened. And productivity growth weakened."[141]

Neoliberalism has arguably started to rot productivism from the inside out. That its policies – sold by and to decision-makers as a way of spurring productivity growth – failed to achieve their stated objectives is one compelling explanation for why, since the 1990s, the productivity concept has occupied an ambiguous space, increasingly crowded by other economic concepts gaining popularity – competitiveness being one of the foremost examples. The latter is not a new idea. Contemporary historians have traced it, for example, to John Rae's political economy, and its emphasis on innovation and invention. In Rae's work, what would today be called "R&D" is the engine of endogenous economic growth and the source of might in international competition. Productivity, specifically that which derives from invention and innovation, is thus intertwined with competitiveness from the earliest theories of both.[142]

It is worth noting that competitiveness is, like productivity, a contentious idea, especially insofar as it is held up as a condition for higher living standards. Economist Paul Krugman, one of the few voices speaking against the concept, has called it "a dangerous obsession." As he wrote in 1994, "it is simply not the case that the world's leading nations are to any important degree in economic competition with each other ... The growing obsession in most advanced nations with international competitiveness should be seen, not as a well-founded concern, but as a view held in the face of overwhelming contrary evidence."[143] Instead, Krugman argues that living standards within a nation are determined largely by "domestic" factors, not international trade. Yet despite a dearth of evidence connecting competitiveness to prosperity, the idea of competitiveness wins people over because it is simple to understand. And it convinces the kind of people who have money and therefore power and influence. Competitiveness "derives much of its attractiveness from its seeming comprehensibility," he writes. "Tell a group of businessmen that a country is like a corporation writ large, and you give them the comfort of feeling that they already understand the basics."[144]

Lately, the productivity concept has ceded some of its limelight to competitiveness, the latter becoming "the new buzzword" in government and business the world over.[145] In my view, the decoupling of workers' incomes and aggregate productivity from the 1970s onward undermined one of productivity's most attractive features, as both a political discourse and a stated political goal: its ability to convince working people and citizens that policies implemented to boost productivity would translate into prosperity for them.

Indeed, there is growing scepticism about the benefits of higher productivity. Continuing the critique started by Braverman in the 1970s, contemporary writers and labour activists have equated increasing productivity with "speed-up" – the acceleration of productive output without any concomitant increases in pay – and have pointed to the divergence of productivity gains and income growth, as well as to the disturbing phenomenon of the "jobless recovery" following the global economic recession of 2008.[146] Even among businesses, there has been a decided de-emphasis on firm-level productivity, as factors like market share and valuation have proven to be better indicators of corporate profit and CEO pay. In niche markets, it can even make sense to keep productivity *down*.[147] In some respects, then, productivity has lost some of its purchase as a governmentality; it no longer carries the strong incentives necessary for the "conduct of conduct."

Against these odds, productivity has not lost *all* of its power in political discourse and public opinion, nor has it become irrelevant as a subject of economic analyses. Such analyses have increasingly come to focus on the impact of exports, education, and demographics (especially aging populations) on productivity growth.[148] Meanwhile, in public opinion and political debate, despite all of the counter-evidence, the notion that rising productivity is automatically good for everyone – or that it can trigger stagnant or slow-growth economies to boom again – persists, despite a spreading recognition that the very machines and technologies introduced in the name of increasing productivity have, by their very existence, the potential to displace or more accurately *replace* human workers.[149]

Instead of being dispensed with entirely, the productivity concept has been kept around, by economists, politicians, bureaucrats, and business leaders, with a caveat: rising productivity does not *necessarily* mean better lives for everybody, but achieving the latter is impossible without the former. In other words, the door only swings one way. Don Drummond conveyed this shift in productivity's importance as follows: "To be sure, productivity growth does not ensure higher wages or greater happiness. But try achieving either or both without productivity growth. Productivity growth at least provides hope and choices to a society. How society uses its spoils is another matter."[150]

We have seen, then, a revision in productivist logic. Productivity no longer promises prosperity; rather, productivity holds prosperity hostage. The disintegration of the old productivity–prosperity connection has not kept banks or governments, think tanks or capitalists, from reminding their publics about the stubborn "productivity gaps" between or within countries. Alongside quarterly job creation and employment figures, productivity indicators have remained steadily employed as weathervanes in the drawn-out, post-recession recovery since 2008. But they have not gone unquestioned.

In December 2012, economists Erwin Diewert and Emily Yu released a paper that claimed to show that Canada's national statistics agency, Statistics Canada, had underestimated the country's multi-factor productivity growth for decades.[151] The basis of their claim was that Statistics Canada's estimates of capital input growth were too high, leading the agency to *under*estimate multi-factor productivity growth. (Recall that multi-factor productivity is estimated as the "residual" growth left over once capital and labour inputs are accounted for. If capital inputs are overestimated, there is less residual left over to explain, and thus less to attribute to multi-factor productivity.)[152]

Statistics Canada economist Wulong Gu issued a rebuttal almost immediately, pointing out four reasons for the discrepancy between official estimates of capital and multi-factor growth and those computed by Diewert and Yu.[153] His defence, briefly: the two approaches measure capital inputs at different *levels*, they adopt different methods of computing the *price* of capital inputs, they involve different levels of *detail*, and, finally, the Statistics Canada approach follows "international guidelines" in producing its estimates, primarily in order to maintain comparability with other countries.

What is so curious about this event in the history of the productivity concept is that it barely registered. Statistics Canada and Gu certainly took it seriously: Diewert and Yu's criticisms threatened to invalidate years of economic analysis and conclusions, and perhaps even the policies designed to respond to the trends such analyses claimed to reveal. But beyond this exchange, which made second-page headlines at best, it was business as usual. Methodological debates seem to continue to fizzle out, dampened by the same "facticity" of productivity indicators that Block and Burns pointed out in the aftermath of the NRP.

The three case studies that immediately follow offer different vantage points on the question of *why* productivity means so much to us even though we do not really know what it means. In the establishment of the Dominion Bureau of Statistics – Statistics Canada's predecessor – in 1918, in the National Productivity Council in 1960, and in the shifting mandate of the Atlantic Canada Opportunities Agency, there are compelling hints that productivity's *moral* and *political* connotations matter more than its empirical make-up – that it functions more, in the language of governmentality, as a technique for government than as a piece of factual information (although its technical efficacy depends on it *behaving* like a fact). It is, of course, not alone in this; there are myriad other numbers and indices, many of them found in the same economic theories and forecasts as productivity, whose normative make-up is as important as, or more important than, their empirical data. Analysing productivity in this manner should be one step in a longer journey. Nevertheless, drawing on the sociology of concept formation introduced earlier, we can see the concept of productivity as an *idea with causal power*, as a concept embedded in a particular metanarrative of The Economy, over and above its existence as a number.

Chapter Three

The Dominion Bureau of Statistics

It is often claimed that productivity growth raises living standards. But how does this actually come about? The most direct way in which productivity improvements benefit people is by raising their real incomes. If higher productivity means lower costs and these savings are passed on in lower prices, consumers will be able to purchase goods and services more cheaply. The increased spending that these higher real incomes allow produces flow-on effects throughout the economy.

Statistics Canada, Canadian Productivity Review, 2008[1]

Measuring Productivity in Canada

The productivity indices developed and published by Canada's national statistical agency rarely make headlines by themselves. The tickers and tables on the websites and in the Business sections of the top national Canadian newspapers (the *Globe and Mail*, the *National Post*, and the *Toronto Star*) are occupied by other numbers: sometimes GDP, CPI, and interest rates, but more often the stark black and red figures representing the movements of the TSX, the Dow Jones, and various other stock markets. It appears that the products and services we produce and consume and the conditions under which we do so are less newsworthy than activities on the trading floor, even though the former affect more people at a more basic level than the latter.

The "Economy" sections of these major newspapers are sub-sections of the larger, more encompassing "Business" or "Financial" sections – an empirical inversion that, while by no means *new*, speaks complicated volumes about the way we think about how production, consumption, income, and wealth are related to one another.[2]

But productivity is not absent from mainstream reportage – not in the least. It may rarely be the central focus of an article – unless there is a marked rise or fall in productivity from one quarter to the next, or a noteworthy "productivity gap." And it is almost always the year-over-year percentage change that is reported and not the actual productivity level, probably because the latter would not be meaningful to the average reader; ordinary people cannot tell the difference between a good productivity number and a bad one, but they can infer that an increase is good and a decrease is bad. In any case, the official labour productivity numbers released each quarter by Statistics Canada are frequently reported as contextual factors in other stories – drawn into more engrossing narratives (detailed below) about shorter workdays in other countries or the benefits of stand-up desks and lunchtime workouts – or cited in editorials diagnosing the ills of the Canadian economy. At a more subliminal level, the presumed link between productivity and prosperity permeates stories, theories, and conversations that do not, on surface, appear to have much to do with productivity at all.

A popular angle in mainstream media and smaller independent websites alike in 2015 was to embed Canadian productivity statistics in articles about working hours in France and Sweden, where two recent events drew international attention. Public servants in the Swedish city of Gothenberg were moved to a six-hour workday without any change in salary, in an experiment begun in the spring of 2014. Around the same time, French employers' federations and workers' unions signed an agreement to ban the use of work e-mail after 6 p.m. Both developments seem to have struck journalists as an opportunity to compare Canadian productivity performance with that of France and Sweden and to assess whether or not similar changes to the organization and boundaries of work were feasible at home.[3]

Periodically, and especially around the annual release of the more complex MFP and TFP numbers (acronyms to be covered further below), bank economists and think tank analysts take to the newspapers to remind readers that Canada "lags" the United States in productivity growth.[4] Their explanations for this persistent gap are many, and even though there is wide agreement around those explanations, solutions to it do not readily present themselves. Some point to Canada's "weak investment" in research and development (R&D) or to Canadian entrepreneurs' lack of the "fire in the belly" that is ostensibly critical to economic growth.[5] Others have pointed to Canada's comparatively larger dependence on natural resources – mainly oil – a sector in which the productivity returns on capital investment are apparently slower to come about.[6] Some urge universities and businesses to form tighter relationships around R&D, while others see weak productivity growth as a sign that the Canadian business tax environment needs to provide more incentives for businesses to set up, stay, and continually invest.[7]

Whatever the exact mix of explanations and solutions, and whatever alternative work arrangements are making waves in other jurisdictions, the productivity concept and aggregate productivity statistics appear in mainstream media – which I am using liberally as a proxy for "public discourse" – in particular and predictable ways. Specifically, productivity and its statistical representations are often found wherever there is discussion of (a) reorganizing work and (b) national (and sometimes provincial) economic competitiveness. These are two separate but occasionally overlapping conversations. In those rarer instances where productivity's importance or relevance is explained directly, it is almost always in terms of its relationship to prosperity – that is, standard of living.

Block and Burns's observations about the "facticity" or taken-for-granted status of productivity, both as an idea and as an accurate, meaningful empirical indicator, ring true. Productivity is not an *argument* made in the public or political arena; it has already been established. Rather, it is used as *evidence* for other arguments. And whether its users stay in the conceptual realm, get technical and cite numerical data, or simply *recite* general truths established through decades of quarterly data releases and related commentary, the productivity concept we encounter in the public record is made possible by the measurement of labour productivity, MFP, and TFP conducted by Statistics Canada.

This chapter explores how measuring productivity became part of the national statistical agency's mandate. Not everything that can be measured statistically *is* measured statistically, and certainly not four times a year or by an internationally recognized standard. How, then, did productivity become something we measure, and something we *must* measure, as a nation? How did the people who first sought to have it tabulated at the national level understand their own actions, goals, and motivations? What sorts of conflicts, controversies, and disagreements, along with consensuses and hegemonies, emerged around productivity's conceptual definition and empirical measurement? What are the legacies of these early engagements with productivity statistics?

When we examine the life of the DBS in the twentieth century, we see that the productivity concept and statistics in use today began to take shape when industrialized nations, working in cooperation, aggressively centralized the collection of statistics and adopted and refined the practice of national accounting – a new (or newly "scientific" and standardized) technique of government – in the immediate postwar period. That aggregate productivity statistics were born in an economic moment that now appears to be unlike any other before or since – in terms of economic growth, median incomes, and income equality – is crucial for understanding how a line was drawn from growth through rising productivity to rising prosperity for all, and why that line was so widely accepted as inherently accurate. Seeing how contingent both the line and the productivity concept are on the accidents and actors of history should highlight why our ideas about productivity, and indeed the productivist ideational regime, are worth reflecting on.

Centralization and Control in the DBS

The previous chapter skimmed the surface of the Canadian (and earlier, Dominion) government's adoption of statistics as a tool for governance. In review, the late 1800s approach of "inventory-making" gradually gave way to scientistic "statistical abstraction" around the turn of the twentieth century, when calls for periodic censuses of population and agriculture were written into law. The first decades of the twentieth century were a busy time for national statistics in Canada, and a time of increasing centralization in the collection, analysis, and dissemination of statistics.

A Census and Statistics Office, first set up inside the Department of Agriculture, was permanently staffed by 1910 and moved into the Department of Commerce in 1912. That same year, a Departmental Commission on the Official Statistics of Canada was called together to study and advise the government on how to transform its existing "hodge-podge" of official statistics into an integrated, efficient *system* of data collection and analysis.[8] Around that time, the British government set up a different Royal Commission to study matters of trade and commerce within and across the British Empire (or more accurately the British Dominions – Australia, South Africa, Newfoundland, and Canada).

The two commissions overlapped in some interesting ways. The trade and commerce minister at the time, George Foster, initiated the Departmental Commission and was also named the Canadian representative to the Royal Commission. But more importantly, while the

Departmental Commission was set up to focus on statistical matters, and the Royal Commission was meant to study trade, the two ended up converging on a mutual concern with economic (specifically trade and production) statistics. The Departmental Commission urged that, in light of the "recent growth of international trade and intercourse," statistics had to be gathered in such a way as to facilitate "true comparisons between Canada and other countries."[9] One of the Departmental Commission's main recommendations was, relatedly, that the collection of industrial statistics – which at the time was a sub-project of the population census – be carried out separately thereafter. This would increase not only the comprehensiveness and quality of industrial production statistics, but also the frequency with which they were gathered and shared. As a "rapidly expanding country," the Departmental Commission argued, Canada could not get by on figures taken only every ten years.[10] The Royal Commission, meanwhile, found the lack of coordination and standardization in the collection of trade data across the British Dominions to be a major problem.

By the outbreak of the First World War in 1914, the Departmental Commission had wrapped up its work and released its final report. The Royal Commission was still going, and its concerns were both altered and amplified by the social and economic upheaval the war had brought. The fighting threatened to completely disrupt and confuse the flows of goods and money within and across empires that were simultaneously breaking into nations. But then again, the trade situation was already in a state of rapid and unprecedented change. Whether one looks at reports from before or after the outbreak of war, one gets the sense that governments were struggling to keep up with the acceleration of production, the intensification of interprovincial and international trade, new alignments of political and economic power, and industrialization in general. All involved in the development of national statistical apparatuses in Canada and abroad appear to have believed that responses to the tumult of the times needed to be based on accurate and comprehensive statistics. And most of them seemed to believe that accuracy and comprehensiveness could best be achieved through centralization. Hence, the Royal Commission recommended a central statistical office for the whole Empire, and the Departmental Commission recommended one for the whole of Canada.[11]

Indeed, the entire story of the DBS in the first half of the twentieth century is one of increasing centralization. As historian Duncan McDowall put it, "if Canada has one abiding claim to statistical fame, it is that the nation has doggedly insisted that the collection and interpretation of its statistics be conducted on a *centralized* basis."[12] From my perspective, centralization (which was certainly not unique to Canada but pursued by its "competitors" as well) was driven by two very apparent motivations. On the one hand, the drive to "bring statistics under official control on a broad basis" after the late 1800s was about increasing *efficiency* within government research by avoiding duplication.[13] On the other, it was about standardization: the creation of "uniform" measures and nomenclature across provinces and, later, international standard terms, definitions, and methods, all with the goal of creating bodies of data, in different departments, provinces, countries, years, and so on, that could be meaningfully compared.

The Departmental Commission hit all these notes – control, efficiency, and standardization – in its final report in 1913, when it recommended the creation of a "central statistical office" to coordinate and unify provincial statistics and an "Interdepartmental Statistical Committee" that would "coordinate with departments" at the federal level. The point of these bodies, according to an unpublished history of the DBS penned by Canada's third Dominion Statistician, Herbert Marshall, was manifold: the "prevention of duplication and of conflicting results"; "better adaptation of statistical materials obtained in one branch to the needs of another"; "uniformity of definitions and methods"; and "supervisions of the various statistical publications with a view to the proper distribution of statistical information."[14]

One cannot read very far into the committee reports, historical monographs, and correspondence in the DBS archives – particularly those produced from 1900 to 1950 – without running into these themes of standardization, uniformity, and efficiency. Thus they were undoubtedly priorities for the newly established bureau, and remained so as it moved through the First World War, the interwar period, the Great Depression, and the Second World War. It was during this same period that the pieces of the statistical, conceptual, and institutional architecture that would eventually support aggregate productivity measurement began to come together. Just as in the American context, a key piece of this architecture was the development of the National Accounts.

"Fanciful Imagination and Prejudice" in the National Accounts

At the time of the Departmental Commission (1912–13), the Census and Statistics Office was collecting a broad but scattershot array of statistics.

Apart from the census of population, this included numbers on production, trade, transportation, labour, migration, and insurance, among others. Such figures were seen as interesting on their own, but they were disjointed and therefore not as useful to government and business as they could be. Different government departments were responsible in an ad hoc manner for each body of data, and there was great and unhelpful variation across the provinces in terms of what information was collected, when, and how. As Canada's third Dominion Statistician, Herbert Marshall, put it, "the whole system lacked overall direction."[15]

Measures and estimates covering the whole Canadian nation were on the horizon – and attempts had been made by British statisticians and economists as early as 1894 – but it would be several decades before Canadian government statisticians had sufficient data, methodological know-how, and epistemological grounds to make a single measure of "national income" or "the national accounts" part of their routine.[16] Perhaps more to the point, it took this long before the government and the country accepted the national income as a meaningful measure of economic activity. Their willingness to accept it had everything to do with their desire, in the 1930s, for a "scientific" confirmation of just how bad the Great Depression was, and similarly scientific evidence that recovery had begun.[17]

Nevertheless, within a year of being created by the Statistics Act of 1918, the Dominion Bureau of Statistics had taken small but important steps towards normalizing the national accounts. Vested with the authority to collect a much broader range of statistics from ordinary people and industry representatives, the bureau began to build "a body of factual data" to support national income estimates.[18] R.H. Coats, Canada's first Dominion Statistician and a pivotal figure in the establishment of the DBS, produced crude estimates of the national income in 1919 for the years 1911 and 1918. But beyond this effort, he was rumoured to have "little interest in or understanding of national income accounts" during his tenure.[19] So progress on the development of national income measures for Canada plodded along in the 1920s. Similar work was under way in the United States, but in both countries the methods were still rudimentary and the measures were widely acknowledged, even by their creators, to be both unreliable and incomplete.

The movement picked up steam in 1932, when the US Senate asked the National Bureau of Economic Research (NBER) and the Department of Commerce to come up with an "all-inclusive statistical picture" of the "contraction" of the economy after the crash of 1929. Simon Kuznets, a member of the NBER's research staff, led the project and ended up setting the standard for national income estimation.[20] The DBS adopted Kuznets's methods for its own estimates late in the 1930s, and used them again for a comprehensive, retrospective study of national income released in 1941.[21] By its own admission, the study "was based largely on the conceptual methods developed by the National Bureau of Economic Research and the United States Department of Commerce," although "British influence," particularly through some British government economists with whom Coats corresponded, "was also important."[22]

At this early stage, the work in all three countries was being done in relative isolation. For example, the DBS had its own methods of industry classification – a critical component of national income accounting – which did not map onto the classification systems in other countries. Still, on both sides of the border and the Atlantic, two mutually reinforcing concepts – "The Economy" as a construct referencing all economic activity taking place within the territorial borders of the nation, and the National Income as its statistical representation – were emerging. They soon slid into the realm of common sense, thanks in no small part to the civil servants toiling in three countries' statistical bureaux.

But the road ahead, particularly in Canada, was not entirely clear of obstacles. When the Royal Commission on Dominion–Provincial Relations of 1937–40 – also known as the Rowell–Sirois Commission – went looking for national income estimates, members found the DBS's numbers wanting. To them, the estimates offered only "the haziest estimation" of Canada's national income; they felt that Kuznets's method failed to translate in the Canadian context because the base data were not the same.[23] The Department of Finance was also dissatisfied with the DBS's national income estimates in the 1930s, believing that idiosyncrasies in Kuznets's treatment of government inputs and outputs underestimated government expenditure at a time when the latter was exceptionally high. The department thus rejected the DBS's figures and opted instead to use estimates from the Bank of Canada, which had been working independently of the DBS on such figures during this same period.[24]

The bank's approach was closer to that of John Maynard Keynes, whose *How to Pay for the War* (1940) is credited with the shift from national income *measurement* to national *accounting* – the latter being a more robust process that sought to grasp income, investment, production, and expenditure, including that which took place in government.

In the 1940s it was more or less the chosen method in Britain and, by the end of the First World War, in the United States as well, while Kuznets's method was falling out of favour nearly everywhere. By several accounts, the seeds for the Keynesian system of National Accounts in Canada were largely sown by one exceptional young economist named George Luxton. A member of the Bank of Canada's research department, Luxton had been "tilted toward" Keynes during graduate school at McGill, and he spearheaded the bank's work on the National Income.[25] His "crude, messy" worksheets formed the foundation of the country's first "modern set of national accounts," which the Finance Department eventually used for policy-setting during the war.

At war's end, the question in every affected country was how to recover economically, heal social scars, and reintegrate soldiers without displacing the workers who had taken over their jobs during the war. And everywhere, the answers were imagined to lie in statistical fact. Accordingly, the DBS's research capacities were greatly and deliberately expanded. As Marshall wrote, "the most important result of the effort to reorganize to meet post war needs was the creation of a Central Research and Development Branch in the Bureau," the "first task" of which was "to reorganise completely the National Income Statistics."[26]

Luxton was seconded to the DBS in 1944 and charged with leading the Central Research and Development Branch. Right away, he introduced the bureau to Keynes's national income and expenditure tables.[27] Although Luxton would die of tuberculosis within a year of joining the DBS – at the tragically young age of thirty – his legacy in constructing the "architecture" of the National Accounts can hardly be overstated. Moreover, his work brought national accounting "into the mainstream of Canadian economic thinking."[28] According to historian Duncan McDowall, Luxton's death "could not have come at a more crucial moment," as every apparatus of government, including his own, was scrambling to figure out "Canada's postwar direction."[29]

But the DBS, like everywhere else, carried on, and it increasingly looked to its neighbours to the south and across the Atlantic for guidance, cooperation, and confirmation. Soon after the war's end, the bureau dispensed with its then-outdated "Tripartite Classification System" of industries and joined a new international effort to develop a standard industrial classification system for the national accounts.[30] The press for standard classifications, along with the adoption of Keynesian tables, can be seen as part of the same international movement towards the "modern" national accounts. It culminated in a September

1944 meeting in Washington, where "experts from the United Kingdom, United States and Canada" settled on the concepts and standards to which Luxton and his colleagues would have to adapt their work. There were many motivations for this international agreement, but it was primarily a manifestation of the very powerful view that standardization "greatly enhances" the "value" of statistical data.[31] Numbers were seen as most meaningful when they could be compared, whether as different series of data collected within the same country or as bodies of statistical material collected in different countries.

For my purposes, the internationally shared architecture of the national accounts is primarily important insofar as it set, and continues to set through periodic revisions, the parameters and possibilities for the aggregate measures of productivity that followed shortly thereafter. One of its most significant accomplishments in this regard was the empirical legitimization of the construct of The (National) Economy, a construct, much like "the nation" itself, with enormous political-economic and discursive ramifications.[32] The development of national accounting channelled Keynesian economic theory into national government and brought the national government and the Canadian people into "what came to be loosely called the 'Keynesian world,' a partnership of private enterprise and state economic management." As McDowall explains:

> This was the high noon of macroeconomics, analysis predicated on an empirically driven overview of the economy as a whole with income, output, prices, and employment seen as the crucial levers of performance. For the first time in Western economic theory, business and government acquired the skill to look *inside* the national economy – to break apart its structure and flows in order to report on its strengths and weaknesses. Hence concepts like gross national product and productivity as well as processes like deflation were developed to provide a stethoscope for assessing our economic wellbeing. In doing so, statisticians and economists equipped Canadians – citizens and policymakers alike – with a new vocabulary of economic citizenship.[33]

From the mid-1940s to the late 1960s, the systems of national accounting were revised and expanded to capture new aspects of production and consumption as deemed necessary, by statisticians and policy-makers, for the fullest understanding of the functioning of the national economy and the factors contributing to growth. Input–output tables were developed to measure inter-industry flows of goods and services, a "massive under-taking" begun in the late 1950s and improved through the 1960s. Enhanced "Industry of Origin" estimates measuring the "real" physical volume of output in specific industries were being produced on a quarterly basis by 1964. In the late 1960s, building on experimental research in the United States, Canadian statisticians attempted to integrate data on "financial flows" into the National Accounts by developing an adjacent set of National Transactions Accounts that traced the movement of financial assets (whereas the main accounts tracked only physical production and services). At the time, the Dominion Statistician Herbert Marshall cautioned that the new accounts represented "a pioneering endeavour. Those who have been concerned with the preparation of this volume," he said,

> are impressed with the potential usefulness of such a wider frame-work of national accounting ... But they would stress that the decisions which have been made on concepts, classifications and arrangement are only suggestions, requiring ratification or reversal in the forum of public discussion; and that many areas of unexplored country have been visited and mapped *with all the inaccuracies, fanciful imagination and prejudice which can be found in the work of the early cartographers.*"[34]

These and other adjustments to the National Accounts, most no less pioneering or controversial than the National Transactions Accounts, were done in the name of "integrating the large mass of economic statistics available within the DBS."[35] And most of them, in some form or another, stuck; given the belief that statistics were most meaningful in comparison with other statistics, the first instance of national accounting practically guaranteed that it would be done again and again. In a sense, then, the production of aggregate income and production numbers created the demand for their own consistent, regular collection and release.

The architects of Canada's National Accounts, and generations of successors thereafter, knew that the data therein were important mainly insofar as they formed the raw material for myriad other economic facts and figures. Indeed, the wider public was, and still is, largely ignorant of the workings and content of the Canadian System of National Accounts (known today, curiously, as the "System of Macroeconomic Accounts"). Instead, they know its most prominent end products: GDP, GNP, and productivity.[36]

"As much knowledge as possible": *The Achievement of National Productivity*

Within the DBS and the Canadian government, as demonstrated earlier in this chapter, the desire for productivity statistics pre-dated the ability to produce reliable ones. The development of the National Accounts in the immediate postwar period finally guaranteed access to the kind and quality of data deemed necessary for valid, aggregate, national productivity indicators. By that point, statisticians and policy-makers had been talking up the benefits and uses of productivity statistics for decades. But Herbert Marshall traced the *"official* recognition in Canada" of the need for "a broadly based system of productivity statistics" to the Interdepartmental Committee on Productivity Analysis struck in 1949.[37]

This committee, a sub-committee of the Committee on Economic Statistics in the DBS, was mandated "to review the conceptual and measurement problems involved in [productivity analysis] as well as the available data sources."[38] It included members of the Bank of Canada as well as representatives from the departments of Agriculture, Finance, Fisheries, Labour, Resources and Development, and Trade and Commerce – or rather, their respective branches of statistics, research, and/or economics. At their first meeting, the members agreed on "terms of reference," including the following mandate: "to discuss the need for productivity statistics; to review work already done in Canada; to define terms; and to outline a possible program or programs for the development of productivity indexes."[39]

The committee's work began with "a thorough and critical review" of the data the DBS could offer such a program, "in order to develop the best possible method of measuring productivity change." Their own understanding of their mandate, role, and significance, as documented in their final report, tells of the dominant framing of productivity in Canadian economic and political thought in the aftermath of the Second World War, and picks up on the shifts and themes at the heart of this book, as identified in the first chapter. Specifically, it rested on the notion and aggregate statistical measurement of The (National) Economy, it drew legitimacy by relating productivity to prosperity, and it emphasized the dire importance of scientific knowledge and expertise in economic policy and planning.

By the time the committee met, the idea of the "whole economy" was evidently a firmly entrenched part of governmentality, one of the committee's primary objectives being "the development of aggregate measures to describe productivity changes at the level of the whole economy and its principal components," although it did set out to provide measures for "individual manufacturing industries" as well.[40] It had not even been fifteen years since Keynes's introduction of "the national economy" to economic thought, yet the notion of a singular, defined Canadian economy was by 1949 an indisputable, statistical fact.

The "need" for productivity statistics was, at the time the committee met, a given. Oddly, a bit of historical sleuthing suggests that Simon Kuznets is to some extent responsible for making it seem that way. Although his method of national accounting lacked staying power, a bit of his thinking had quietly worked its way into mainstream economic thought. Using his US national accounts data, he came up with a historical series that showed that as the economy grew and productivity rose, the lowest and highest incomes converged. Taking this finding as indicative of a fundamental and universal law, he theorized that "income inequality would automatically decrease in advanced phases of capitalist development, regardless of economic policy choices or other differences between countries, until eventually it stabilized at an acceptable level." His findings, which clearly mark a critical leap forward in productivist thinking, were widely embraced, and "the philosophy of [Kuznets's] moment," as Thomas Piketty writes, "was summed up in a single sentence: 'Growth is a rising tide that lifts all boats.'"[41]

Statisticians and economists in government in any country with a national accounting program were evidently convinced by Kuznets's theory and data, if not his method, that understanding the mechanisms of economic growth held the key to predicting and, with "informed" policy, increasing prosperity for all. The Interdepartmental Committee, justifying its own existence in its final report, declared that productivity research "throws light on the effective utilisation of capital, labour and natural resources upon which success in maintaining and raising our present standard of living largely depends."[42] In support of this claim, the committee explained that "gains in productivity spread through the economy in a variety of ways, such as higher wages, shorter hours, increased profits, lower prices and increased quality of products."[43]

Its report again plucked at the theme of prosperity, as well as the day's steadfast belief in scientific expertise in government, when it considered the strain the early days of the Cold War were putting on the Canadian economy:

> The need for productivity information is high-lighted [sic] at the present by the fact that Canada is faced with an enlarged and accelerated defence

program which is being superimposed on an economy already at a high level of operation, quite unlike the situation prevailing in 1939. It is essential that industry and governments do all they can to raise the level of production of the economy with existing resources, since this is the only means by which the economy can sustain heavy defence programs and yet maintain present living standards, insofar as that is possible.

Here knowledge about productivity is, therefore, of prime importance. In addition, it is essential to obtain as much knowledge as possible of manpower requirements with respect to our strategic industries. Productivity measures, [sic] would provide an indication of manpower needs at various levels of defence production, and this would help to establish a sounder base both for planning future defence production and assessing the strain of such production on the economy's manpower resources.[44]

This particular understanding of productivity – as a characteristic of the economy and an indicator of economic success and prosperity – was validated by a growing international community of economists and public servants whose work revolved in one way or another around the national accounts in industrialized countries. Through the 1950s, the DBS's closest co-conspirator in productivity research was the NBER, which it "carefully studied" to inform its own plans.[45]

Productivity and Industrial Harmony

One part of the US experience seized the committee's attention more than others: the uptake of productivity analyses in collective bargaining. From their perspective, it appeared that "measures and analyses of productivity have become increasingly important in industrial relations in recent years." Specifically, they noted that "both parties to collective bargaining have sought to relate wage increments to such measures" and that "many industrial relations programs such as those covering wage incentives, job evaluation, quality improvements, employees [sic] selection and training, etc., are directly or indirectly designed to improve labour's contribution to increased industrial efficiency."[46] Thus productivity measurement and monitoring seemed to be of use, if not benefit, to both workers and employers. This apparent dovetailing of interests seemed to present a new opportunity to improve employee–employer relations.

Indeed, the picture the committee painted in its report was one of industrial harmony in the United States. "There are many examples," they wrote, "of the useful and constructive role which unions have played in helping to increase efficiency at the plant and industry level." Indeed, their observations led them to posit that efficiency and productivity could actually be increased *through* "improved industrial relations" – that employee–employer harmony, productivity improvements, and rising living standards were mutually reinforcing components of economic growth. Key to capitalizing on this fruitful relationship, with productivity at the centre, was, according to the committee, the provision and analysis of productivity data at the aggregate, national, *and* the industry and firm levels. Again developments in the United States were cited as "evidence that both management and labour are making extensive use of the information provided by these studies."[47]

This thinking would give rise to the series of labour–management conferences and the standalone Productivity Council covered in the next chapter.[48] It was also an obvious carry-over from the days of Taylor, Mayo, Rockefeller, and Mackenzie King. While these four characters lacked the same desire for aggregate national accounting data – and certainly had nothing of the sort at their disposal – they had nevertheless contended that productivity improvements depended on peace and cooperation between capital and labour. And although they targeted their proposition at the level of the individual firm, it was also pointed at "the nation." After all, even Taylor had been driven to study productivity out of a concern for "national efficiency" and "waste."[49]

Working Hard: National Productivity as Labour Productivity

The DBS sub-committee also shared with Taylor and his contemporaries a narrow focus on labour productivity. After defining productivity as a "ratio of input to output," the committee's report explained that standard practice in productivity research was to take "the quantity of labour … as the input factor in this ratio." They believed at this time that it was "impossible" to "measure" or "add … together in any meaningful sense" the other "inputs," such as capital. Limiting the scope of productivity analysis to labour productivity was, the committee explained, the practical response: "Information on man-hours is needed in any case by most firms for cost-accounting and pay-roll records, hence it is easier to obtain than other statistical information. Further, as a result of measurement, it is the most homogeneous factor common to all firms … Finally, it provides evidence that is tangible and easily understood of the extent to which economic progress reduces the need for human effort." Thus, they concluded, "the measurement of man-hours seems to offer the most useful information for the least expenditure of time and effort."[50] Realizing how this narrow focus on labour might be interpreted by the literate public, they offered a caveat: "There is no implication in this output per labour input measure, however, that labour is solely or even mainly responsible for either gains or losses in productivity ... The term 'output per man-hour' or its reciprocal 'unit labour requirements' is preferable to the popular term 'labour productivity' since the former are more precise descriptions of the measurement and are less subject to misinterpretation."[51]

These few lines in the committee's report show that members *knew* that the language and concepts they were using to analyse productivity would filter down into everyday understandings, not only of productivity as an indication of national economic performance, but also of the significance to that performance of working people's efforts and relationships to work. They took pains in their internal reports to stress that labour productivity was merely a practical, utilitarian focus that did not imply that labour was the only or most important factor in economic performance. Further justification for the labour-centric definition, as well as productivity measurement in general, came in the form of scientistic appeals to objectivity, validity, and reliability, and the claim that government policies *had* to be grounded on a solid base of empirical research.

The Science of Productivity, Planning, and Policy

For members of the sub-committee, obtaining "as much knowledge as possible" about productivity was not an abstract exercise in understanding. Its purpose was explicitly to inform government economic policy and planning – especially "policies designed to maintain and increase productivity levels" – which were at that time "limited" by a "scarcity of information on industrial progress and the lack of careful analysis."[52] They urged that there be "careful compilation and interpretation of statistical data" and "competent analysis of the conditions affecting trends indicated by statistical series." They pointed to some particularly urgent "needs" for comparative data on cross-industry variations and historical changes in "productive efficiency," including data that would enable them to compare individual firms at single points in time as well as data that could track single firms over multiple points in time.[53]

Turning their attention to one of the most pressing economic problems of the time (according to the federal government), they posited that information on productivity would be helpful for understanding "under-employment" and "whether certain segments of the labour force might be encouraged to move to actually or potentially more prosperous regions."[54] Thus, in the early days of aggregate productivity research, the idea began to circulate that people could and should be shuffled about to meet the needs of "the economy," a territorially bounded whole whose performance at the national level was accepted as more important than the coherence and stability of everyday life.[55]

These same assumptions, priorities, and justifications carried over into a "Productivity Research Section" established within the DBS in 1961. A commissioned report authored by political scientist Imre Bernolak (who would go on to lead productivity research organizations in Canada, the United States, and Central and South America) described the new research section's responsibilities as follows: "developing, co-ordinating, testing and analyzing a variety of matching input and output measures for productivity purposes."[56] The work was more technical than that of the 1949 committee; as Bernolak reported, the Research Section planned to construct a series of input and output tables for individual industries that could be scaled up to the aggregate level, as well as assemble historical production data into coherent data sets on which to do longitudinal analyses.

But the researchers saw it as equally part of their mandate to settle on terms of reference – or rather, to *set* the terms for all future productivity research. "An essential part of the work will continue to be the classification of concepts and definitions," wrote Bernolak, such tasks being "required by the complex nature of productivity measurement."[57] In studying "a vast variety of input and output concepts, definitions and actual statistics as well as their interrelationships (and any existing gaps) throughout the different industries in the economy," the Research Section was simultaneously "improving the conceptual and practical coordination of different areas of statistical measurement."[58]

Like the 1949 sub-committee, members of the Research Section believed that their work, and the knowledge they generated, was absolutely essential to government policy. "The common and basic purpose" of their efforts, according to Bernolak, was "to throw light on the effectiveness of the utilization of available resources, its changes over time and its variations between and within industries." But the broader purpose was explicitly about governing, and doing so within a productivist, that is, growth-focused, regime. In Bernolak's words: "It is expected that the quantitative measures which are being developed by the Bureau, together with supplementary qualitative information, will not only contribute to filling gaps in the understanding of economic growth in general and of the growth or decline of individual industries in particular but also assist in improving the accuracy of forecasting production and employment."

The technique of "forecasting" on the basis of statistical data was relatively new at the dawn of the 1960s, and had been highly controversial in the Canadian government. For example, the DBS once squared off against the Department of Trade and Commerce and the Rowell–Sirois Commission over the production of population predictions during and after the Second World War, with the department fighting to discredit and discourage what it called "crystal gazing" on the part of the DBS and the commission.[59] But it appears that by the 1960s, using statistics to predict the future had stepped over a line from fantasy to facticity, and was a perfectly acceptable practice for Canada's statistical bureau – particularly in the case of employment and production forecasting.

The new Productivity Research Section also inherited the earlier sub-committee's interest in comparative data, which they "expected to indicate at least some of the reasons why productivity is advancing faster in certain industries than in others."[60] The focus on labour productivity carried through as well: the input–output tables were to "consist of man-hours and numbers employed [as] measured on both 'hours paid' and 'hours worked' basis [sic]." Their rationale for the two different measurements was that "the first [hours paid] is an economic and, more specifically, a 'cost' measure while the latter [hours worked] is a technical concept." Speaking again to the need for data-driven economic policy (and highlighting the changing connotations of "the economy"), they explained that "both [measurements] are needed because, on the one hand, all production is carried out in an economic setting and all the problems involved are basically economic, and, on the other hand, because the solutions to many of the problems are of a technical nature."[61]

Indeed, many of the limitations faced by the sub-committee were still in place when the Research Section began its work. For example, the 1961 researchers continued to worry that a single measure of productivity was inadequate – that "no one particular productivity measure ... could provide all the information sought." Although they could *imagine* a single, all-inclusive measure, the data and methods at their disposal were not sufficient to develop one. Instead they had to settle for "a series of ratios and indexes ... prepared for the various uses."[62]

Like the 1949 group, Bernolak's researchers realized that their limiting of "input" data to the outlay of labour was problematic. And they wanted to do better. Alas, Bernolak admitted, "in the field of capital input measures the work of the Productivity Research Section has been limited to overall conceptual problems. The feasibility of incorporating capital input in Canadian productivity measures cannot be determined until the results of an experiment aimed at the development of capital stock estimates is completed by the General Research Staff."[63]

For the time being, the Research Section did what it could do to at least improve the labour statistics in its reach. To that end, it helped plan the 1961 Census "for the purpose of securing labour input data which can be used as benchmarks in improving the quality of man-hours estimates derived from the Labour Force Survey."[64] (In 1965 the DBS would make use of the improved man-hour data for a report titled "Indexes of Output per Person Employed and per Man-Hour in Canada, Commercial Non-agricultural Industries, 1947–63." The newly developed labour input data were matched, for the first time, with data on output by industry of origin from the National Accounts.[65])

The ongoing concerns regarding labour-centric analyses and comparability aside, Bernolak's report shows evidence that statisticians in government were also anticipating and confronting somewhat new and different problems in productivity research in 1961 than they had in 1949. For one, they began to seriously consider the conceptual and technical difficulty of separating out, yet still capturing, the contributions of "non-production workers" (i.e., managers) in production processes. Moreover, they were stymied by the "conceptual and statistical problems" of measuring productivity "outside the field of goods-producing industries." How were they to measure, they asked, "the real contribution of the insurance and banking businesses to the economy? Or, how to measure the output of a privately owned television station?"[66] On the one hand, they were dealing with a rapidly reorganizing, expanding, and evolving economy – new jobs and industries were cropping up before their eyes at a pace they had never seen. On the other, they were just realizing what previous statisticians had failed to think about.[67]

Yet productivity research in the DBS was also making great strides on the conceptual and technical fronts. Bernolak reported that efforts at "global measures" (i.e., aggregate productivity measures) were well under way at this time. Also, an "Analytical Test Project" had been established for the purpose of obtaining or creating data to test, willy-nilly, for correlations of productivity with firm size, earnings, and anything else that the researcher's mind could come up with.[68] The objective in doing this was to "enable the individual establishments to compare their performance with the rest of the industry, pinpointing some of the areas where changes could be made to increase their productivity."[69]

Still, the bureau was a few steps behind the pioneering productivity research coming out of the United States. While the DBS toiled to assemble the right capital stock and man-hours data to fill the basic models of productivity growth it had adopted in the 1940s, the cutting edge of statistical economics was figuring out how to incorporate more qualitative aspects of labour and capital, such as the education level of workers, as well as additional inputs like technology, materials, and energy.

"More of an analytical product": TFP and MFP in Canada

One of the first to widely advance a workable model of productivity beyond labour and capital inputs was the Harvard-educated American economist Robert Solow. A professor at the Massachusetts Institute of Technology, in 2014 he would review Thomas Piketty's *Capital* positively, and criticize economists who defended the wealthiest 1 per cent of Americans against those who dreamed of a more equal distribution of wealth.[70] But back in the 1950s, Solow was working on a theory that would soon produce a widely accepted measure of productivity growth – the "Solow Residual," also known as total factor productivity (TFP) – and contribute to the "growth accounting framework" that was more or less the standard approach to productivity analysis in the twentieth century.

The TFP or Solow Residual is, in the simplest of terms, the proportion of measured productivity growth that exceeds the growth in capital and labour inputs; it is a residual because it is "left over" after subtracting capital and labour growth from output growth. It is not so much an explanation of economic growth as it is an admission that there is more at play in determining productivity than the combination of capital and labour. This basic idea would be taken up by many other economists in Solow's time, including John Kendrick, Dale Jorgenson, and Zvi Griliches, all of whom would, in the late 1960s and 1970s, advocate the expansion of the National Accounts to better capture inputs, outputs, and changes in productivity.

But Solow's contemporaries made important (and sometimes controversial) innovations on the TFP idea and its measurement. Kendrick, whose 1961 *Productivity Trends in the United States* was heralded as "the most comprehensive survey of productivity trends in the United States ever made," was among the first to challenge the dominant interpretation of the Solow Residual.[71] The latter was usually taken as a proxy for technological change or innovation, such that whatever growth could not be attributed to capital or labour was attributed to technology. According to James Livingston, Kendrick believed, in contrast, that "the forces underlying growth in productivity" were "more complex than mere changes in technology." They depended, for him, on the existence of a "socio-economic organization or 'institutional' framework that either enables or promotes the pursuit of efficiency."[72]

Jorgenson and Griliches went further in their 1966 and 1967 essays, arguing that estimates of the residual were so vastly overblown that there had actually been almost *no* growth in TFP, whatever it meant, over the last several decades.[73] Their work left business people and economists scratching their heads, as it seemed to suggest that the rapid technological change they had witnessed in their lifetimes had not improved productivity in the least. However, Jorgenson and Griliches's enduring point was merely that the measure of TFP or the Solow Residual was imperfect – that it needed some tinkering in order to *truly* capture the causes of productivity change. Others, like Robert J. Gordon, attempted to move beyond the work of Jorgenson and Griliches to account, for example, for the impact of knowledge and research (foreshadowing interest in R&D) on productivity gains.[74]

In any event, after Solow, attention turned in statistical economics circles to TFP, and any serious attempts at productivity measurement in the 1960s and 1970s had to do more than simply count man-hours and capital stock. Yet it was not until the 1980s that the DBS's successor, Statistics Canada, produced its first TFP estimates (which the agency refers to as multi-factor productivity, or MFP).

John R. Baldwin and Wulong Gu, statisticians with the Canadian government, have traced the history of MFP measurement at Statistics Canada. As they tell it, interest in "concepts that went beyond labour productivity" spiked during the slowdown in labour productivity growth that affected North America and "developed countries" elsewhere – a point to which I return below. Recognizing the work of Solow, Jorgenson and Griliches, and Vancouver economist Erwin Diewert, Statistics Canada moved to "expand" its productivity program to "include additional inputs and developments in the economic literature on productivity measurement." Its "Multifactor Productivity (MFP) Program was launched in 1987."[75]

Baldwin and Gu, presumably expressing the general view at Statistics Canada, note that MFP is "more of an analytical product" (reflecting here the agency's shift towards seeing itself as a "service provider" that offers "products" to "clients" and "customers") than simpler measures of labour productivity. Specifically, they propose that MFP involves "particular assumptions about the production process" that do not factor into labour productivity estimates.[76] Not only, then, is MFP more complex than labour productivity; it is also understood by Canada's national statistical agency as more theoretically grounded, more abstracted from the kind of reality the ordinary person can grasp, and, in a sense, more removed from the way productivity is understood in everyday life.

And since the launch of Statistics Canada's MFP program, work on improving such estimates has only gotten more intense, and the measures more complex. Jorgenson and Griliches led the development of more robust and specific estimates of capital inputs, and national statistical agencies gradually adopted the "constant quality index of capital and labour input" they had recommended in 1967. Significant efforts were targeted at bringing Canadian and American data and methods in line with each other, and then in 2002 the Organisation for Economic Co-operation and Development (OECD) published a manual for productivity measurement that set international standards to enable greater comparability.

The OECD guidelines advanced what is called the KLEMS growth accounting framework. KLEMS (an acronym that is sometimes used interchangeably with MFP) stands for K-apital, L-abour, E-nergy, M-aterials, and S-ervices, and is shorthand for a framework for national accounting (and therefore the productivity estimates based on those accounts) that contains detailed data on all of these input and output factors at the industry level. Although the OECD explicitly states that its productivity manual is not meant to be "prescriptive," its objective was nevertheless to "improve international harmonisation," and to that end it emphasizes the advantages of "KLEMS type" data. The latter, says the report, are the most "desirable ... when countries have a choice in constructing new measures or developing a system of indicators."[77]

Statistics Canada embraced KLEMS, and in 2013 announced that it would, "as part of the [next] System of National Accounts historical revision" (a process the agency undergoes every few years), improve "the consistency of the industry productivity KLEMS database."[78] The agency's adoption of KLEMS was not out of the blue; like the international efforts of the previous century, the OECD manual's content was

directed and informed by an international working group, in this case
the Statistical Working Party of the OECD's Industry Committee, as well
as an "informal expert group." In the latter, Canada was represented by
Industry Canada and former Statistics Canada employee Rene Durand.
(Jorgenson, Griliches, and Diewert were *not* among the experts listed in
the group.)[79]

Following the release of the OECD's guidelines, other bodies were
established to further the KLEMS approach. From 2003 to 2008, the
EU-KLEMS project, funded by the European Commission, assembled
and analysed KLEMS data for twenty-five of twenty-seven EU member
countries as well as for Canada, the United States, Australia, Korea, and
Japan. In 2010, Jorgenson launched the World KLEMS Initiative (WKI), a
project that aims to generate industry-level KLEMS data sets for as many
countries as possible. As of 2015, it had assembled data from the EU,
Latin America, and Asia. Like the DBS's productivity researchers, the
architects of the World KLEMS Initiative see productivity measurement
as one of the most powerful tools in the project of economic governance,
as well as a key to policies that lead to economic growth and, in turn,
prosperity. It is decidedly, and unsurprisingly, a productivist project.
The insights the WKI is meant to provide, according to Jorgenson, "are
essential in assessing changes in comparative advantage and formulating growth policy."[80] The unprecedented comparability of the data is
especially advantageous, Jorgenson notes, as "international differences
in the sources of growth have become central to the development of new
directions for policy."[81] What KLEMS represents, then, is a technique of
productivist governmentality; it draws authority and legitimacy from
its scientific expertise, and it reinforces the already dominant idea that
productivity growth leads to economic growth, which is the foundation
for better standards of living. The WKI is just one of many institutions
furthering this idea and technique of governance.

While work on MFP estimates and KLEMS data sets spread glob-
ally and intensified locally, Statistics Canada did not cease all work
on labour productivity. In fact, it has continued to release quarterly
labour productivity estimates. Controversy about productivity research
methodology since the 1980s has attached itself mainly to MFP – as in
the case of the exchange, noted in the introduction, between Diewert,
Yu, and Gu – while labour productivity numbers have continued to figure in mainstream media as the most accessible, least dubious measure
of how hard or how efficiently Canadian industry is working compared
to its "competitors."

The Squeaky Wheel of Productivity

The timeline of developments in productivity research – from the early advances made in aggregate measures, to the expansion of TFP and MFP, to the international effort to amass comparable KLEMS-type data – can be mapped, perhaps not surprisingly, onto concurrent ups and downs in measured productivity and economic growth. That is to say, major ground is usually broken in productivity measurement when productivity slumps or slows according to extant measures. This "squeaky wheel gets the grease" scenario constitutes somewhat of a feedback loop, where noteworthy estimates that come out of a particular method of measuring productivity trigger increased interest in the revision of that same methodology.

What all of this tells us is that from its very early, exploratory stages, statistical productivity research has responded to discrete, historically contingent problems, with an eye to informing government policy *and* business practice – and at times, seeing into the future for both groups. It has always corresponded with productivist logic, in that it is always and everywhere discussed as a means of understanding and furthering economic growth. This logic and the goal(s) it assumes for statistical inquiry are unthinkable without the idea of a singular, national economy in/on which to apply them. It seems that in the 1960s, the number one problem was keeping up the pace of productivity growth realized at the end of the Second World War, on the widely held assumption that this, and the broader economic growth it would ensure, was the key to the dramatic rise in prosperity in countries that had recovered from the war. Accordingly, the priority was on *increasing* efficiencies (and thereby productivity), at the level of both individual firms and industries and the National Economy. And, given the way that the characteristics of extant data pushed government statisticians towards labour costs as the easiest and most understandable proxy for productivity, thinking about increasing productivity naturally collapsed into thinking about how to get workers producing things quicker.

Then, in the 1970s, "the existence of a productivity crisis became a major political theme in the United States" – and in Canada as well. Coverage of labour productivity exploded in major newspapers. Behind the scenes in government statistical bureaux, work was under way to shift the focus away from labour productivity and draw attention to the myriad other factors that contribute to the productivity of firms, industries, and national economies. But outside the world of statistical research, a "broad campaign ... by business and political leaders ... seized on declining rates of productivity growth as proof of the need for national policies to restrain wages and limit the growth of state spending."[82] Closer to today, the worldwide economic recession of 2008 is repeatedly referenced as the impetus for the World KLEMS Initiative, as the notion of continuous and limitless economic growth is increasingly called into doubt by a growing body of research on economic and environmental sustainability and technological unemployment. Paradoxically, the question of how to actually increase productivity without displacing workers is more of a mystery now, even though its measurement is ostensibly more refined than ever.

As Janice Gross Stein has argued about efficiency throughout the twentieth century, productivity was, in certain times and places, compelling enough to be considered a worthwhile end in itself rather than a means to some higher end. But the body of correspondence, reports, memorandums, and technical manuals in the DBS archives, taken as a whole, shows that there were actually several prized ends to which productivity was assumed to lead. All were guided by some telling assumptions about the internal logics and dynamics of The Economy. It should now be clear – perhaps even tiresome – that productivity has been considered the linchpin of prosperity throughout the former's life as a statistical economic indicator. Indeed, it still is – just note the quotation from Statistics Canada that opened this chapter.

Once productivity was understood as a determinant of national wealth and living standards, it logically became "necessary" – an "urgent need" – to monitor it, measure it, pick it apart, and find the root cause of its variations. It also became reasonable to hope that, if productivity improvements were correlated with employers' profits, employees' incomes, *and* national economic performance, capital and labour could realistically work as *partners* in production rather than as adversaries. And so in the 1970s, attention started to focus on how improving productivity could be used as a goal at the firm level, and also as an "objective" incentive built into collective agreements – in other words, it became understood simultaneously, and rather awkwardly, as both an outcome of *and* a necessary condition for industrial cooperation. This point is taken up in the next chapter.

Chapter Four

The National Productivity Council

Governmental interventions are important because they have effects. They seldom reform the world according to plan, but they do change things. They may be resisted, but not from spaces or positions outside power. In place of the familiar and often spatialized dichotomy, power here, resistance there, the analytic of governmentality draws our attention to the ways in which subjects are differently formed and differently positioned in relation to governmental programs (as experts, as targets), with particular capacities for action and critique.

Tania Murray Li, 2007

Nineteen hundred and sixty was not a year which most people will remember with any great nostalgia. It saw no major catastrophes, but it was full of anxiety and tension at home and abroad. Here in Canada, attention was focused on the slowing up of the nation's economic growth and the consequent spread of unemployment ... The postwar era of prosperity when a ravaged and hungry world would buy Canadian goods at any price we chose to set are long over. The revival of industry and agriculture in Europe and Asia has meant fierce competition for domestic as well as foreign markets. Whether Canada can resume its former rate of growth and provide employment for all its people depends largely on whether we can meet this competition by increasing productivity and reducing prices. There are encouraging signs that Canadian business is now responding to the challenge. Governments are also responding, in their own way, to the seriousness of the times ... Some of [the Diefenbaker cabinet's] measures, such as the establishment of the Productivity Council, the efforts to expand foreign sales, and the Senate investigation into manpower problems and the nature and causes of unemployment, are thoroughly commendable.[1]

Globe and Mail, December 1960

Thanks to the statisticians tapping away on the computers added to the DBS less than a decade before, and to the government's willingness to fund them, the health of the 1960 Canadian economy was a precise, scientific fact rather than a gloomy mood informed by anecdote. The numbers cascading out of the bureau's offices in Tunney's Pasture, the government complex in Ottawa, brought with them a new vocabulary of economics; The Economy, gross national product, gross domestic product, and productivity all emerged, sweeping up smaller measures and local economic production into a national picture; "employment" and "unemployment" were now aggregate measures rather than just descriptors for the general condition of one's neighbour. Blocks away from DBS headquarters, in the confluence of these burgeoning lexicons and data sets, the National Productivity Council (NPC) was born.

This chapter explores the little-known details of the NPC, drawing on the ideas of governmentality and productivism to interpret and understand its origins, accomplishments over its short life, and replacement by the Economic Council of Canada (ECC) in 1963. Many of the NPC's "techniques" are, at a glance, peculiar – for example, its near-exclusive focus on hosting seminars with management, labour, and government – and the records available in Library and Archives Canada suggest it was a confused and internally conflicted organization.

Once we situate the NPC as a form of governmentality in a longer history of the productivity concept, productivity statistics, and productivity councils, and in a wider frame of the discursive and political-economic conditions of the 1960s, the peculiarities make some sense. The NPC is a powerful case study of the productivist ideational regime in which productivity has acquired its meaning and has had its effects. What went on in the council highlights the contested but nevertheless dominant assumptions about productivity's relationship to prosperity, nationhood, and progress. It offers insight into the lasting discursive association of productivity with labour – and with "working hard" especially. It highlights the divisions between ostensibly benign productivity-boosting initiatives and controversial, politicized ones.

It suggests, moreover, that the political elevation of increased productivity and economic growth as national goals has been closely linked to the preservation of a particular economic and social order, and to the protection of particular interests. For this reason especially, it is not surprising that the NPC was more of a public relations campaign for productivism than anything else. Much of its time was spent figuring out how to get working people to *buy into* productivity as a personal, corporate, and national goal, when many at the time resisted, associating the term with technological change, displaced labour, and alienating work. In pursuit of its legislated mandate to "promote and expedite continuing improvement in productive efficiency in the various aspects of Canadian Economic activity," the NPC spent most of its effort getting workers to acquiesce to changes to production that might ultimately devalue their labour or render it redundant.

The Cold War Context

In part, the new council's emphasis on discussion, research, and public relations reflected a general public and governmental distrust of anything that looked like ideology in economic planning. This distrust, and the limits placed on the NPC's mandate, had much to do with the Cold War and the unprecedented (and since unmatched) economic growth of that period. But the times were also marked by serious ideological tensions between the communist, totalitarian model guiding the Soviet Union and other Eastern Bloc countries, and the liberal capitalist model espoused by the United States and its allies. Canada can be included in the latter group, even though it was and continues to be a welfare state, with a more influential socialist (and social democratic) tradition. It was home to a more tightly regulated capitalism that saw government intervention as the best guard against *actual* socialism.[2] Still, it can be said that across the West, liberal ideology reigned; in the United States, national legitimacy hinged on maintaining freedom, prosperity, and social mobility (or at least loudly purporting to do so) while also ramping up production. Economic growth was paramount, and government intervention to that end was acceptable, but it could not come at the expense of the individual's liberty or opportunities.[3]

Although this period was a high point (soon to be over) in government intervention in economic life, any such intervention had to appear to express rather than direct the population's will, lest it be branded totalitarian, authoritarian, or socialistic. The rhetoric surrounding these ideas was more subdued in Canada than the United States, but it still erected rigid boundaries around the acceptable role of government in economic affairs. At the same time, governments found themselves with new tools at their disposal to direct and manage economic activity with a level of precision they never had before.

By 1960, near what would be the end of postwar economic expansion, all of the DBS's newly created data told the Diefenbaker government that the economic landscape was shifting. Ordinary Canadians would hear this too, not least from the major newspapers, which increasingly focused on the slowdown of the Canadian economy. Stories about rising unemployment and the problem of retraining appeared alongside news of recovery and growth in overseas industries and in-depth coverage of foreign ownership of Canadian businesses.[4] Letters to the editor complained about selfish business people hoarding profits and intractable unions hampering efficiency. All of these topics were "dominant national issues evoking widespread comment" that the government would ignore at its peril.[5] When trade and commerce minister George Hees appeared touting a "rosy" view of the economy, readers and editors responded with criticism.[6] They wanted to be levelled with, and notwithstanding concerns from some corners about "government tinkering" in the economy, they wanted to see action. Recommendations abounded. The Royal Commission on Canada's Economic Prospects (1957) recommended ceding direction of economic policy to an "advisory committee of economic experts," as did a plan from the Liberal opposition labelled the Pearson Plan.[7] The Co-operative Commonwealth Federation (CCF, Canada's socialist, labour, and agrarian party) urged that there be some form of "economic planning."[8]

But in the Cold War the word "planning" was contentious – and in some circles, downright profanity – in economic discussions. Of course, the "free" market was then, as it is today, propped up and directed by a complex web of government interventions. Still, politicians and other officials who proposed economic policies were always vulnerable to the liberal capitalist accusation that they were treading into "socialistic" or "communist" territory. Many averted this by branding their policies as non-interventionist measures that simply made room for the market to do what it was inclined to do.[9] As the records of the NPC below will attest, even while the Soviets were viewed as the enemy, the Soviet Union was being held up as an example of what increased production and productivity could do for living standards. (This is a testament to the hegemony of productivism – no matter what political economic regime we look at, the assumption that economic growth is good and vital to social progress is there.) The challenge facing Canada and other liberal Western countries was to replicate or exceed the Soviets' level of production while maintaining the democratic freedoms set out in their constitutions.[10]

These boundaries between acceptable liberal policy and dangerous centralized control demarcated the tight space in which Hees proposed a tripartite committee of government, labour, and management. That proposal would eventually come to fruition as the NPC, which was a Diefenbaker government initiative (one of several) aimed at what had been identified as the most pressing economic challenges of the time: the "twin problems of structural unemployment and Canada's relationship with international markets."[11] Although it was widely recognized that structural unemployment – "caused substantially by the introduction of new technologies" – would not be solved without a "complex of policies involving training programs for displaced workers, [and] adjustment of monetary and fiscal policies," the NPC was touted in public communications as a direct response to unemployment. It appears to have been assumed that figuring out how to increase productivity in Canadian industry was *de facto* the same as figuring out how to reduce unemployment. The connection was rarely made explicit, but Diefenbaker proposed that "productivity" – by which he likely meant *output* – "had not kept pace with the increases in the labour market."[12] In other words, Canadian industry could not employ all who were willing to work because it was not producing enough. The solution that followed was to boost productivity, and the NPC was meant to find out how a country could do that.

A Council in "the National Interest"

The bill to create the NPC hit the House of Commons in 1960, promising to "expedite," "improve," and "expand" economic activity in the midst of what was, by that point, widely regarded as an economic slump. In the preamble to Bill C-52, the NPC was presented as a means "to provide expanding opportunities for increased employment and trade and rising national standards of living." It was plainly "in the national interest" to establish such a body immediately.[13] The exact mandate laid out in the bill was vague. Although it included numbered lists of "objects and powers," it was limited (discursively, not legally) to the hazy tasks of "fostering and promoting" the following:

- the development of improved production and distribution methods,
- the development of improved management techniques,
- the maintenance of good human relations in industry,
- the use of training programs at all levels of industry,
- the use of retraining programs to meet changing manpower requirements,

- the extension of industrial research programs in plants and in industries as a means of achieving greater productivity, and
- the dissemination of technical information.

It was also granted authority to "organize, assist and enlist the aid of committees, teams and other groups in the implementation on a national, regional or industry basis of programmes designed to give effect to any of the objects" listed above. Despite being hemmed in by various taboos about government intervention in the economy, the NPC was thus to have great latitude so long as it stuck to *encouraging* increased productivity.[14]

Hees stood in the House of Commons to explain that the bill followed through on a suggestion that Diefenbaker had made at a conference on employment earlier that year. He assured the House that Diefenbaker's "specific proposal, which outlined the need for such a council and the functions it might undertake, was accepted by leaders from commerce, industry, labour, finance and education." He boasted that the NPC would be "a completely new development for Canada," one that "pioneer[ed] in new fields of Canadian economic development."[15] But truthfully, the idea of a productivity council was not at all original; the NPC was designed largely out of a perceived need to have the same government bodies as other "advanced" nations and then justified, after the fact, as an answer to Canada's unique unemployment situation.

Granted, Hees did not try to take credit for the idea. Instead, he used the record of productivity councils in other countries to advocate for a Canadian NPC. "Productivity Councils have been very successful, both in the United Kingdom and in Europe, as instruments in raising industrial efficiency," he explained. Calling up examples that will be explored in this chapter – such as the Anglo-American Council on Productivity and the British Productivity Council – Hees reported that in the United States, Britain, and Europe, "representatives of both management and labour [were] working together with the common aim of increasing productive efficiency in industry as a whole."[16] In fact, he told the House, "similar activities are carried out in practically every European country," and even in Asia, India, Pakistan, Japan, Iran, Lebanon, and the Philippines.[17]

Speaking to the major economic concerns of the day – trade deficits and increasingly competitive markets – Hees insisted to MPs that "in view of the progress made by other countries in the field of productivity,

Canada cannot ignore this field of endeavour." The country had to take productivity seriously "for the benefit of all Canadians."[18] Bringing in the additional concern of unemployment at home, he made his pitch: "I am convinced that we in Canada can achieve equally successful results if Government, Management and Labour will co-operate fully to make Canadian products competitive in both quality and price ... If our products are competitive, as to both price and quality, with goods produced in other countries, they will be sold, and Canadians will be employed producing more of them."[19]

Notably, only once in the legislative act that launched the NPC into existence is the word "employment" mentioned, and it occurs in the preamble: "In order to provide expanding opportunities for increased employment ..."[20] Yet in the Senate debates following the act's introduction, Conservatives in Diefenbaker's cabinet placed the NPC under the rubric of "measures to combat unemployment" and sought to convince the House that "the Council was an important Government measure designed as one remedy for the serious unemployment problem." Opposition MPs did not buy it. They argued that the government was "deliberately and falsely claiming that the Council could deal with the unemployment situation" and that in reality the bill had "no relationship whatsoever to the current and immediate unemployment problem." But the bill passed, and the NPC made it out of Parliament with its attachments to unemployment intact.[21]

This controversy highlights the fact that, from its inception, the NPC was informed and influenced by the productivity councils established in other countries in response to the need to rebuild war-damaged industries *literally* from the ground up, amid local social and labour unrest. In contrast, when the NPC was introduced to the public and pitched to MPs, it was branded as a solution to problems of a different sort – namely, unemployment and trade imbalances. Yet the NPC's establishment effectively cast these two problems as matters of productivity, and even as *determined* by "productive efficiency."

This adaptation of the productivity council model to objectively different circumstances reflected the breadth of productivity as a concept: because it was discursively linked with a variety of economic processes and problems, a council charged with promoting productivity did not have to limit itself to any single economic issue. The adaptation might also be a sign that the *form* of the productivity council itself – the assembly of labour, management, and government – was appealing to the Diefenbaker government for reasons over and above its actual potential impact on unemployment and trade. Or it might indicate that the administration viewed unemployment and trade deficits as somehow determined by industrial relations and cooperation, and the tripartite productivity council model promised to improve at least that. Hees's House of Commons statement suggests the latter interpretation: he claimed that the NPC was "an important first step," in "close co-operation between Government, Industry and Labour ... toward our goal of a good job for every Canadian."[22] In any case, my objective here is not to dwell on the motivations of historical actors. What matters more is the milieu in which their actions took place.

"The progress made by other countries"

There is no single point of origin or precursor for the NPC, but several small initiatives arguably paved its way. Just as with the development of productivity statistics, the United States was an instigator in pushing productivity to the centre of economic development, foreign policy, and industrial relations. In 1946 the Truman administration convened a conference on productivity with the same tripartite (labour–management–government) participation as the NPC would have fifteen years later.[23] The conference was part of what historian Andrew Carew has called the postwar "battle of production" – the desperate effort to "overcome the immediate crisis of postwar scarcity" by regaining and exceeding the standard of living, manufacturing output, and trade that had existed before the Second World War. But once that urgent problem was relatively under control, the mechanisms and initiatives developed to deal with it were "gradually transformed into a permanent fixation with productivity as a technical problem."[24] Worldwide, from the end of the war onward, a parade of councils and conferences, bringing labour, management, and government together to hash out their differences, were assembled and unleashed at the productivity problem, which was now framed as a matter of industrial cooperation towards economic growth rather than a matter of economic reconstruction.[25] So, with productivity now a "permanent fixation," the appearance of a productivity council over a decade later in Canada is not so surprising.

As Carew documents, the global emergence of productivity councils began with a cooperative effort between three groups: the British government; the British Trades Union Congress (TUC), which was a labour umbrella group; and Americans associated with the Marshall Plan.

The latter was the program of US aid to Europe after the Second World War, one of whose primary objectives was to weaken communist influence in the European labour movement; indeed, one of its lasting effects would be to split that movement into communists and social democrats.[26] Together with the British government and the TUC, the Marshall Plan's architects created the Anglo-American Council for Productivity (AACP) in 1948, but the three founding parties were not on equal footing. The British participants, according to Carew, understood that the "flow of Marshall Aid" depended on the American government being convinced that British industries were running as efficiently as possible. They saw the AACP as a means of "correcting American misconceptions of British industry," and agreed to its establishment.[27] For the British, it was an "information programme" that would dispatch news of their postwar reconstruction efforts; for the Americans, the AACP was a vehicle for teaching British industry about "productivity American-style."[28] Its actual activities included sending delegates from each country to the other to visit plants and firms and gather information; designing and running a publicity campaign to expose British productivity weaknesses; and assembling sub-committees to conduct comparative studies of specific aspects of productivity in each country.

Many of these activities were carried out under the banner of a program launched by the AACP within a year of its inception: the US Technical Assistance and Productivity Program, soon to be known simply as the Productivity Program. It was a key piece of the Marshall Plan, organizing upwards of 1,500 "productivity tours" in which delegates from European countries visited American factories to learn American "know-how."[29] It also began to disseminate what Carew calls "productivity propaganda" across Europe.[30] Soon, there were plans "to convert the AACP into a permanent national productivity centre – the British Productivity Council – with a professional staff engaged in a long-term programme of work." According to Carew, "the Americans wanted to export" this model "to all western European countries, and in the course of 1950 they began to exert pressure in each participating country for the creation of a national productivity centre through which American managerial values and techniques could be disseminated."[31]

However, the Americans' plans met resistance, especially in Germany and Italy. Labour groups there were concerned that focusing on productivity would lead to layoffs and other pressures on workers. They objected to what they saw as an unfair emphasis on labour over capital, dredging up the old economic theoretical debates over the productivity of each.[32] But such criticisms were ultimately marginalized, I argue, because they fell outside the dominant postwar ideational regime. That ideational regime was productivism, but with a newly prominent twist: the goals of productivity and economic growth now hinged on industrial relations, in the optimistic belief that workers and employers had a joint interest in economic growth and could be compelled to work together to achieve it.

This thinking was a continuation of the scientific management and human relations perspectives explored in chapter 2. Carew points out that although both were most influential in the 1910s, 1920s, and 1930s, "the ideal of harmonious, pluralistic industrial relations based on elaborate collective bargaining routines under enlightened capitalism became the subject matter of a growing literature even in the late 1940s."[33] By then, the anti-communist, anti-Bolshevist "belligerence" from the first Red Scare through the 1930s had given way to a subtler "collaborationist industrial politics," but Cold War antagonisms and anxieties were still very much alive. The project of encouraging economic growth still hinged on discouraging or simply disempowering unions, but this was to happen first by maintaining social order and industrial peace, and second by effectively inducing workers to help design the managerial processes that would control them.[34]

"Labour–management cooperation" was the buzzword in the years around the AACP's operation; thus the unique thrust of the AACP did not come out of nowhere. Movement towards the collaborationist model in the United States was led by Clinton S. Golden, a former radical socialist who served as chief labour adviser to the Marshall Plan. It was largely thanks to Golden, who had more than a pet interest in productivity and industrial relations, that productivity took on such a prominent role in European recovery and US international relations. In fact, in 1942, Golden argued in *The Dynamics of Industrial Democracy* (with Harold Ruttenberg) that "the pursuit of productivity" should be at the centre of industrial relations. In that book, productivity is presented as an apolitical goal that is in everyone's interest and is therefore uncomplicated by the political squabbling that affects other industrial issues.

The authors' thinking is characteristic of the productivist thought of the period: increased productivity meant more goods; more goods meant more sales and trade; more sales and trade meant higher profits *and* higher wages; and all of these factors both depended on *and* engendered "labour–management co-operation." Following this logic,

Golden and Ruttenberg saw productivity as an especially powerful weapon in "waging the cold war": economic dominance would be achieved not only through sheer production levels but also through cultural dominance, because economic success would be seen as the natural outcome of a liberal capitalist economy built on cooperative industrial relations.[35] It would not be long before this vision of productivity-centred industrial relations was institutionalized in a new form of collective bargaining: "productivity bargaining," which began in earnest with an "epoch-making agreement between the [United Auto Workers] and General Motors."[36] That agreement is one of many productivist threads linking the statistical elaboration of productivity with its manifestation as a consequence of industrial relations in the NPC.

Productivity Bargaining: A "Staircase to Prosperity"

At the 1946 US Department of Labor Conference on Productivity, the role of productivity statistics in collective bargaining was a subject of considerable debate. As Block and Burns have shown, union representatives worried about which measures of productivity would be used to determine wage levels. Businesses balked at the notion of guaranteed wage increases eating into their profits. Representatives from the Bureau of Labor Statistics, meanwhile, "pleaded that BLS measures not be used in collective bargaining unless management, labor and the BLS had sat down together to create commonly agreed upon measurement procedures."[37] Like Harry Magdoff, whose concerns about the reliability and meaning of aggregate productivity measures appeared in chapter 2, BLS representatives urged caution in the interpretation of the aggregate productivity indicators.[38]

Nevertheless, "the idea of linking wages gains to productivity" gained traction, and four years later it was put to the test when General Motors "devised the idea of linking wages to productivity and prices in the context of a long-term agreement."[39] As Carew explains, the contract "gave workers an annual wage increase tied to anticipated productivity gains ... in return for which management expected its authority at the point of production to go unchallenged."[40] The UAW–GM agreement, for Block and Burns, was "the critical step in moving the aggregate productivity concept from academic and government studies into the policy arena"; it "became a model for other industries with strong unions, and 'productivity bargaining' became a key component of the new system of labour relations."[41] Productivity bargaining appeared to solve many problems. It appealed to analysts who had been calling for "a rational and objective basis for wage determination." It also worked for employers, who, like General Motors, were not keen to take "a stance of total opposition" to their unions, but also did not want to make bargaining a "free-for-all."[42]

The emergence of productivity bargaining should, then, be seen not as a "win" for either labour or management, but as one more mechanism influencing the distribution of remuneration and control over the labour process within industrial relations. It fits within a longer narrative that includes the managerial revolution and follows the overlapping but separate struggles between workers and employers over wages on the one hand and working conditions on the other. Gains made on one front sometimes meant sacrifices on the other.[43] This is why, within the diverse groups that have historically made up "labour," divisions have periodically emerged over the question of which fight – wages or control over working conditions – unions should focus on winning. Viewed in this book's terms, these divisions are between the productivist desire to benefit financially from higher production and the anti-productivist desire to turn productivity gains into leisure. The productivist desire has a vested interest in perpetual economic growth, on the assumption that a bigger and bigger pie means bigger and bigger pieces for labour. In contrast, the anti-productivist desire – for less work and a modest amount of stuff – could be achieved without perpetual economic growth. It is apparent that the productivist impulse in the 1950s was stronger, as the productivity agreements that took shape then were about wages, not hours.

Although predictions of a coming "leisure society" (in which technology would liberate people from menial work and everyone had more free time) had proliferated in the interwar years, it was as common to hear that increased leisure represented a social problem rather than a utopia. Proponents of a shortened workweek were often ideologically aligned with syndicalism – Bertrand Russell is a prime example – while those who wanted to preserve a liberal capitalist or even socialist order with work at the centre warned that people would not know what to do with extra free time and would fall prey to vice. Where Russell remarked on the absurdity of a society built on "overwork for some and starvation for others," others in his era were concerned that people would waste their time and money on pursuits that did nothing for the individual or common good.[44] Academic treatises on "the leisure society" and "the leisure problem" continued to square off against one another well into the 1980s, but thanks to the productivity bargaining of the 1950s, and to the hegemony of productivist thought, organized labour in the West fought less and less over work time and more and more over remuneration.

In addition, just like scientific management at the turn of the century, productivity bargaining effectively turned workers' and managers' attention away from how surplus value gets *shared* towards *increasing* the surplus so that there would be more of it to go around, which in the process would shrink or at least bury class conflict.[45] Carew's research on the Marshall Plan led him to conclude, similarly, that "unresolved class tensions were ... channelled into a general quest for productivity and economic growth," and "what were really political issues were transformed into problems of output."[46]

The UAW–GM agreement, which "first cemented the link between wages and productivity in the United States," entrenched a particular understanding of *how* higher productivity benefited ordinary working people. It contractualized the promise that increased productivity would mean higher pay and purchasing power; meanwhile, the hope that increased productivity would result in more leisure time and freedom quietly and slowly died – within collective bargaining at least – over the 1960s and 1970s. Thus, a very specific interpretation of "prosperity" – one that limited prosperity to consumption wages and in some ways pulled life deeper into the market – came to dominate talk of productivity's benefits to working people.

Productivity's benefits to industry – to the employers that made their money in it, and the governments that saw their tax revenues and international economic competitiveness as dependent on it – remained tied to healthy industrial relations. Productivity bargaining seemed to wedge productivity into labour–management relations in a civilized, constructive, and orderly way, creating a "moving staircase to prosperity" that everyone was eager to climb aboard.[47] "American propaganda in Europe" proudly proclaimed "that the wage-productivity equation was a central and standard feature of US collective bargaining," and a model for other nations and industries to follow.[48]

The American and European story partly unearthed here reveals that productivity is not necessarily or inherently a productivist concept. It would be possible, for example, to settle on an adequate level of productivity for specific industries or economies and then stop trying to grow or produce more. The more efficiently a society produced what it needed, the more free – that is, *liberated* – time that society's members would have.[49] People could work less and consume a bit less. But they would still have more than the bare necessities.

The story so far also helps make sense of the shape that the Canadian NPC took upon its establishment in 1960, especially with regard to its emphasis on industrial relations and public "awareness" campaigns. Indeed, this longer history helps account for the emergence of a Productivity Council at all, considering that the biggest challenges facing the Canadian government at that time, from most perspectives, were not matters of productivity *per se*. Knowing how the links between productivity and prosperity were reified and strengthened by the spread of productivity bargaining will help establish the fundamental assumptions on which the NPC was built.

The National Productivity Council in Canada

From the outset, the NPC appears to have been a Rorschach inkblot for people who believed it was the answer to their own particular prayers and who sought to influence its direction. In 1960, when the NPC bill was still just an idea, assistant deputy labour minister George Haythorne wrote to Hees and applauded him for having "raised this matter" of productivity. He noted that "the department of Trade and Commerce has been giving it active consideration and has been approached by a number of sources who have requested that we take an active role in preparing a comprehensive program ... to foster productivity and education of both management and labour."[50] He reminded Hees that "it is the declared policy of the Government to foster expanding employment opportunities, in cooperation with employers and employees" rather than relying "entirely [on] the private sector of the economy."[51] He closed by recommending that the NPC develop a comprehensive plan before consulting with employers and labour.[52]

Around the same time, Haythorne wrote another letter to John A. Roberts, assistant deputy trade and commerce minister. Roberts was not a council member – none had been appointed yet – but Haythorne seemed to believe he would have some influence over the NPC's mandate. "I thought it might be preferable to approach the question of productivity and technological change indirectly rather than directly," he wrote. "As you know, both the employers and workers are sensitive about these matters for different reasons. They might, on the other hand, both agree that co-operation among the three groups [referring to labour, management, and government] is essential in promoting employment."[53]

Haythorne may not have known at the time that he would be named to the NPC as a government representative and would have plenty of direct influence on the council's activities. At the end of April 1961, more than five months after the NPC was approved in Parliament, Prime Minister Diefenbaker announced the names of the council's members. The twenty-four men and one woman were drawn from four spheres: big business, representing "industry and commerce"; "agriculture and other primary industries," represented by the heads of resource companies and the like; the Canadian Labour Congress (CLC) and several smaller craft unions, representing "organized labour"; and the "public at large," represented by a mayor and more business people.[54] There were also several "government experts" from the Department of Trade and Commerce, the Department of Labour, and the Department of Mines and Technical Surveys as well as the Defence Research Board.[55] Reporting on the announcement the day after it was made, the *Ottawa Citizen* mused that, other than the government representatives, it "sounded in part like a blue-chip list of Canadian tycoonery."[56] This echoed labour's criticisms, including most prominently those of Claude Jodoin, president of the CLC and member of the council, whose concern was that the NPC was dominated by executives of large corporations and that labour had had little say in who was chosen. Even the council's chairman, George DeYoung, was president of the Ontario company Atlas Steel.[57]

The first six months of the NPC's official existence – from April to September 1961 – were spent conducting meetings, planning future activities, soliciting research and expert advice, and fielding inquiries and requests from business people, labour groups, government departments, and the general public. These activities evidently looked like busywork to the outside world. By the sixth month, pressure had begun to mount for the council to show the public what it had accomplished. Chairman DeYoung wrote to NPC government representative B.G. Barrow to say that he had "been pressured considerably by the newspapers and some members of the government to hold a press conference at which we would disclose to the public the things we are going to do. As you may have read in some newspaper releases, the editors are beginning to call us a failure."[58]

It seemed that the council's detractors – largely individuals and groups who believed that the last thing the country needed was another council pushing paper around – were smugly watching their predictions come true. But by the end of the year, the council had made *some* headway in planning a series of labour–management–government seminars to be held across the country. The conferences, lasting two or three days each, would bring together union representatives, employers and managers, bureaucrats and politicians, and academic economists, to speak to one another about productivity. Teams were at work in each province and by January 1962 were sending progress reports back to council. While these teams tried to pull things together locally, the NPC worked to coordinate the conferences from Ottawa, debating in council meetings over such details as whether to invite the press, whether special efforts should be made to have women representatives, and various logistical matters.

The plans came together slowly. According to historian Daniel Coates, whose dissertation is the only history of the NPC, progress was partly hampered by disagreement between labour and the other members.[59] This interpretation – which will get more attention in what follows – is borne out in the archival records, but it also seems that the council simply got bogged down figuring out exactly what function it was meant to perform, reaching consensus on what "productivity" itself meant, and ultimately navigating the political minefield around its very existence. George Hees touched on this difficulty when he spoke to members at a council meeting in January, acknowledging "that in the past year it has been a very difficult problem to get down to concrete terms [and to] introduce the idea of Productivity." Nevertheless, he said,

> the main idea is to get people "productivity minded." There have been a number of new jobs – 80–90 thousand according to Dominion Bureau of Statistics. These have been made possible to a large extent by the ideas getting quietly out. I think it is important to instil the word productivity in people's minds. Labour–management across the country are getting the idea ... I think we are working on real labour–management government cooperation, it is paying off in what we can see in increased job figures in industry.

Hees was almost certainly overstating the council's impact. The press's attention was not on productivity but on the interpersonal drama within the council – Jodoin's political skirmishes with other members, which would eventually lead to his resignation, and disagreements between business and government representatives over such matters as whether it would be better to have more or less competition in Canadian industry.[60] The media revelled in the discord. The council's role in job creation was also dubious; there was no way of knowing whether the new jobs added over the year had anything to do with NPC activities.

Labour–Management Seminars and the Mission to Europe

It would be March 1962 before the NPC did anything but generate gossip. That month, it held the first labour–management seminar in Kingston, Ontario, at Queen's University. The seminar, like the others that would follow across the country, gathered employers and industry leaders together with government employees, delegates from local and national unions, and academics (mainly economists) armed with research papers, discussion papers, and literature reviews on productivity. Representatives of the DBS were almost always on hand, offering reports on the progress of aggregate productivity statistics (and the challenges in creating such figures).

At this first conference, two ideas of lasting significance were raised. First, according to a recollection presented at a later seminar in Vancouver, it was unanimous that the NPC needed to include "economic studies on a broad scale" within its scope. Second, it was recommended that the council organize a tour of Western Europe – a "productivity mission" – to learn about industrial relations there, and specifically to understand how relations between labour, management, and government either facilitated or thwarted increased productivity.

The NPC took the latter recommendation to heart immediately, and sent thirteen delegates, led by J.A. Roberts, on a two-week, six-country European tour in the summer of 1962. Several weeks after their return, Haythorne presented its preliminary findings at the second labour–management seminar at Dalhousie University in Halifax. Overall, Haythorne told the mixed audience, the mission found harmonious relations and cooperation between unions, employer associations, and governments, each of which "accepted" the role it had to play in fostering economic growth and productivity. Haythorne's remarks had something for everyone: while unions were "freely recognized for many years as the mouthpiece of workers," he assured the crowd that "the free acceptance of unions is matched by a full acceptance of employer organizations." The knowledge the NPC inherited from its Productivity Council predecessors about the secret to productivity was thus backed up by first-hand evidence: although unions and employers "tend to have opposite positions" on "wage rates and hours of work," this had "not prevented them from co-operating closely where [it] is to their mutual advantage and to the advantage of the community as a whole."[61]

Skirmishes broke out over subsequent proposals that Canada seek to emulate the "employer associations" and "management–labor agreements" found in Sweden and Switzerland.[62] Critics called such measures "economic planning" in order to conjure up thoughts of "the totalitarian model of the communist countries."[63] Proponents were forced to proclaim their commitment to protect private property and profits, so long as a reasonable portion of the latter were reinvested in production.[64] These disagreements aside, Haythorne was largely preaching to the converted; the theme of cooperation seeped into nearly every presentation given over the two-day seminar. Herbert Lank, the president of DuPont Canada, gave a speech outlining "management's viewpoint" on economic growth and productivity, which was essentially that cooperation at all levels "is the only sure way we are going to be able to strengthen the inseparable links between morale, efficiency and productivity."[65] D.W. Ambridge of the Abitibi Power and Paper Company pointed to labour and management's "common objectives" in discouraging the social ills of "uneducated teddy boys, beatniks, bank robbers, pimps or prostitutes."[66]

If there was any disagreement about the cooperative pursuit of productivity specifically, it was on the part of labour. But this was more than a simple difference of opinion about the collaborationist model. By the time of the Halifax seminar, a major schism had opened up between Claude Jodoin, the CLC's representative on the NPC, and the rest of the council. Jodoin had been pushing for some time for a broader mandate for the NPC. He believed that productivity had to be approached as one concern among many rather than as the sole factor by which all other economic problems were determined. His criticisms, judging by the meeting minutes archived by the council, went unheeded for many months.[67] But when the mission to Europe returned, Jodoin was vindicated: it concluded that "attempts to improve productivity must be undertaken as a component of broader economic and social programs."[68] Even DeYoung was finally swayed by the idea that "some form of economic planning was both desirable and necessary," and he recommended "a broadening of NPC powers" to his government.[69] When cabinet failed to act, Jodoin resigned from the council.

J.A. Daoust, the papermakers' representative, used his time at the Halifax seminar to comment on Jodoin's departure, attributing it to Jodoin's feeling "that the scope of the Council was too restricted in its terms of reference to deal with economic problems now causing deep concern."[70] In the rest of his speech, he was on the defensive about labour's role in industrial relations. "We are not militant unions," he said. He admitted to having "militant discussions" among members, but assured attendees that these were "on a high plain [sic]" and that, when it came down to it, labour would be civil and cooperative regarding goals that were in everyone's interest. At the next NPC-sponsored seminar at the University of Saskatchewan in January 1963, the CLC was still willing to participate, sending William Dodge, executive vice-president, to deliver a paper. He referenced the European mission's findings – namely, that "the nations which appear to have found the solution to unemployment and the secret of steady economic expansion are also those which have highly developed systems of labour–management consultation and co-operation" – but steered largely clear of the controversy around Jodoin and the NPC's mandate.[71]

The rest of the discussion in Saskatchewan revolved around the production issues of rationalization, technology, and automation; the labour market issues of education, and redundancies and retraining; the industrial relations issues of collaboration and formal labour–management–government structures; and the need for research into all of these topics.[72] From Saskatchewan, the seminar moved on to Montreal in May 1963. Similar themes dominated the presentations and break-out discussions: technology and redundancies, vocational retraining, and the need for a more comprehensive economic development plan. On the latter note, none other than George DeYoung spoke at length. By then it had been two years since NPC members were announced to the public, and DeYoung seemed to have felt that it was time to reflect on the council's progress. The narrative he used to explain its change of direction to seminar participants foreshadowed – quite explicitly – the dissolution of the NPC and the establishment of its successor. Recalling the many different tasks given to the council, from "find[ing] new processes and products which we could sell to other countries and compete better at home," to "study[ing] the problems of how to improve human relations in industry" and "the human issues created by our rapid technological advance," he admitted that it was "apparent" early on that "the productivity aspect of economic development could not be isolated from the many other factors which impinge upon the economy."[73]

Although as mentioned, DeYoung initially failed to get a broader NPC mandate past cabinet, the government soon came back with its own policy allowing the council to take on some economic planning functions. Shortly thereafter, they revised the plan and came up with a bill to create an entirely separate council, but the Diefenbaker government was defeated – just weeks ahead of the Montreal seminar – before the bill could pass. However, the next government – the Pearson Liberals – proposed a new body that would carry out much of the same responsibilities as the redirected NPC. When the bill establishing the new Economic Council of Canada (ECC) passed on June 1963, the NPC "ceased to exist," and its secretariat was "absorbed" into the ECC.[74]

But after a short summer break, the labour–management seminars continued under the direction of the ECC, with the fifth picking up in Vancouver in October. The topic on everyone's mind was the effective replacement of the NPC by this new body, which was widely understood as a consequence of the former failing to accept that its focus on productivity was too limited to adequately address Canada's economic problems. Walter Koerner, a British Columbia businessman, philanthropist, and ECC member, gave an address about the background of the seminar. In it, he told the story of the NPC as if it had been doomed to fail from the outset:

> As soon as the National Productivity Council came into being in 1961 it became clear at these early stages that the objectives of the Council seemingly could not be satisfactorily solved because the essential atmosphere for approaching common goals was absent or treated lightly by both sides ... Also missing, as I indicated early in 1962, was the fact that the N.P.C., as then constituted, did not concern itself with current trends of research into economics, socio-economic, financial, external and internal trade, and various educational questions. The need for tackling problems of productivity improvements was therefore more complicated because it was to be carried out in isolation from problems of growth.[75]

Koerner's point that the NPC had failed because it tried to "isolate" productivity from "problems of growth" is a productivist point. It is clear that in his view, productivity is a concept *embedded* in productivist logic; productivity only matters insofar as it contributes to growth. Channelling the productivist ideational regime, Koerner sought to convince his audience that a body that subsumed productivity growth into a larger economic growth agenda would be more successful because it would be conforming more closely to how the economy actually worked. He nevertheless admitted that "the N.P.C. did achieve pioneering results,

and its work was very important." Especially important from his perspective was the NPC's role in "prepar[ing] the ground regionally and
nationally for the functions which are now to be taken over by the new
Economic Council of Canada." But one thing was certain: "from now
on, productivity under the new Act will be viewed in the context of our
whole economic life."[76]

Koerner's remarks suggest that the NPC's demise had been predictable from a very early stage. And indeed, there had been much discord over its short life. The rest of this chapter zooms in on several of
the most enduring controversies within the council and explores the
shifting understandings of productivity at the heart of them. The idea
of governmentality comes into play here as it helps us articulate these
divergent interests and perspectives in the terms provided by Tania Li:
we find an array of "subjects [who] are differently formed and differently positioned in relation to" the NPC, its mandate, and productivity
thinking, some as "experts," some as "targets," with varying degrees of
presumed responsibility for productivity levels, and "with particular
capacities for action and critique."[77]

Defining Productivity: "Differences in Value"

The archives of the NPC are comprised primarily of two types of files:
council meeting minutes, and proceedings (papers, speeches, and
schedules) from the labour–management seminars. The most striking
(and amusing) parts of both are those in which council members or
conference participants discuss the meaning of productivity. They did
this often, and not just in the early stages of the council's life. At an NPC
meeting in January 1962, council member George Metcalf, president of
Loblaws and Toronto's designated industry representative, asked the
group: "What does productivity mean to you? To me it means more
work – creating more jobs." No one answered him for a few moments,
and then Norris Crump, the CPR's president, launched into an incoherent
story. "Referring to Mr. Metcalf's statement," he began, "productivity
means a lot of things to different people. While in Rotterdam a while
ago I happened to notice a cobblestone road – men were on their knees
laying stones as they did a hundred years ago."[78] What seemed like the
beginning of a story about automation and productivity trailed off into
near nonsense, and the discussion moved on.

It picked up again when members heard from an advertising agency
tasked with developing promotional materials for the NPC. As the

group brainstormed ideas for pamphlets and slogans, they offered a glimpse into their collective thinking – heterogeneous as it was – on productivity's meaning. The assistant deputy trade and commerce minister, B.G. Barrow, rattled off some ideas: "more productivity – more jobs," "being more competitive," "export[ing] more from the home markets ... It means more for everybody." A moment later, he piped up again: "Productivity means progress." Haythorne echoed Barrow's line – the government's line – that "higher productivity means more jobs." Businesswoman Anna Speers jumped in too: "Mr. Chairman," she said, "I find myself thinking about Mr. Crump's English slogan 'productivity is above all else an attitude of mind.'"[79]

If the foregoing reads like a motley assortment of catchphrases, that is because it is. There is no indication in the archival records that the NPC ever reached a consensus or settled on an official definition; in fact, there is no record of any serious, sustained attempt to do so. This was reflected in the variety of definitions put forward in public. For example, DeYoung had publicly coined the definition "work smarter and get on with the job," while Hees had been mostly consistent in his understanding of productivity as "obtaining the best possible use of all the factors of production and distribution."[80] At the labour–management seminars, participants offered their own definitions. DuPont Canada president Herbert Lank ruminated on its "interesting connotations" and "sophisticated shades of meaning" and tried to persuade his fellow delegates to "try to confine ourselves to its less abstruse meanings and remain closer to the familiar generality expressed in the dictionary." For Lank, this meant that productivity should connote "efficiency," "technology" and "Labour-Management co-operation" – "loaded words in some circles not too long ago, but matters of general concern today."[81] Dr Andre Raynauld, the head of the Department of Economics at the University of Montreal, took the newly created TFP concept out for a spin, proposing that participants at the fourth seminar in Montreal ought to care about the productivity that was responsible for economic growth *apart* from increases in population (labour) and economic resources (capital). "Thus defined," he said, "productivity refers to production increases which cannot be attributed to labour or capital but to more general phenomena," a category that "may include anything we wish."[82] One of the break-out working groups from that same conference reported back to the full assembly that they found that "'economic development' could be discussed more easily than 'productivity' since there is a more basic understanding of the term."[83]

This sort of stumbling over definitions and terms of reference was eventually cited as one of the reasons the NPC did not survive. At the fifth conference, in Vancouver, DeYoung delivered a speech as the president of Big Algom Mines Ltd. In his view, the NPC's greatest struggle was "resolv[ing] differences in value" attached to the productivity concept. His summary of this struggle, below, points to the clash between productivism and anti-productivism – between those who believed greater productivity meant greater prosperity and those who associated it with redundancy. He also references a time when productivity was not immediately understood as a means to economic growth – when it was, first and foremost, a matter of making "the most effective use" of resources:

> When the Productivity Council began its deliberations nearly three years ago, I was most interested in the fact that all those around the tables were convinced of the importance of productivity improvement ... If we were going to redress our balance of payments, if we were going to compete against nations which were quickly coming to industrial efficiency and spreading their goods throughout the world, if we were going to feed, clothe and house a growing population, and improve our standard of living, it would have to be done through improved productivity. That is, in one broad definition, to make the most effective use of all our resources. We found, however, that the road was not a simple clear pathway.
>
> One must always realize the difference in values that people in various walks of life have. So, while the word "productivity" meant a better way of life – a constantly improving standard of living – to some of us, to others it meant slave labour, unemployment and speedup. Time was needed and a forum was needed to resolve these differences in value ...
>
> As we felt our way slowly toward a common understanding between our representatives, the need for accepted definitions and reliable statistics became felt. We didn't even have an accepted measurement of unemployment – only the fear of the word and the state.[84]

DeYoung's use of the word "value" is telling. It suggests that the struggle to define productivity was a matter of divergent interests, beliefs, and desires rather than an objective matter of finding the *right* or *true* definition based on an assessment of all the facts. Granted, for the NPC, it was at least partly an objective matter – the gatherings of experts on productivity were a means of getting all the facts into a single discussion – but the most enduring challenge in the seminars was reconciling the seemingly incompatible perspectives of people and groups who *wanted* productivity to mean very different things and, accordingly, wanted very different things out of the NPC. All of this is quite consistent with the tenets of Somers's historical sociology of concept formation: productivity can be seen in the NPC seminars and meetings as a relational, intersubjective concept embedded in a productivist ideational regime. That regime is not entirely insulated from alternative ideas – for example, ideas about work-sharing and more leisure; however, it is strengthened in the fraught process of purging or simply rendering irrational – unthinkable, unsayable – those alternatives. The NPC eventually recognized that productivity's definition depended on whom you asked, and that there was no one definition that satisfied everyone. In this way, a straightforward definitional question was quickly revealed to be a political one, which then cascaded into debates over the morality of the current political economic order. Most of these debates, however, did little to challenge productivism or the desirability of economic growth.

"We have no alternative": Productivity, Technological Change, and Unemployment

At all five conferences and the NPC's regular meetings, one controversial topic never failed to pop up: the relationship between productivity, technological change, and unemployment. Even before the NPC bill landed in the House of Commons, those who knew about it were cautious about how the word "productivity" would impact public perceptions of the council. Specifically, they worried it would be associated with technological unemployment. Haythorne had hinted about this in his aforementioned 1960 letter to J.A. Roberts, in which he effectively proposed that the NPC make the more palatable idea of labour–management cooperation its primary mandate, with productivity lurking somewhere behind the scenes.[85] It appears that the council, too, was aware from early on that productivity was controversial because, logically, increasing it might initially lead to *fewer* jobs if labour-saving technology introduced to boost productivity replaced workers. (This, despite the government's insistence that increasing productivity was a way of combatting unemployment.)

At first, the CLC's Claude Jodoin was the only one taking issue with the productivity focus. He warned his fellow council members that "in some groups and trade unions there is not too much enthusiasm" and even "some reluctance" about the NPC.[86] But at a meeting just before the first labour–management seminar, the group invited W.R. Dymond, a representative from the Department of Labour, to provide an overview of the country's "manpower" situation. Dymond's presentation described not only the numbers of unemployed in various regions and industries, but also the level of skills and education among them. Council members were especially concerned about the fact that 43 per cent of employed Canadians and 75 to 80 per cent of the unemployed had "only primary school education or less."[87] They spent a considerable portion of the meeting fretting about the 43 per cent in particular.[88]

The manpower data roughly inventoried the number of workers "displaced" by productivity-enhancing technological change and, since it provided some additional demographic details, helped clarify what it would take to redirect displaced labour to new jobs.[89] This information set the tone for the NPC's engagement with the productivity concept in meetings and seminars to come, drawing attention to the potentially volatile disagreements over whether higher productivity was in workers', employers', or government's interests, and whether it was a cause or a consequence of unemployment and slow economic growth. But Dymond did not answer these questions, and by the end of its mandate, neither, arguably, did the NPC.

At the fourth seminar, in Montreal, several working groups broke away from the main event to discuss an important and controversial question: Who is responsible for the effects of technological change? Answers varied, predictably, with some advocating for employers to invest in retraining displaced workers, others placing the responsibility with government, and one group concluding that "the individual has the key responsibility ... No one can reduce human problems or anxieties if the individual himself is not prepared to help."[90] During the presentations, a debate stirred around the similar question of whose interests should prevail when it came to planning for greater productivity. The strategy of choice, no matter who spoke, was to present one's own constituency's interests as though they were universal – not to mention critical for economic growth. Indeed, *no one* thought outside the productivist vision of continuous economic growth. Some, like J. Claude Hebert, even tried to pre-empt anti-growth arguments, arguing that employers should not be asked to "unnecessarily employ more people," for example, by implementing a "shorter work week," as this would have grave (but unspecified) consequences for "the future welfare of our economy."[91]

For Hebert, as for most of the seminar's presenters, some redundancy was "inevitable." Yet most, including Hebert, also agreed somewhat contradictorily that the goal for government, employers, and Canadians at large was "full employment." According to Peter Victor, "economic growth was originally adopted as an objective of government policy" in Canada precisely to ensure "full employment in the post–World War II era."[92] At the NPC seminars, technological unemployment was viewed as a *temporary* mismatch between people and jobs – as an unfortunate detour on the way to full employment.[93] No one was willing to entertain the idea that productivity gains might lead to less work in a *good* way. Even those who were happy to see workers displaced by machines or more efficient processes wanted to see those workers employed doing something else in short order.

Also speaking at the Montreal seminar was René Paré, President of the Societé des Artisans. He reported that Quebec's Economic Advisory Council (active from 1943 to 1944, and again in 1961), pursuing "the most complete utilization of its material and human resources," sought to ensure full employment. Paré explained, evoking a humanism (and a religiosity) that was rare, albeit not entirely absent, at the seminars, that "man is the primary natural resource and that he must be thoroughly used," but "it is essential that we appreciate that man is also a soul, a human being, a citizen, a creature made in God's image, to whom it is important to give a medium in which he and his dependents can live properly."[94]

In his report on the Mission to Europe at the Halifax seminar months earlier, Haythorne had also discussed the importance of full employment in the context of productivity improvements. He reported that the mission had consistently found four "principal objectives" in the productivity plans and labour–management relations "in all six countries." The first was full employment, which Haythorne believed would mutually benefit labour and management. But at the third seminar, in Saskatoon, the head of the University of Saskatchewan Department of Economics and Political Science, A.E. Safarian, cautioned his audience about the pursuit of full employment. "Full employment is not a sufficient guarantee of rapid economic growth and rising living standards," he said. What the country needed more was "maximum improvement in the productivity of our resources in those industries which are growing most rapidly and are most productive."[95]

What should be gleaned from the foregoing is the deeply held assumption that full employment was relevant to productivity on two levels.

First, the unemployed were cast as inefficiencies in the economy – as wasted human resources, the antithesis of high productivity, to be avoided because of the costs to human dignity and social cohesion as well as the financial costs to governments and businesses. Second, it was understood that increasing productivity, particularly by improving production technology, might put people out of work. These connections were rarely *explicitly* drawn and discussed in the seminars and NPC meetings, but the discussions that did happen evince that participants internalized productivity's potentially negative impact on employment. Many, particularly business representatives, sought to redraw the connections, proposing that short-run displacement would lead to more jobs "in the long run." The idea that the goal could be less work *and* less unemployment (via a better distribution of work) was entirely absent.

Whither Work? Productivity and Social Justice

No one at the seminars floated the "leisure society" thesis, at that time in vogue, that boosting productivity could mean the end – or at least the serious curtailment – of work, at benefit of a more leisurely population. Instead, the reigning idea was that ordinary people would enjoy vaguely defined improved living standards. The only type of idleness brought about by productivity gains would be unemployment, and every effort was made to assure sceptics that even this would not last. Lank, for example, urged his audience to consider that "automation has its bright side too": "in enlightened hands," it could "bring tremendous social and economic benefits in the form of higher productivity, an accelerated pace of general business activity and improved living standards for everyone." He admitted that those in the room, and the groups they represented, were "all morally bound to work towards relieving whatever inequities automation may produce." But, he argued, "we have no alternative in this competitive age but to accept the automation of processes wherever it will serve us best."[96]

By the final conference in Vancouver, the whole issue of labour–management cooperation had been reoriented to revolve around this one dilemma: how to ensure that the benefits and costs (excluding a drastic increase in leisure) of "inevitable" automation and technological progress were distributed evenly among workers, employers, and government. All three parties, as DeYoung put it, had to decide "where the responsibility lies for redundancy, obsolescent skills and training needs in our advanced society."[97] Safarian, after tempering the promise others saw in full employment, offered similarly sobering thoughts on productivity's presumed benefits to ordinary people:

> All major decisions on raising productivity and growth rates involve real sacrifices to part or all of the community for at least a period of time. Most decisions ... also involve changes in the distribution of income between groups ... The point which must be grasped is that growth at [sic] rising living standards inevitably involves change, and change falls unevenly on different groups and at different times ... At this point ends and means merge, and the question becomes not simply "how to expedite economic growth?" but the broader question – "what is growth for and for whom?" This is not a question for technicians or bureaucrats, or even for politicians alone. It is one the entire community must have some part in answering.[98]

Viewed as part of a longer history of the productivity concept, this discursive shift at the NPC seminars represents a considerable rupture in the long-standing association of productivity with prosperity. Yet it does not mark a break with productivism. If anything, what we see in the struggle to make different views on productivity commensurate is the power of the productivist ideational regime to fix the horizons of possible solutions. Simply put, there was no space for anyone to seriously consider a future in which the economy stopped growing. But the problem of the unevenly distributed costs and benefits of increased productivity became more difficult to sidestep, and the notion of a simple relationship between productivity and living standards could not be accepted on faith. At least, that was the conclusion drawn by some participants. For others, and for many outside the seminars, the connection held fast.[99]

For the NPC, the social justice problem was gigantic – not at all the kind of thing a twenty-five-person council drawn from disparate regions and constituencies could settle in a meeting, let alone several meetings. But the impossibility of answering Safarian's moral questions about economic growth does not preclude us from assessing what the NPC did accomplish. When it came to tangible actions and effects, beyond hosting the tripartite seminars, the council made headway on one objective: convincing the public that its mandate was in their interest.

"Creating a climate of increased receptivity"

The bill that established the NPC gave it two types of responsibilities: first, *fostering*, and second, *promoting*, economic growth and productivity.

Newspapers and public forums emphasized the fostering role – what the council could actually do to "stimulate" increased productivity.[100] In contrast, at the recorded NPC meetings and especially the seminars, nearly everyone's attention was on the related socio-political problem of how to grow an economy without growing inequity at the same time. The twenty-five-person council, however, appears to have left this high-level question to the academics and industry and labour representatives, while in meetings and correspondence among government officials it concerned itself with *messaging*. "The main thing," as Hees said, "is to get people productivity minded."[101] The NPC wanted to influence how their work would be received by the outside world, *and* they believed that productivity itself was a "state of mind" they could inculcate. In practice, these two fronts often merged; over the course of the group's initial meetings, public resistance was identified as a major obstacle in the way of productivity growth.

Accordingly, the NPC drew in public relations and advertising experts to help them. It was not so much that the NPC abandoned or ignored the question of how to increase productivity without also increasing unemployment. Rather, they accepted, as did most seminar participants and consulted experts, that *some* "displacement" of labour was inevitable, and devoted their energies to severing the mental connection between productivity and technological unemployment, to quell workers' fears and open the way for comprehensive plans for economic growth.

Granted, Hees had been up front about the NPC's public relations aspect from the very beginning. Speaking in favour of the NPC bill in 1960, he noted that both the British Productivity Council and the Anglo-American Council for Productivity had learned, through their experience, that "the major influence which such an organization could exert was on the climate of opinion about productivity."[102] Indeed, a central claim in Carew's history of the Marshall Plan is that its "greatest achievement and the factor that has had the most lasting effect on labour" was its "role in developing among European workers a consciousness – indeed, an acceptance – of the need for an ever increasing level of productivity."[103] This precedent is probably why, late in 1961, before any of its other major initiatives were under way, the NPC sought the aid of the Canadian Association of Advertising Agencies and the Canadian Advertising Advisory Board.

An archived letter between those two advertising bodies describes a "public relations programme" to be designed and implemented on behalf of the council. In pursuit of its mandate to "promote a national unified effort toward increased productive efficiency and a higher rate of economic growth," according to the letter, the NPC hoped "to develop an acute awareness on the part of the public that:

(1) We are in a struggle and that the struggle is not among ourselves, but with the various trading areas with which we must compete;

(2) The battle is won by teamwork in the workshops, the planning rooms, the research labs, the sales organizations and management offices;

(3) There is a need for greater sharing of responsibilities, sacrifices and rewards;

(4) There is a need to remove impediments to renewed growth by smoothing out the personal affects of dislocation and change;

(5) There is a need for increased skills and adaptability of the work force because of the effects of accelerating technological progress;

(6) If we are to grow, we must be competitive; and if we are to compete, we must be efficient; and if we are to be efficient, we must have the best methods, products, plant facilities and organization.

In creating public "awareness" about these six tenets – most of which, especially 4 and 6, were obvious expressions of productivism – the council reportedly hoped "to create a climate of increased receptivity for higher individual performance and more effective teamwork." A potential slogan was put forward: "putting the U in productivity."[104] One member even enthusiastically proposed that the NPC adopt "some crazy symbol or cartoon" to represent them.[105] At a meeting the following month, the council welcomed an advertising salesman from Toronto. He presented them with a draft brochure called "LET'S GET RICHER," and a debate broke out about the definition of productivity. This was the point at which B.G. Barrow and Norris Crump shared their rather disjointed thinking on the matter, and they and others tossed out possible ideas and pitches for a public relations campaign. "What we want in a promotion campaign is 'how' to get across what we want the people to do or what we are going to do," offered A.R. Harrington, a business representative. "We have to get it out to the people what we can do for them."

Their more specific suggestions about what to say reveal, first, what members thought the general public was inclined to believe about productivity already, and second, the message they wanted to get across. Council knew that productivity was associated in the public mind with being overworked, or worse, with technological unemployment. To counter this belief, they wanted to persuade people that, as George Haythorne put it, "higher productivity means more jobs." His colleague, Barrow, emphasized that "the job concept is [most] important." Harrington agreed: "Unless we get this across we won't be successful." So the council's success hinged from the outset on cementing in the public mind the connection between productivity at the industry and national level and employment and prosperity for the individual – although at no point did they seek or make use of empirical data to prove the link between increased productivity and jobs. It was merely assumed. Moreover, NPC members wanted ordinary people to hear the message that everyone, including them, had a role to play. Haythorne proposed another slogan along these lines: "Let us all pull together."[106]

The advertising representative eventually grew agitated by the discussion as it jumped from topic to topic. Before taking his leave, he made one final point: "We work less in this country than in the U.S. We have to come out of this. Can we in this country persuade people to do it[?] ... You don't get rich by having more time off." "I don't think there is any more purpose in my sitting here," he said, and exited the meeting. Even the chairman, George DeYoung, was tiring of the public relations game, which he found "most annoying" and "very frustrating." The council unanimously agreed to strike an Advisory Committee on Public Relations, and the discussion moved on.[107]

There are no examples of published pamphlets, posters, or other promotional materials in the NPC records at Library and Archives Canada. Internet searches turn up nothing, even for the ECC. There is, in other words, no indication that the NPC ever released the campaign it was working on in 1961. It seems that the only way the public came to know about the NPC's activities was through the newspapers. Although as mentioned, the media tended to fixate on the micropolitics between council members and between the constituencies they represented, stories about the NPC still brought the productivity concept into public discourse, and ensured its association with employment, competitiveness, industrial relations, and prosperity.[108] But by late 1962, it had become increasingly clear to council members that productivity was inadequate, unsuitable, or both, as a focus for government economic development efforts. This realization is evident not only in the seminar participants' and NPC members' arguments for a broader mandate (discussed above), but also in the resistance they perceived and noted, on the part of workers and organized labour, to the very word "productivity." It is impossible to say which of these factors contributed most to the NPC's dissolution – which was certainly precipitated by the fall of the Diefenbaker government as well – but it was no coincidence that the body that came to replace the NPC dropped the word from its title.

Business representative Eric Benson noticed the shift in terminology at the Vancouver meetings, which took place just as the NPC's activities (but not all of its precise "techniques") were being transferred to the ECC. Rather than ignore the elephant in the room, he pointed it out and offered his interpretation to his fellow delegates:

> I have a sneaking hunch that along with the formation of the Economic Council, two words are being quietly down-graded. One is "productivity" – because someone is afraid of the possible irritation to various elements in the Trade Union movement who might relate it to an unfortunate connection with speed-up. The other is "planning" – because of possible general apprehension in the ranks of various management groups ...
> I will go along with the semantics, but in the long haul the entire success of the Economic Council's work will depend on the satisfactory resolution of these two terms.[109]

Unlike the NPC, the ECC was not unduly hampered by its name. "The Economy," now a given, did not ignite partisan or class divisions like "productivity" did. No public relations campaign was needed to warm up the public to a new or contentious idea. The ECC tackled many of the same "problems" as the NPC, and in many respects went deeper than the earlier council ever did.[110]

Nowhere are the ECC's early priorities – nor its initial approach to productivity – more clearly or officially stated than in a report it released in 1966 titled "Economic Goals to 1970." The report reflects the five basic goals assigned to the ECC upon its establishment: "full employment," "a high rate of economic growth," "a reasonable stability of prices," "a viable balance of payments," and, finally, "an equitable distribution of rising incomes."[111] (Note the assumption that incomes would continue to rise.) It identified rising productivity as a key component of economic growth, which was itself dependent on a growing population and, in turn, a growing labour force. It shared the postwar confidence that productivity was "at the heart of [a country's] economic welfare and the prosperity of its people" and assumed that productivity gains were "the essence of economic growth" and "the real source of improvements in average living standards."[112] It accepted labour productivity as the measure of productivity that mattered and was most reliable. Its admission that productivity measurement was subject to error and technical difficulty did not discourage it from offering quite detailed predictions of the country's "potential pro-ductivity" in the years to come – even assessing prior performance as "below potential."[113]

Curiously, among the reasons for poor productivity performance listed in the report, there is one glaring omission: labour relations, even *poor* employer–employee relations, are not counted. This is in marked contrast to their centrality in the NPC's work. The ECC identified six other factors that, in its view, made "very important contributions" to the goal of "increased productive efficiency": "increased investment in human resources to improve knowledge and skills"; "improved mobility of resources"; "greater specialization and better organization of production"; "swifter and more effective technological advances"; "enlarged investment in fixed capital"; and "more initiative and enterprise ... under the spur of competition and the lure of higher returns."[114]

It seems that industrial relations – and the whole "collaborationist" model of productivity growth – had been jettisoned in the process of folding productivity into the larger objective of economic growth. This is not an inevitable or logical shift, but rather an indication that *something* – in the broader culture, in economic discourse, in govern-ment prerogatives – had changed in such a way that labour relations, once identified as the linchpin of productivity growth, were now so insignificant they hardly warranted mention. This is particularly odd given that union membership was mostly steady through the 1960s, and that the middle of the decade saw a massive wave of strikes and labour unrest across the country; thus, it is not as if industrial relations were not in the zeitgeist.[115]

The ECC did not completely sidestep the issue of industrial relations, however. In the late 1960s through to the 1980s, it periodically produced studies of labour–management relations.[116] But industrial relations were irrefutably sidelined in the ECC's founding terms of reference. The newspaper coverage of its establishment devotes little attention to the topic of labour relations, concentrating instead on the spectre of "economic planning."[117] Although some of its initiatives still brought representatives of organized labour into conversation with academics, employers and policy-makers, the ECC operated as an "advisory" body that drew on "expert" research instead of seeking consensus through town hall–style stakeholder sessions.

In plain, the switch from the NPC to the ECC represented a shift in governmentality – a change-up in both the thought and the techniques applied to economic growth. Knowing that the NPC struggled with a productivity-centric mandate, it is reasonable to conclude that the ECC subtly distanced itself from productivity and industrial relations simply to avoid the same pitfalls as had beset the earlier council. But does this abandonment of NPC objectives and format mean that the council had no lasting impact, or that its fundamental assumptions died along with it? Certainly not. The productivist thought to which the NPC conformed continued to guide the ECC, becoming even more pronounced and targeted. But the new body did have to renegotiate the role of the productivity concept, interpreting it as a means to an end – economic growth – rather than an end in itself.

The NPC and the Conduct of Conduct

The NPC is an ideal case study of governmentality. The economic theory and lay assumptions about productivity that informed its practical activities are clear examples of what Dean summarizes as "thought as it is embedded within programmes for the direction and reform of conduct." The genealogy in this chapter sought to show where the NPC came from, as well as the dynamics and tensions that entrenched certain ways of thinking and marginalized others over the course of its existence. I have wedged the council into this book's longer narrative in order to draw attention to the contingency of the NPC's techniques, and the deep roots and wide-reaching effects of the council and its thought-made-technical.

In following the model of the Marshall Plan productivity councils, the NPC took on the discursive association of productivity with industrial relations and worked from the assumption that the quality of employee–employer relations determined the productivity of firms, industries, and nations alike. As previous chapters showed, there were other configurations of the productivity concept that could have determined the NPC's choice of techniques, including theories that placed more emphasis on the productivity of capital. But especially after the First World War, the dominant ideational regime focused interventions on labour productivity and directed the reform impulse towards workers' performance and attitudes. Success in this regard hinged on highlighting the "natural" or "logical" alignment of workers' and employers' interests and exhorting both to cooperate towards their shared better future in a growing economy.

There were alternative ways of making the link between productivity and well-being: instead of embracing the assumption that increased productivity would mean "more jobs," the council could have oriented itself towards a world with less work; but by then there was a pervasive fear of what ordinary people would do if they found themselves with more free time. The "ghosts" Weber saw in his day – the "dead religious belief" in the Protestant work ethic – haunted those who laboured and those who governed them well into the twentieth century, such that a world without menial work was posited as dangerous and sinful instead of liberating and humane. Only material rewards, a diminished threat of unemployment, and a steady increase in consumption power would sufficiently endear Canadians to their government's national productivity plan.

The NPC's techniques had an ambiguous relationship to the work of the DBS. On the one hand, the council was regularly presented with progress reports, empirical studies, methodological tracts, and theoretical essays by DBS representatives. Those technocrats often warned about the shortcomings in their productivity statistics, but they also boasted about the importance of such statistics for economic growth, government policy, and the welfare of Canadians. As Simon A. Goldberg, Assistant Dominion Statistician, said in his address to the Dalhousie seminar, "productivity statistics are at the apex of the system of economic statistics."[118] But the statisticians' reports almost always included some attention to the productivity of both labour and capital, and they *never* provided any empirical evidence of the assumed link between productivity and living standards. They merely peddled the same truisms as the business people and politicians attending the seminars alongside them: productivity would practically guarantee economic growth, employment, higher incomes, and lower national debt.

The NPC's gravitation towards public relations as its chosen technique illuminates something very important about its historical and political context. In that tight space between liberal economic governance and centralized economic "planning," the council's most obvious course of action was to seek to subtly influence the public mind – to educate Canadians about the importance of productivity to their own well-being, and to instil an understanding of productivity as dependent on harmonious, cooperative industrial relations. This is the space in which many, if not most, government apparatuses have found themselves over the seventy years since the Second World War: having to govern without appearing to exercise anything but the will of the people. So the NPC and other government bodies sought to shape, ever so subtly, the people's will. Given that the NPC collapsed after three years – all three marred by slow progress, confusion over terms of reference, disagreement among members, and poor public perception and press coverage – and was never fully revived in the ECC, we might reasonably conclude that it failed in this crucial task.

However, the survival of productivity as one widely accepted factor in economic growth suggests that the NPC did not fail completely. In a way, the council merely discovered that productivity was a term best left in the background, along with "planning," as it needlessly raised the question of *who* was more responsible for productivity growth, and stoked fears of technological unemployment. Moreover, although no one involved in the NPC or in the establishment of the ECC could have predicted the decline in Canadian unionization rates after 1970, the ECC's movement away from industrial relations foreshadowed the decreasing significance organized labour would command vis-à-vis economic policy in the new council's final decade. By the 1970s and especially the 1980s, industrial relations and organized labour would be cordoned off as *political* concerns, to be dealt with outside the politically neutral, self-contained, and externally driven national (and later global) economy.

The government activity carried out under the banner of "economic development" would expand in the 1980s, retaining both the productivist impulse and the productivity concept (albeit in the supporting role it held in the ECC). It would be increasingly devolved into *regional* efforts to bring provincial economies in line with national averages without relying too heavily on federal transfer payments to redistribute the national income. The ECC helped kick this process into gear with discussion papers and policy backgrounders on regional differences in productivity and other measures of economic performance.[119] As the next chapter will show, the productivity concept was marginal to regional economic development discussions for a relatively brief period after the 1970s, but it has enjoyed a revival of sorts in the twenty-first century, alongside the flashy, compelling, and now ubiquitous concept of *competitiveness* and the subtler but no less influential discourse of *opportunity*. Understanding the effects of these concepts on the productivist ideational regime – Do they fit within it? Do they challenge it? Are they complementary or competing? – is imperative if we want to make sense of economic thought at the beginning of the twenty-first century.

Chapter Five

The Atlantic Canada Opportunities Agency

As many economists tell us, we are entering a new economic age ... The new economy is producing goods and services at a very different employment level. The production of the economies of the western world has exceeded pre-downturn levels, but still some 25 million to 30 million people are left unemployed ... In addition ... there are those over 45 and 50 years of age whose skills may have become obsolete and are no longer needed in the new economic society. We must be aware of the potential disaster for the western world if we ignore the victims of this new age [and we must] alleviate the potential misery of those who will not fit into the new age ... Another potential, but very real, danger is that when employment of the individual becomes endangered those who still have jobs become less and less willing to share their affluence through tax contributions which really provide the safety net. These people see themselves endangered and develop a survival-of-the-fittest mentality.

– Senator Alasdair B. Graham (Cape Breton), Senate Debates,
20 December 1983

Long before the first Dominion statistician and the NPC – and decades, even, before the first economics journals offered a space for reflection on the concept of productivity – the British North American colonies of Canada (Ontario and Quebec), New Brunswick, and Nova Scotia joined together to form the Dominion of Canada in 1867. Not surprisingly, neither the nascent notion of productivity nor the goal of economic growth as such played a part in Canada's Confederation or the discussions thereof. But in just over a century, both would move to the centre of relations between the provinces and the federal government.

The federal structure of fiscal responsibilities and obligations, and the terms governing the movement of people, goods, and money across provincial borders, have at times thrust the provinces' productivity performance into the middle of heated debates over who-owes-who-what via what channels. These debates emerged, for example, around the terms of Confederation itself in 1867, and around the issue of federal transfer payments (the dispensation of surplus federal tax and tariff revenues back to the provinces), especially in 1982, when such "equalization measures" were written into the Constitution Act.[1]

But until fairly recently, negotiations over the provinces' rights and obligations towards one another, and the terms of reciprocity between the federal government in Ottawa and provincial governments elsewhere, revolved around the uneven distribution of natural resources, the labour force and population, and taxes and tariffs. At some point, post-1980, productivity presented itself as a useful word for expressing all of these factors in a single concept and measure. This was to direct attention away from the initial, historical distribution of various resources towards how efficiently provinces used their endowments, which fit very well with the laissez-faire "market fundamentalist" governmentality of the time.[2] Instead of seeking to redress injustices of the past or mitigate power imbalances in interprovincial and intergovernmental relationships, the government and wealthy parties that wished to hang on to their wealth could focus on helping weaker provinces work harder and do more with less.[3] The evolution of government agencies with "regional development" mandates offers a window onto this mentality as it developed in the Atlantic provinces.[4]

This chapter looks specifically at the Atlantic Canada Opportunities Agency (ACOA), a body established in 1987 with a mission to "increase opportunity for economic development in Atlantic Canada and, more particularly, to enhance the growth of earned incomes and employment opportunities in that region."[5] Nowhere in the act was there any mention of productivity. Today, however, the agency's *top* priority is to foster "greater productivity." The closest the original act came to productivity was in two lines that delimited the ACOA minister's mandate, which tasked him or her with facilitating "improvements in locally based productive employment." Not until much later did the agency make "growth in productivity" its most important objective. Productivity, in other words, has become a target in itself again, as it was in the NPC's day, as opposed to an outcome or condition of other improvements; it is now seen not as a fixed quality of certain jobs (as is implied in the agency's initial focus on "productive employment"), but as a feature of industries, labourers, and entire economies that can and should be continuously improved. If ACOA's transformation is any indication, the old association between productivity and such negative potentialities as technological unemployment appears to have faded from memory, at a time when technological advances seem even *more* capable than ever of delivering a world where fewer and fewer humans are needed to produce the goods and services we all need (and those we simply want).

In this chapter, I draw on the agency's archival records, historical parliamentary debates, newspaper archives, and over twenty years of ACOA's reports to Parliament, asking when and why the focus turned to productivity (and improvements thereto). What I find is a revised productivity concept, the lineage of which extends through the NPC, the DBS, and the early economic thought covered in previous chapters, but which is noticeably different. Most importantly, the long-standing, direct discursive link between productivity and prosperity has been replaced with an indirect one that connects productivity improvements with increased *opportunities*. ACOA's more localized vantage point on this discursive change highlights how shifting understandings of productivity and productivism are translated into policies and programs that touch the ground where people live, work, and encounter "the economy." To contextualize these insights, we must situate ACOA as one of the latest manifestations of an evolving regional development governmentality that dates back to Canada's birth.

Unequal from the Outset

Confederation raised all kinds of questions about equality between the ten provinces and three territories that would eventually comprise Canada, and between the three to five "regions" into which the country is discursively and at times practically divided. Confederation did not come easy, and was a "tough sell" in Nova Scotia in particular.[6] Pro-Confederates, touting the benefits of interprovincial rail, improved trade, debt allowances, and centralization, came up against staunch resistance from anti-Confederates who worried about the small province's sovereignty in an agreement dominated by bigger, economically and politically more powerful provinces to its west. But the pro-Confederates eventually won out, and the groundwork was laid for the country we now call Canada. Since 1867, as Canada has added two more eastern provinces, four to the west, and the three territories, the question of Confederation's costs and benefits has arisen again and again.

When Nova Scotia and New Brunswick first linked up with Ontario and Quebec, the two easternmost provinces were already less well-off than the others. The best available historical estimates of national and provincial income suggest that there was inequality at the time of Confederation and in the decades thereafter, with the lowest wages and incomes in Nova Scotia and New Brunswick.[7] In addition, as historian Patricia Thornton has shown, "a steady net loss" of population "was already well underway" in the Maritimes at the time of Confederation. There is ample evidence that the terms of Confederation only exacerbated these existing inequities, obliging the Maritime provinces (joined by Prince Edward Island in 1873) to pay for many benefits that never came to fruition, limiting their authority to levy taxes, making it even easier for labour to move to the more prosperous provinces, and weakening the Maritimes' established and highly beneficial trade relationship with the northeastern United States.[8]

The British North America Act (BNAA), which laid out the terms of Confederation, established a fiscal compact between the provinces and their new federal government whereby the latter would levy taxes on the provinces and tariffs on interprovincial trade in order to finance its considerable new programs and projects (e.g., the nationwide postal service, an intercolonial railway, and the census and statistics). Each of the provinces would receive a subsidy to pay for government operations, and the federal government was obligated to dole out any surplus revenues in additional "transfer payments" to the provinces on a per capita basis (not, notably, on the basis of financial need). It would also assume the provinces' debts. These subsidies and transfers accounted for most of the Maritime provinces' revenues in the first decade after Confederation, with New Brunswick drawing "92 per cent of its revenue from Ottawa, ... Nova Scotia 81 per cent," and "Prince Edward Island 75 per cent."[9] Early on, Maritime politicians had bargained hard for "better terms" – higher subsidies, transfer payments, and debt allowances – and won some small concessions. But twenty-five years after Confederation, their provinces were still struggling. Wages and incomes remained comparatively low, out-migration "reach[ed] epidemic proportions in the 1880s and 1890s," and the decent economic growth the Maritime provinces had enjoyed through the 1880s gave way to stagnation in the 1890s.[10]

As historian Richard Starr has noted, the dominant view around this time was that "the level of public services in each province should be dictated by the level of wealth." But "eventually," Canada "rejected that ungenerous way of thinking," and in the postwar era, a needs-based fiscal transfer system began to take shape, along with "equalization" policies.[11] The system was quite straightforward: given that the low tax base in some provinces "constrained [them] from providing the necessary level of services," the federal government "collect[ed] a bit more in taxes than they require[d] for their purposes" and redistributed the surplus "to ensure that all Canadian citizens [had] a semblance of equality in health, education and other services provided by provincial governments."[12] What Starr considers "generous" was also, and not coincidentally, decidedly *not* productivist. The early fiscal transfer system conveyed no assumption that well-being or equality depends on economic growth, nor did the system's architects assume that the provinces' economies or the national economy should or could grow continuously.

The Maritime provinces played a crucial role in the emergence of the arrangement and of the ideas propping it up. Indeed, it was largely because of strong advocacy (and threats of separation) from the Maritime provinces that the system was established. Starr traces the idea of equality through redistribution to Nova Scotia premier Angus L. MacDonald, who called for a kind of equalization program in 1938. The impetus for such measures had been growing during the Great Depression, when the provinces faced insurmountable health and social welfare costs, so much so that the federal government struck a Royal Commission on Dominion–Provincial Relations in 1937. In the order-in-council calling for the commission, the Mackenzie King government advocated "a re-examination of the economic and financial basis of Confederation and of the distribution of legislative powers in the light of the economic and social developments of the last seventy years."[13] The Rowell–Sirois Commission, as it was known, responded to overwhelming evidence and presentations from the provinces indicating that the latter could not cover the costs of their constitutional responsibilities.

The five commissioners and about a dozen staff members spent three years travelling the country, interviewing various provincial authorities, soliciting advice, and commissioning expert research. By many accounts, the body's findings and recommendations shocked a nation that was not yet fully aware of the wide disparities in income and well-being between the provinces. In its 1940 final report, it recommended that the federal government collect more taxes, assume responsibility for unemployment insurance and other programs then under the purview of the provinces, and begin giving grants to the poorest provinces to help them cover the costs of social programs and services still in their control. The weight of its evidence – particularly heavy after the Great Depression – seems to have compelled the government to act, and the Canadian people to support it. Thus began several decades during which the redistribution of wealth among the provinces, while not entirely *un*controversial, was a normal part of Canadian governance.

In 1957 the St Laurent government introduced the country's first formal "equalization payments" program, and in 1982, the *right* of the provinces to "sufficient revenues to provide reasonably comparable public services at reasonably comparable levels of taxation" was enshrined in the constitution. All parties – federal and provincial – were thus committed to the "principle" of equalization.[14] But by that time, in Starr's account, the system was already beginning to weaken under attack from neoconservative governments at all levels. Mirroring similar arguments against welfare to individuals, some argued against regional equalization on moral grounds, claiming that it was not fair that wealthier provinces should subsidize those that failed to thrive. Others sought to convince Canadians that regional transfers actually worsened inequality in the long run.[15] Even some Maritime and Atlantic politicians came to believe that equalization payments were a shameful handout that damaged the entrepreneurial spirit in their provinces: "the help that hurts."[16]

At a deeper level, the discourse around equalization – visible in the constitution itself – was changing; productivist ideas were becoming hegemonic. The productivist ideational regime was taking shape. The Rowell–Sirois Commission's sole concern was that the provinces be able to afford the social services and programs for which they were responsible. The equalization scheme introduced in 1957 (in the Federal–Provincial Tax Sharing Arrangements Act) spoke to the same concern. These ideas were evidently hardly controversial, and aside from a few assurances that they did not amount to Soviet-style "centralization" in government, they needed very little help to gain approval in the House of Commons. None of the provinces wanted to renege on their obligations to their residents, nor did they wish to see their counterparts doing so. The recommendations and proposed legislative changes only needed to point to the need for "reasonably comparable public services" in order to underscore their importance. Thus, there was nothing in the Rowell–Sirois Report or the 1957 equalization bill about promoting economic development or expanding "opportunities." But twenty-five years later, in the Constitution Act of 1982, the concept of equalization would be firmly attached to economic growth and entrenched in pro-ductivist logic. It would foreground the objectives of "promoting equal opportunities," and "furthering the economic development to reduce disparity in opportunities," as if a minimum standard of public ser-vices was not valuable enough without some prospect of it increasing provincial incomes.[17]

Productivity and Regional Inequality

The shift in thinking about regional inequality and equalization described above stemmed from deeper changes in how The Economy was understood – recall here (from chapter 1) that the notion of a sin-gular, fixed economy was only just coming into existence in the mid-dle of the century. Although today Canadians sometimes think of the provinces as having their own separate, bounded economies, trading among themselves within the larger national economy, this image of self-contained spheres of economic activity, with boundaries that lined up with provincial geography, was embryonic in the 1950s. At most, the provinces were understood to have economic *characteristics* that warranted certain kinds of treatment by the federal government. Introducing the 1957 measures to the House of Commons, then–finance minister Walter E. Harris surmised that the task before the government was the "reconciliation ... of the differing factors of economics, geog-raphy, race, custom and religion" across the Canadian provinces.[18] The tax-sharing "equalization" measures proposed in the new bill prom-ised to preserve the federal system and look out for "the national inter-est" without curtailing the rights of the provinces to do as they pleased in the areas under their jurisdiction. (Payments were thus to be given with no strings attached.)

A curious assumption runs through Harris's remarks on the bill that is at odds with the assumptions underlying later equalization schemes and regional development rhetoric. The assumption, at the end of the 1950s, was that the provinces were naturally and even immutably endowed with different levels of wealth – "differing factors of economics" – and, accordingly, there was less interest in incentives for economic growth in weaker regions, and less concern that equalization payments would create "dependency" on the part of receiving provinces. Indeed, as Starr found in his research, Harris's predecessor as finance minister, Douglas Abbott, was of the same mind. He had once opined that "no federal-provincial fiscal arrangement can alter the facts of geography or change the location of rich natural resources, but federal-provincial arrangements should be designed to moderate, rather than aggravate, these regional inequalities of wealth and resources."[19]

A mere thirty years after the first formal equalization plan, this sentiment would be marginalized by the influential idea that the equalization system created parasitic and damaging interprovincial relationships, perpetuating inequality and holding all of the provinces back from their full economic potential. As one conservative MP put it in the 1980s, equalization was appealing only to people who "don't like success."[20] The diminishing support for equalization over the 1960s and 1970s fits with the broader narrative, introduced in chapter 1, of the rise of neoliberal thinking – or market fundamentalism – in Canada and across the world.

A bit of a refresher might be helpful here. Neoliberal governmentality and market fundamentalism prioritize entrepreneurialism, competition, freedom (especially for business), and laissez-faire economic policy (or, at least, the appearance thereof). They tout the market's ultimate power to provide the necessities and perks of life to all who are willing to work for them. There is little room in neoliberal thought for the notion that provinces (or people) might be structurally disadvantaged and there-fore deserving of structural support. Instead, the reigning view of social, political, and economic relations is that, so long as government does not meddle in economic affairs, provinces (and people), acting freely, com-petitively, and entrepreneurially, can prosper and, through their compe-tition and prosperity, induce presumably boundless economic growth. In this way, neoliberal thinking and market fundamentalism are *expressions of productivism*, although they are not the only ones.

Much has been written about the tenets of neoliberal and market fundamentalist thought and their effects on governance and everyday life.[21] But the Canadian experience with regional inequalities and with the interventions (or non-interventions) designed to address those ine-qualities highlights an important bit of neoliberal discourse that has yet to be examined in any great detail: the discourse of *opportunities*. The case explored here, of the Atlantic Canada *Opportunities* Agency, is an insightful starting point. It serves as a "paradigmatic case" of the economic opportunities discourse emerging in the 1980s, and because it has survived well into the second decade of the twenty-first century, it offers insight into how that discourse has evolved through several major fluctuations in the Canadian and global economy.[22] But for my purposes, it is most important for what it reveals about productivity and the productivist ideational regime.

In short, I find three striking developments. First, productivity has become one of the primary markers by which provincial economies are judged and ranked in terms of their importance to the National Economy and/or the drain they represent on its limited resources. The "deservingness" of a given province vis-à-vis federal transfer payments has, in a twist of logic, come to depend on its ability to show solid productivity growth and to exhaust *all* extant "opportunities" for increased productivity rather than on demonstration of need.

Second, and relatedly, governments that once expended most of their energy looking inward for ways to increase employment and incomes have, especially in the twenty-first century, turned outward. This is not to say that governments have come to invite foreign investment and international business; in Atlantic Canada especially, developing local business (encouraging "start-ups" and lauding the "small business owner") is the stated goal. But there is still an international dimension; start-ups are considered most successful if their products and services reach the export market. Pointing to the development of a new "global" economy, governments have thus made it their job not to protect or increase the prosperity of their people, but to help them gain a competitive edge – even if it means lower wages and less work, at least in the short term – against "low-cost" producers in other countries. Once the dust finally settled after the collapse of the NPC, productivity emerged, unmoored from the damaging concepts of technological unemployment and speed-up, and rose to prominence as an indispensable component of global competitiveness.

Third, I find additional evidence that the historical connection between productivity and prosperity has been redrawn. As noted, governments and mainstream economists have gradually begun to treat productivity not as a guarantee of prosperity, but as a necessary condition for increased average incomes and standards of living (the same can be said for economic growth). As Don Drummond, quoted earlier, put it, "productivity growth does not ensure higher wages or greater happiness. But try achieving either or both without productivity growth."[23] ACOA seems to have accepted this point, and no longer promises to deliver better living standards and prosperity – just economic growth. All of this will lead to a question: Can the productivist ideational regime be said to be dominant, still, despite these changes? Are we still looking at the same basic constellation of ideas and narratives?

Institutionalizing Opportunities

Comparing the mid-century finance ministers' statements about federal–provincial relations to the dominant obsession with "opportunity" from the 1980s onward, one can see a slow but drastic transformation of the way in which provincial wealth and economics are understood by the state (defined broadly) and its citizens. The proclamations of Abbott and Harris – that the federal government had to do something to "mitigate" the consequences of unevenly distributed resources – stemmed from a Depression-era sensitivity to inequality and poverty, and anticipated what Starr has called "the era of good intentions." Starr dates the latter to the election of John Diefenbaker in 1957, and the reign of a *"Progressive* Conservative" government that would take many of the crucial first steps towards a Canadian welfare state. Over the next half-century, as the power to govern shifted from the Diefenbaker government to the Pearson (and then Trudeau) Liberals, Canada would see the introduction of needs-based transfers to the provinces and regional development agencies (and related bodies). The influence of productivism was certainly there, but it was not so powerful as to render unthinkable redistributive efforts that did not depend on economic growth. In large part, this is likely because the Canadian economy, like the US economy, *was* growing at unprecedented rates. The tax base was such that the government could afford to spend money in "underdeveloped" areas without attracting too much criticism from the net givers.

The reader interested in a detailed historical review of these agencies and payment systems should consult Donald Savoie's 2003 report, *Reviewing Canada's Regional Development Efforts*. In that work, which was produced for the Newfoundland and Labrador government's Royal Commission on Renewing and Strengthening Our Place in Canada, Savoie argues that a shift occurred between the 1960s and the 1990s. Specifically, programs "initially designed to benefit have-less provinces" and "alleviate regional disparities" slowly turned their gaze to "national unity."[24] But running parallel to this shift was another – the one I began to trace above: the "guiding principle" of the earliest equalization and regional development efforts was *need*, but over time and political-economic changes, they began to take up the discourse of *opportunities* instead. I argue that this shift points to the intensification of productivism, in Canadian governmentality, and in general: the expansion of the productivist ideational regime and its successful "embedding" of other economic and social ideas about taxation, fairness, redistribution, equality, and so on.

As Savoie's review makes clear, the earliest regional development agencies (RDAs) devoted significant resources to basic economic infrastructure in the Atlantic provinces. They funded highways and electricity plants, partly in the belief that a foundation of adequate infrastructure was a matter of regional equality, but also on the assumption that such a foundation could give provinces the leg up they needed to achieve economic growth on par with the wealthier provinces. The latter assumption became more pronounced as the first RDAs were dissolved and replaced by new ones. The Department of Regional Economic Expansion (DREE, later bisected into the Department of Regional *Industrial* Expansion or DRIE and the Industrial and Regional Development Program) maintained the focus on infrastructure needs, "but with an important caveat." As Savoie summarizes, DREE "would focus on slow-growth regions, but look to growth areas within these regions to promote economic development."[25]

Savoie connects this change in priorities to several influences. First, he notes the growing popularity of the "growth poles" theory of economic development – the notion that economic growth was optimally and realistically going to be clustered around key industries and areas – an idea that shaped the way DREE targeted funds. Second, he suggests that Ontario, Quebec, and the Western provinces began to complain that they, too, deserved infrastructure funding. They drew on an emerging discourse of "competitiveness" to bolster their case, arguing, perversely, that whatever the federal government did for one region it ought to do for all regions. They managed to divert attention away from the uneven playing field and towards the intentionally uneven supports, and they convinced the federal government to establish RDAs in their provinces. By the 1970s, the majority of regional development funding was being spent west of New Brunswick.[26] Third, Savoie points to the rise of "the neo-conservative school," which sought to shrink government and diminish its control over (some) economic affairs – to "get government out of business," in popular parlance.[27] Regional development was, according to this school of thought, an intervention in a National Economy that would otherwise sort itself out fairly through competition and freedom. The confluence of these ideological and political factors, which are part of an evolving neoliberal governmentality, destroyed DREE and the short-lived bodies (e.g., DRIE) that appeared in its immediate wake.[28]

One of its successors, however, remains: ACOA, established in 1987, the same year DRIE was disbanded. Unlike DRIE, which prioritized the establishment and development of specific industrial operations ahead of the broader development of entire regions (validated, again, by the "growth poles" concept), ACOA (and the parallel agencies established in other regions around the same time) was meant to take a more holistic approach, directing funding and other kinds of support to businesses across the region. In part, this new approach stemmed from an emerging consensus, driven by the results of new economic and policy research, that most economic growth came from small and mid-sized businesses. Policy-makers had concluded that the "smokestack chasing" of DRIE and earlier bodies had failed – and would continue to fail – to incite economic growth and expand employment in depressed areas.[29] Buoyed by the increasingly influential neoliberal goal of "liberating individual entrepreneurial freedoms and skills," Canada's governments set their sights on a new kind of regional development – one that apparently eschewed direct government aid in favour of "creating the conditions" and "expanding the opportunities" for economic growth.[30]

Accordingly, ACOA was established in 1987 with a mandate to improve opportunities, and a title that ensured this focus would not easily be abandoned. It was there to help businesses establish themselves through seed funding and general assistance with coordination, and to be an advocate for the region with the federal government. Media coverage of the agency's founding, combined with the records of parliamentary debates, speaks volumes about the anxieties of the time and the ideational regime within which ACOA had to make sense and find legitimacy with the population. Many warned that allocating federal money in this way would create an unhealthy dependency, on the part of receiving provinces, on the national government – a rather curious worry, considering that similar bodies were established in Ontario and Quebec and on the prairies around the same time. Even among Atlantic Canadians, their media, and their MPs, there was a deep, related worry that ACOA would hand out money left, right, and centre and thus become a drain on federal tax revenues. Moreover, there were predictions that the agency would become one more ballooning bureaucracy being strangled by its own red tape.

The Mulroney government sought to pre-empt these worries immediately, beginning with the official announcement of ACOA's establishment. First, it assured Canadians that the agency would *not* receive any new funding. Rather, Mulroney announced, its "top priority is to work towards a more effective use of the generous funds already set aside for the development of the Atlantic Region." Furthermore, went the government line, ACOA would ensure "the development of businesses rather than the uncontrolled growth of the public sector" by "eliminat[ing] obstacles that stand in the way of private-sector growth" and "strengthen[ing] our competitiveness by lightening the burden of red tape and regulation."[31] The news release issued by the Prime Minister's Office emphasized the agency's commitment to "long term economic development" and its "coordinating mandate over all federal activities" in this regard.[32]

Still, by early 1988, the regional papers would surmise that ACOA looked "like a cumbersome bureaucracy – 189 employees already and counting towards 380." As the Halifax *Chronicle-Herald* concluded, "all that can be said definitively about ACOA today is that its wheels grind slowly."[33] Later that year, debate broke out in the House of Commons over a proposed amendment to the Government Organization Act delimiting ACOA's mandate and institutional structure. Jack Harris, a New Democratic Party MP from Newfoundland, proposed that the description of ACOA's role should include, among its objectives, "reduc[ing] the economic disparity between Atlantic Canada and other regions of Canada." Addressing the House, he said:

> Mr. Speaker, this is probably one of the most important motions before the House at report stage … [It] is the core and the essence of what we in this party think the Atlantic Canada Opportunities Agency ought to do … Why is the Government afraid to put into the legislation a commitment to the reduction of regional disparity? It may or may not want to answer that question, but I have my own interpretation of the Government's action. It has developed an agency which does not have that goal. This is an agency that is basically designed to assist business and economic development. It has no goal to reduce the regional disparity between the Atlantic Region and other regions of the country that are more prosperous. Without that objective, we simply have another agency to assist business and enhance the economy.[34]

Ultimately, Harris's motion was defeated. Most MPs, including many from the Atlantic provinces, disagreed with putting regional inequality so front-and-centre. They were quite satisfied with the original wording, which merely committed ACOA to "support and promote opportunity for economic development of Atlantic Canada, with particular emphasis on small and medium-sized enterprises."[35] Denis Cochrane, an MP from Moncton, New Brunswick, expressed the views of this majority as follows:

> I am much more anxious to promote opportunities than to go about measuring disparity ... We are anxious to build upon what exists, and upon the opportunities that are presented in Atlantic Canada. This is more productive than making an effort to write a report and provide statistics that will really have no meaning ...We want to put the staff time, energy and effort toward expanding our opportunities rather than measuring negative factors.[36]

Moreover, he said, "we do not want to entitle a certain region or a certain province to a given amount of money under this program. Rather, we want all Atlantic Canadians to have the opportunity to chase after every economic opportunity that presents itself."[37] Conservative MPs added to Cochrane's points, the most bombastic among them being the minister of international trade, John Crosbie, whose remarks, though increasingly hyperbolic, are only a slight exaggeration of the assumptions underlying the rejection of Harris's amendment. He began by reinforcing the primacy of "opportunities" in the new agency's mandate. "If the people are more alert, more on the ball, more active and have more initiative in Nova Scotia, PEI, New Brunswick or Newfoundland than in the other places," he proposed, "then they deserve to have a response to their initiatives." In his view, ACOA was meant "to give entrepreneurs, risk-takers and those who have initiative a chance to move ahead."[38] He closed with this dramatic dismissal of the NDP motion:

> The few remarks of [Mr Harris] were simply a poem against success. He sounds as though he did not like success, as though he were against the people who are successful. The implication of his remarks is that the people who are successful should not be assisted by this agency. Has one ever heard such absolute tommyrot? Should this Agency only give assistance to those who have never had success in their lives, those who have been completely unsuccessful up until now?[39]

Crosbie did not need to be so shrill. His vision of ACOA – as a reward system for those who "dare to try" rather than a delivery system for "welfare" – was already the accepted vision for the new agency, and it would remain so.[40] This foundational and lasting commitment to opportunities and individual enterprise is important here because it shaped the terrain on which the productivity concept would eventually re-emerge and find a home. The story of how productivity came to matter to ACOA adds an additional, perplexing, and related layer to the agency's history, and offers one perspective on the most recent ruptures and continuities in the productivity concept and in the productivist regime in which it has long been embedded.

Establishing the Atlantic Canada Opportunities Agency

Savoie, a Canadian scholar of public administration and frequent adviser to federal and provincial governments, wrote the 1987 report that effectively led to ACOA's creation. At the request of Prime Minister Mulroney, Savoie "had discussions" with business people, academics, political leaders, policy-makers, and ordinary Canadians about how Atlantic Canada could grow its economy and improve standards of living for its population. He claimed to have found, through these discussions, "a deeply felt desire to break away from dependency on government," as well as wide recognition "that the dependency syndrome offers little prospect for improving economic opportunities, particularly for the new generation."[41]

He was careful to distinguish his object in the report – regional economic development – from the question of "regional equity in public services and income," arguing that the two had "become confused and it is important to separate them in our thinking and to keep them apart."[42] Indeed, he pointed out, federal transfer payments had largely taken care of the equity issue. With that matter settled, attention had to turn to "creating, developing and strengthening the private sector." Atlantic Canada would have to eschew the "smokestack chasing" of earlier initiatives and, according to Savoie, focus on "developing new endogenous companies, enhancing existing business, developing new products, and expanding into new national and international markets."[43]

All of Savoie's specific recommendations about mandate revolved around this commitment to business *development*. Savoie's sights, and the agency's in turn, were set on establishing businesses – *small* businesses, to be precise. Informed by MIT economist David Birch's 1979 essay "The Job Generation Process" – which Savoie called "the most widely read and quoted article in the history of industrial development" – Savoie and most governments of his day were convinced that small and medium-sized enterprises (or SMEs), not big corporations, were the biggest job creators. Accordingly, economic development efforts turned towards the problem of getting small businesses up and running, encouraging people to be entrepreneurs, and lifting some of the bureaucratic and financial burden from those who "dared" to start a small business. Savoie strongly recommended that ACOA take a "long-term view," and he made some recommendations about the need for "innovation" and "human resources development," but there was very little in his vision for ACOA that dealt with the sustainability or even the performance of businesses. It was enough to simply get more of them going, to get Atlantic Canadians to seize on the available opportunities for business. Savoie did not make a single mention of productivity.

The act establishing ACOA created an agency that closely mirrored Savoie's vision; its object was "to support and promote opportunity for economic development of Atlantic Canada." It was to focus on "small and medium-sized" businesses, developing "entrepreneurial talent," and enhancing "economic prosperity" in the region. The original act, like the version that is in force as of 2014, does not include the word productivity, although it does make two references to "productive employment" in its delineation of ministerial responsibilities.[44]

Even in the parliamentary records from 1986 to 1990, although there are many mentions of productivity and many exchanges about ACOA, there is only one discussion that suggests that it is ACOA's responsibility to improve productivity in the region.[45] In October 1989, an MP reporting to the House of Commons quoted Prime Minister Mulroney as saying the following about the Agency: "ACOA is about the future, about helping business people improve productivity, exploit new technology, develop new markets and create new jobs. ACOA represents a new approach and a new commitment on our part to Atlantic regional economic development."[46]

Yet in its first one-year report to Parliament, covering the period 1989–90, the agency did not mention productivity at all. A section on "Catching the Wave of Global Trade" presaged a shift towards trade and "competitiveness" that would fully take hold nearly twenty years later, but the emphasis was overwhelmingly on helping "get the Atlantic Region's new pioneers into business."[47] The minister's introductory letter reiterated ACOA's commitment to small businesses and entrepreneurs, especially new start-ups, which it helped in "developing management and marketing skills."[48] This commitment to business start-ups was all-encompassing; "everything that ACOA has done and will continue to do," according to Mulroney, was about "renew[ing] the 'Atlantic Entrepreneurial spirit.'"[49]

ACOA at the End of the Twentieth Century

In 1991, perhaps spurred by the new decade, perhaps by the "severe recession" that had set in around 1990, ACOA (and outsiders looking in) began to reflect on its achievements to date.[50] Long-serving senator Alasdair B. Graham, originally from Cape Breton, asked in June 1991 for a list of its major accomplishments. Graham, whose collection at Library and Archives Canada is also the primary holding of ACOA's records, saved the document he received in response. In it, there is nothing at all about productivity, either in the rundown of the agency's objectives or in the accounting of its achievements. There are only job numbers and qualitative reports about increased support for entrepreneurs, procurement of federal contracts, and "strengthening the environment for business growth."[51]

Savoie, who had remained central to the agency throughout its first four years, wrote another report that reviewed ACOA's efforts to date and made recommendations for the way forward. My reading leads me to conclude that although it took some time, it was this 1991 report, titled *ACOA: Transition to Maturity*, that thrust productivity into the agency's official communications and its strategic plans and priorities – the latter of which were increasingly expected of government agencies through the 1990s and 2000s, as a matter of greater accountability. Savoie remarked that although "solid progress has been made," the agency still faced serious challenges. The "global economy" was making its tasks more complex, as was "deindustrialization" and the concentration of "new technologies" in "high-growth areas." Unfortunately, Atlantic Canada displayed a lack of innovation and the "lowest levels of technological intensity," and it also had the lowest levels of economic output and growth.[52] In Savoie's view, if the region was "to be competitive," it would have to meet the following "key challenges": "the continuing decline in productivity in the region's manufacturing and service industries"; "the quality of the labour force"; "the application of technological innovation"; and, echoing the politicians and pundits of decades past, the region's dependency on the federal government.[53]

To help the region overcome these deficiencies, Savoie recommended that ACOA focus its energies on two key "themes." The first was entrepreneurship, because, so he reasoned, "if the region is to prosper," it had to be Atlantic Canadians who "provide the energy, the skills and the imagination to conceive and organize economic activity."[54] But the second "overall theme" is slightly more important to the story building here: Savoie wrote that "ACOA should focus its efforts on making Atlantic Canada more competitive":

> In this regard, it should aim to increase the region's productivity levels over the next five years ... It is hardly possible to overstate the importance of productivity for Atlantic Canada. The global economy imposes its own discipline and unless a region becomes competitive, it will simply not prosper ... There is thus an urgency for Atlantic Canada to turn its attention to productivity and ACOA is the one agency ideally suited to take the lead ... If there is one goal that the four Atlantic Provinces have in common, it is to increase their productivity.

This direct link between competitiveness and productivity would resurface many times in ACOA's future communications and initiatives – that is, being competitive is often framed as a matter of being at least as productive as other regions and countries. Savoie had a few ideas about how ACOA could help the provinces pursue this common goal: it could prioritize "promoting innovation and technology transfer, human resources development, increasing cooperation with the private sector and the universities, strengthening the region's research and development capacity and even its infrastructure – notably transportation." In sum, he suggested, "these two overall themes should form the basis of ACOA's vision of how it would like to lead Atlantic Canada for the next several years."[55]

Judging by ACOA's report to Parliament in 1992, these recommendations were not swiftly adopted. According to John Crosbie, then the minister responsible, the agency's primary objective was still helping small businesses and entrepreneurs in "developing and marketing innovative ideas." ACOA president Peter B. Lesaux noted then that the agency had undertaken "an intensive corporate planning exercise." It would have had access to Savoie's report and recommendations for this purpose, but the "seven strategic priorities" on which it settled did not include increasing "the region's productivity levels" as Savoie suggested. None of the seven – "Innovation and Technology Transfer, Entrepreneurship Development, Trade and Investment Promotion, Procurement and Industrial Benefits, Human Resources Development, and Investment Support and Diversification" – said anything whatsoever about productivity.[56]

The next time ACOA reported to Parliament it was 1993, and the accepted format had changed from one-year reports to five-year reports. In its review of activities from 1988 to 1993, the agency still devoted only scant attention to productivity. It recommitted itself to a definition of equity as "meaning equality of opportunity," and it again stated its mission "to foster, in a strategic partnership with the people of Atlantic Canada, the long-term economic development of the region through the renewal of the Atlantic entrepreneurial spirit."[57] This time, however, it began to place more emphasis on the influence and role of the federal government. And it was in pointing to *national* economic priorities that the agency first made productivity an explicit piece of its objectives. Its "strategic priorities," it explained, were "shaped by national priorities and by annual consultations with Atlantic Canadians." As such, they had been "refined through the years to reflect the Agency's mandate and the *national concerns of increased productivity and competitiveness in the global marketplace* [italics added]."[58]

However, like the previous reports, the 1993 report did not include any measurements of Atlantic Canadian productivity, either in its introduction to the region's economy or in its accounting of ACOA's "impact" on that economy's performance. At the end of the next five-year period, in 1998, a change was under way, but productivity was still peripheral to the agency's understanding of its mandate. Specifically, ACOA minister John Manley's introductory letter points to an increased emphasis on competitiveness – that is, on ensuring "that the resources which facilitate and accelerate competitiveness are available to everyone, everywhere." The report outlines ACOA's "evolution" over its second five years – for example, it had forged more partnerships, adopted a more "diverse and sophisticated" approach to small business assistance, and focused increasingly on "'value for money.'"[59] The 1998 report took up 1993's interest in competitiveness, which it sought to measure and improve so as to ultimately "respond to the myth that Atlantic Canada is not a competitive location for investments."[60]

In the 1998 report, productivity makes an appearance only in the context of one (new) strategic priority: "Business Management Practices." Revealing the long legacy of the human relations and management schools, the agency was convinced that "enhancing management skills in SMEs leads to an increase in survival, growth and productivity." It took extant evidence that "Atlantic Canada ranked poorly against benchmarks for management efficiency" as an explanation for why "the region's SME survival rate is lower than the national average."[61]

But by the next report, in 2003, productivity had jumped the walls of the business management initiative and was running through almost every other strategic priority area, from the very first paragraph of ACOA minister Allan Rock's introduction: "The defining characteristics of Canada's economic success over the past five years have been increased productivity, improved international competitiveness, better trade performance and greater foreign direct investment. At the centre of this has been a growing emphasis on technology, innovation, skills and learning."[62]

Minister of State Gerry Byrne, who also provided an introductory letter, opened his remarks with the proclamation that "increasingly, in Atlantic Canada, the drivers of the region's productivity and competitiveness are its ideas, talent and ingenuity." Moreover, "Atlantic Canada's ability to compete in world markets now, more than ever, depends directly on its capacity to innovate productively."

Both ministers wove this new explicit emphasis on productivity into the agency's historical mission to foster entrepreneurship. Calling up the old association of productivity with prosperity, they praised ACOA for its commitment to make new "trends" – such as "the growth of new, knowledge-rich industries" – "pay dividends to the people, businesses and communities of Atlantic Canada."[63]

In the main report, the new emphasis on productivity was attributed, as it was in 1998, to a shift in national priorities. But in 2003 it was specifically traced to the federal government's "Jobs and Growth Agenda." This apparently unofficial agenda was built around "improving Canada's economic performance through greater productivity, increased international competitiveness, and enhanced trade and foreign direct investment."[64] In 2001, ACOA identified as one of its "key results commitments" the "improved growth and competitiveness of Atlantic small and medium-sized enterprises, leading to increased productivity, earned incomes, and job creation."[65]

Throughout the 1990s, productivity rarely appeared in ACOA's communications without competitiveness. Outside the agency, debate swirled around the competitiveness of the Atlantic provinces *and* the competition *between* them for ACOA funding. A 1991 speech from the head of one prominent think tank, the Atlantic Provinces Economic Council (APEC), offers a glimpse into the rhetoric around competitiveness at the time. APEC was all for stoking the competition between the region and its "global competitors," but curiously, it was also of the view that competition between Nova Scotia, New Brunswick, PEI, and Newfoundland and Labrador was counterproductive and should be eliminated, preferably through some form of regional economic cooperation, if not full economic "union." (The proposal that the four Atlantic provinces or the three Maritime provinces amalgamate into one mega-region tends to surface every few years.) Citing the prevalent "concern that the gain of one province necessarily occurs at the expense of another," APEC argued that "pre-competitive cooperation" among the provinces could "enlarge the pool of potential investors" in the region.[66] In other words, APEC believed that the benefits of competition could be preserved and the negative impacts mitigated if the provinces cooperated to make a bigger pie first and *then* fought over the pieces.

Productivism from Above

Looking at some of the speeches and other communications from the federal government over the 1998–2003 period, it is clear that productivity was enjoying a significant resurgence in Canadian governmentality more generally, often in relation to economic competitiveness. ACOA minister John Manley, for example, gave a speech in 1999 titled "Putting People First: Productivity, Growth and Living Standards." The understanding of productivity advanced therein reveals something very important for making sense of the way ACOA absorbed productivity into its collection of priorities. Echoing the decades-old productivist beliefs that guided the DBS's productivity research and the NPC's strategies and objectives, Manley told his audience that "productivity – the measure of the efficiency with which people, capital, resources and ideas are combined – is the most important determinant of our standard of living."[67] Just like the NPC and the DBS, however, Manley could not avoid the *"cui bono?"* question of who would gain and who would lose from productivity improvements. He admitted this was a relevant thing to ask, but he pleaded for Canadians' patience and trust:

> There is no question that there are Canadians who wonder where their place is in the productivity agenda beyond lower wages. I hope that I can convince Canadians that a productivity agenda need not mean lower wages, more hours worked and greater hardship. With time and a concerted effort, the government and the private sector acting in partnership, can make sure that all Canadians see an increase in their standard of living.

To underscore the necessity of productivity improvements despite these risks to wages, work time, and work effort, Manley appealed to his audience's insecurity and enmity. The country was now "in [a] fight for a share of the global economy"; its international "friends" were also its "competitors" in everything from tax regimes to intellectual property rights. Competing – and winning – would depend on establishing the best "conditions" for businesses to set up and make money. Again, the message was that high productivity cannot guarantee jobs and income gains, but low productivity most certainly drives investors away, pushes existing businesses out, and leaves Canadians with no jobs and lower wages. As I put it in chapter 2, productivity has been transformed in political discourse from the guarantor of prosperity to its abductor.

Manley probably did believe that productivity was the cornerstone of better living. Indeed, everyone working in government to advance the "productivity agenda" likely felt that such efforts were the key to greater prosperity. But productivity's growing association with competitiveness, and the absorption of this association into productivist arguments for economic growth, points to a developing governmentality that was – and still is – a bit nefarious. ACOA's evolving understanding of how productivity growth happens and how it affects ordinary people's lives offers one perspective on the impact the productivist ideational regime has on public policy and governance.

ACOA and Productivity in the Twenty-First Century

In the first decade of the twenty-first century, ACOA continued to put productivity at the forefront of its agenda. In its five-year report covering 2003–8, ACOA minister Peter MacKay again emphasized the synergy between the agency's "work to develop a more innovative, productive and competitive regional economy" and the federal "government's goal of a prosperous and united Canada."[68] But beyond this, his remarks, and the material that follows in the main report, hint at the importance of several increasingly prominent concepts structuring productivity's role in regional economic development discourse.

At the forefront is the growth in "international competition from low-cost producers" and the importance of *being* competitive. To the agency, "it was becoming increasingly evident" in the late 1990s "that globalization and the rise of the knowledge-based economy were pushing Atlantic Canada toward what economist Michael Porter and others called the new 'paradigm of competitiveness.'" In this (not-so-new) new paradigm, in ACOA's interpretation, "prosperity ... would be based on productivity, rather than on labour or natural resources."[69] It had evidently accepted these propositions, crediting them with the adaptation of its business programs after 2003 "to focus less on support for the acquisition of capital assets and more on the assets associated with productivity – innovation, marketing, international trade and human resources development."[70] (It is unclear how capital came to be understood as anything other than a factor of production and therefore productivity, but it is likely a conclusion unquestioningly taken from the "competitiveness paradigm" literature.)

Part of the impetus for change, according to the report, was that unemployment in Atlantic Canada had dropped to historic lows, thereby outdating ACOA's founding mandate of creating jobs and boosting employment. The agency ostensibly needed to shift its focus "from helping business to create employment to stimulating growth in productivity, competitiveness and earned income." Accordingly, it reported that it was now focused on "fostering research and development, technology adoption, business skills development, and trade and investment."[71] It had also begun to try to reorient its activities towards the "factors that contribute to lower levels of productivity in Atlantic Canada (relative to the national economy)" – which at that time included "firms' ability to innovate," "R&D spending," "business skills," "international trade," and technology adoption. Not coincidentally, it was in this 2008 report that ACOA first included charts measuring productivity alongside those depicting GDP, employment, income, and exports. It developed programs to help small businesses increase their productivity through the acquisition of labour-saving technology *and* the application of better human relations and management practices.

Thus, it appears that the agency circled its wagons to target low productivity and its causes over a decade after Savoie, its architect, urged it to do so. It took up Taylorist and human relations assumptions about productivity, which by this time were so entrenched and taken for granted that they needed little justification. It put productivity explicitly at the centre of several initiatives and strategic priorities and even in its stated mission. It did not try to cover up the shift or pass it off as a continuation of the same project in new terminology. As its spokespeople made clear in the 2008 report, "although high-quality jobs will continue to be important to the economic security of individuals and families going forward, the focus of ACOA's work will need to shift ... Thus, the agency will give increasing emphasis to growth in productivity, competitiveness, and earned incomes."[72]

In 2014 the ACOA website lists "three strategic areas of activity" that are obvious outgrowths of the change in direction from 2003 to 2008. Productivity is there in the first strategic area – "Enterprise Development" – which targets "improved growth and competitiveness of Atlantic enterprises with emphasis on those of small and medium size; and fostering the development of infrastructure leading to increased productivity, earned incomes and job creation." The second strategic area, "Community Development," encompasses the agency's efforts to improve communities' "infrastructure and strategic planning capacity," which in turn is supposed to improve "employment opportunities" and trigger "economic growth." The third is ACOA's "Policy, Advocacy and Coordination" activities, which mainly entail "ensuring regional influence" on federal policy.[73]

The imperative of economic growth runs throughout the agency's current mission and mandate, but on the website – the organization's public face – growth is noticeably unaccompanied by its usual partner concepts of prosperity, well-being, quality of life, and national unity. It advances a perfect example of what Serge Latouche calls "growth for growth's sake."[74] It is, then, a productivist government agency. But more specifically, it is a *neoliberal* productivist agency, because it pairs growth for growth's sake with laissez-faire ideas, enterprise, and individualism. It has managed to shed its old associations with such *social* goods as living standards and prosperity (or, at least, social understandings thereof) and even *jobs*, and it has strengthened its attachment to specific individual benefits, most prominently "earned incomes." Yet all of the tenets of the productivist ideational regime are still *there*. All that has happened is an adaptation of an extant ideational regime to new circumstances – exactly the kind of plasticity that Somers expects ideational regimes to have.

For anyone who believes in society (unlike, for example, neoliberal icon Margaret Thatcher, who deemed society a fiction), ACOA exemplifies not a *different* ideational regime, but merely a *worse* version of productivism than the versions that hinged social welfare on productivity growth. It now de-emphasizes even social welfare and makes productivity either a good in itself or, at most, a condition for potential individual gain.

One additional example of neoliberal thinking in ACOA's mandate is its orientation towards infrastructure, which earlier policies controversially excluded. Soon after the agency was established, House of Commons debates over its role frequently homed in on the question of whether it should directly fund infrastructure projects (e.g., building new bridges and highways to improve trade routes). Somehow, infrastructure ended up falling outside the scope of "opportunity" – despite the obvious case that could be (and was) made that having the necessary infrastructure is a condition, and thus a critical opportunity, for economic development and competitiveness – and it was decided that ACOA would not fund such projects directly.[75] The more recent iterations of the agency's priorities, listed above, bring infrastructure into its mandate, and the agency claims to be "investing in infrastructure projects." However, it does not actually make the investments; rather, it helps communities access funding from the federal infrastructure program, Building Canada. And in most communications, ACOA makes it clear that it will only *help communities help themselves* when it comes to infrastructure. This self-described role as a "facilitator" that "creates conditions" and "fosters" certain economic activities conforms to neoliberal ideas about how governments should relate to and act towards The Economy.[76]

One of the conditions deemed necessary for economic growth, beginning in the late 1990s but particularly after 2000, is the presence of a "skilled" labour force. Accordingly, ACOA has put increasing emphasis on helping businesses train their employees. To its small business "clients," it says that in order to "become more competitive," "your employees have to be well trained." It extends financial support to businesses so that they can undertake training programs, and it partners with universities and colleges to support "skills development." The right training and skills appear, in ACOA literature, as indispensable components of business, economic, and worker "adaptation" to "today's economy."[77] For ACOA and most Canadian government bodies, skills – and the proper match between extant skills and extant jobs *and* future skills and future jobs – are now critical for ensuring productivity and economic growth.

This emphasis on skills has much in common with the idealization of full employment that emerged at the NPC seminars in the 1960s. In that thinking, unemployment was economically inefficient and wasteful, not to mention socially harmful. Then as now, political leaders contemplated ways to retrain and redeploy those workers made redundant by technological advancements and – increasingly towards the end of the twentieth century – those whose jobs had been outsourced to low-wage jurisdictions (when entire employers did not relocate them-selves). In both time periods, concerns of this nature were informed by labour force statistics, initiated by the DBS, measuring employment status, education, and location – recall, for example, the NPC worrying what would become of the precisely 43 per cent of unemployed, under-educated Canadians.

Continuity and Change in Productivity and Productivism

Given the similarity of concerns from the 1960s to the 2000s, we might ask what it is about productivism that is actually different between the DBS, NPC, and ACOA case studies. There is a mix of continuity and revision, with the same issues and tensions augmented by new concepts and assumptions. One such mix concerns the relationship between the labour force – and labour productivity – and economic growth. The productivist ideational regime remains intact, but the way it orders and interprets workers, employers, and productivity is different. Whereas discussions of economic growth during the time of the NPC revolved around the assumption that productivity growth, and thus economic expansion, hinged on harmonious industrial relations, today's discus-sions trace productivity to the *quality* of labour itself, regardless of how well it "gets on" with employers. "Quality," meanwhile, has come to mean *skills*.

The shift away from industrial relations makes sense, given that the period between the NPC and ACOA saw a sustained pattern of *de*industrialization in North America, driven by technological unemployment, the rise of cheap production overseas, and the resulting decline of industry and rise of the service sector in the West. (The extent of deindustrialization depends on how the latter is measured. If it is measured in terms of the *volume* of goods produced in the country, Canada has actually not seen much of a decline between the 1960s and the 2000s.[78] But if it is measured in the value of the goods produced [as a share of GDP], or in terms of the share of total employment – arguably the only two measures that actually matter to human well-being – manufacturing has indeed seen a substantial decline.)[79]

Accepting that deindustrialization has occurred in the most meaning-ful ways, we can also assume that government and business in Canada lost their definitive, isolated target for productivity improvements, and faced a conundrum: if harmonious industrial relations were no longer a viable route to productivity gains (because big industry itself was no longer the driving force of the Canadian economy), to where could they redirect their interventions? The obvious choice might have been capital investment and technology – the "other" inputs in the production process – but, perhaps unsurprisingly, the idea of turning entirely away from labour and workers was not a popular one among employers and government. Instead, the answer was to continue to focus on labour and individuals, but rather than their cooperation with employers, the targets for intervention became their *initiative* and *entrepreneurialism*, and later their *skills* and *training*. The linchpin of productivity, particularly at the level of regions and provinces, became, from the 1990s to the 2000s, the population's ability to seize available "opportunities" and to adapt to changing demands for specific skills and capacities. And this, it turns out, can mean small business owners seeking lucrative new markets, large enterprises locating and extracting natural resources, and unemployed or seasonal workers accepting whatever jobs are available within a 100-kilometre radius.[80]

The specific language of "skills" (as opposed to, say, education) is relatively new. For ACOA, and indeed all levels of government in Canada, the obsession with "skills development" has gone hand-in-hand with anxiety about "skills shortage" and "skills mismatch." These terms refer to a scenario where employers cannot find workers with the skills they need, either because there aren't enough of them, period (shortage), or because they are idling elsewhere, in places where established industries need different kinds of skills. Shortages and mismatches alike are seen – much like generic unemployment was in the 1960s – as an inefficient use of human resources and, therefore, a threat to productivity. The practical example of these scenarios, in 2015, is the demand for manual labour and service workers in Alberta's oilfields, which pulls workers with the requisite skills away from the Atlantic provinces, where demand for such labour is lower and where the jobs pay less. (Although, that same year, oil prices dipped below 45 dollars per barrel, and the province was facing imminent recession. Nevertheless, these interprovincial dynamics, combined with the relatively poor job prospects for graduates of humanities and social science programs, have posed a real challenge to the idea that Canada is a "knowledge economy.") The term "skills" directs attention to qualities of individual workers and aggregate qualities of the labour force as a whole. Skill is different from "education," which in the 1960s was the NPC's greater concern.[81] Education can be a quality of the individual worker and of the labour force, but it also refers to a comprehensive system under government control and a public institution, and thus it is arguably less individualistic than skill.

Relatedly, among today's economists, labour leaders, employers, and politicians, unlike those of the 1960s, there is no expectation of full employment. Granted, they rarely talk about persistent structural unemployment either, lest it discourage the unemployed from trying. We hear positive words instead, like "job creation." In any case, the productivist objective is merely to ensure a match between available jobs and available skills. Meanwhile, the rhetoric around retraining the unemployed, much like that around regional inequality, has taken a slightly more individualistic, laissez-faire turn. Notwithstanding the tangled web of social services and income and employment supports (aka "welfare"), rhetorically it is up to the unemployed person to solve his or her personal unemployment problem, just as it is up to the provinces to pull themselves out of stagnation. The role of government is now explicitly, discursively limited to establishing the opportunities and conditions for unemployed people (and lagging provinces) to retrain, to refashion themselves into the kinds of workers (and provinces) whose skills are valued in today's economy, on the hope that the private sector will invest in them when they do.

Politicians and public interest groups have pointed to the Atlantic region's poor record of employer-sponsored and on-the-job training, imploring businesses to take on some of the training costs that currently fall to universities, colleges, and governments. But aside from a federal grant designed to split training costs with businesses, not much has been done to compel employers to train employees. In contrast, ACOA and other government agencies do more to laud entrepreneurialism and direct resources towards programs that ostensibly facilitate self-employment. In Atlantic Canada especially, the small business owner is the hero of the day, lionized as the ultimate expression of ambition and determination and not the offspring of necessity.[82] Past governments, after the postwar heyday of state-funded "make-work" projects ended, may not have actually involved themselves in finding work for displaced workers either. But as was evident in the accounts from the DBS and the NPC, they at least kept up the rhetoric of *feeling responsible* for their "reintegration."[83]

The discourse of opportunities has also changed how the productivist ideational regime envisions the National Economy. Unity in the National Economy today stems not from redistribution and equality of income and services, as it arguably did in the age of generosity covered in Richard Starr's work, but rather from the willing and entrepreneurial participation of all provinces in a competitive process against one another and "global competitors." We are talking, here, about the convergence of liberal individualism, market fundamentalism, and productivism, which has given rise to the belief that productivity and economic growth do not necessarily lead to prosperity for all, but do lead to a set of *opportunities* to prosper, for which people and communities of all sizes must compete. That is the understanding of economics that underpins ACOA's various programs and public relations, and indeed the activities of many other government apparatuses around the turn of the twenty-first century. The productivist ideational regime, though it has changed, is alive and well and structuring the way we think about and seek to manipulate productivity in Canada.

The narrative in this book has shown productivity's evolution from a simple notion of inputs and outputs, to a consequence of industrial relations, to a complex statistical indicator, a currency for opportunities, and a strategy for global competitiveness. At the same time, it features the consistent presence of productivist thought and, in the postwar era, the constraining influence and remarkable adaptability of the productivist ideational regime. This constant has ensured that productivity has generally been understood as a *good* that only gets better as it increases. This understanding has been powerful enough to deflect even the most damning counter-evidence – from the law of marginal utility, to the rise of technological unemployment, to the divergence of productivity and average incomes after 1970.

But, as the next chapter will show, as the productivity concept – in particular, its statistical measurement – adapts to new evidence and environments, and as it is modified to account for economies and societies much different from the ones that birthed it, it tends to become increasingly complex and arcane. It is still undeniably a goal (productivity) and a status (being productive) to which many ordinary people aspire, but as an economic indicator it has little connection to how workers and even businesses experience production, consumption, and exchange. The productivity concept itself will adapt; it will find a place to embed. However, it is impossible to say whether either the measurement of aggregate national productivity or the productivity–prosperity connection, both so central to the case studies here, will survive as they drift further away from their original moorings.

Chapter Six

The Decline of Productivity?

The position taken here is that there is no 'true' measure of productivity or production for a group of diverse products; that measures of production and productivity should therefore not be considered 'approximations' to an ideal 'reality'; and that a clearer understanding of the specific purposes for which they are to be used and of the questions that are being answered must dictate the method used to construct them. The more clearly the purposes and the meaning of these measures are understood, the more valuable they are.

– Harry Magdoff, 1939

Statistics and the techniques that produce them have some ironic tendencies. In pursuit of a better grasp on "reality" as humans experience it, they expand to capture more of what is already ostensibly measurable, and transform that which is not measurable into that which is. But in so doing, they get further and further away from "reality" as humans experience it. Moreover, most statistics are originally sought for a specific purpose; they are believed to be instructive, to tell their users what they should *do*, to help them advance towards a particular goal or value. And they often do help us, albeit subject to ideological debates and competing interpretations.

But the more statistics are "refined," the more they can take on lives of their own. Their collection becomes a goal, and a value, in itself. As Block and Burns's examination of productivity showed, complex aggregate measures can end up being meaningless even to the statisticians who produce them – and they mean very little anyway, to an ordinary person deciding how to live, where to work, what to buy, how to satisfy a need. Statisticians and social scientists have long known about the "ecological fallacy" – the false attribution of characteristics to individuals on the basis of aggregate (group) data, that some "information loss" occurs when statistics are aggregated – yet institutional reliance on aggregate social and economic indicators has never been higher.[1]

There are, however, signs of growing scepticism about the dominant economic indicators of our day and the concepts that underpin them. Productivity is one such concept and indicator. Although the genealogy and case studies in this book emphasize productivity's remarkable staying power – the power of the productivist ideational regime – they also point, however preliminarily, to two menacing cracks in productivity's foundations, both of which call into question the relevance of productivity as a way of assessing our socio-economic situation.

The first crack is due to the increasing "flakiness," to borrow from Harry Magdoff (introduced in chapter 2), of productivity statistics: the development of ever more arcane indicators that, in attempting to "account" for more and more factors, mean less and less in terms that ordinary people (and statisticians alike!) can understand. The challenges of measuring the total output of a national economy – let alone monitoring changes over time or comparing different subsets within a national economy – have led to statistics that are manipulated, imputed, weighted, and recoded until they are many times removed from the thing they initially measured.

The second crack is due to the widening gap, detailed throughout this book, between aggregate productivity and average wages. This is a significant problem for the productivity concept because it undermines the productivist connection between productivity and prosperity: the thing that makes productivity worth measuring and that justified its pursuit and perfection in the first place. Productivity has thus lost not only some of its scientific legitimacy, but also some of its normative power. In the simplest and only slightly hyperbolic terms, there is a marginal but growing sense that *aggregate* productivity is *meaningless*, because it is so abstracted from our everyday lives, and *pointless*, because knowing more about it will not improve them.

The First Crack: Reliability and Validity

Scaling Up Productivity

The productivity concept in Adam Smith's pin-making example is fairly easy to understand. Productivity increased when more pins were produced in the same or less time than before. Whether the worker was simply rushing to work faster, streamlining her movements to work more efficiently, or working on a production line to divide up the labour, increasing the rate of production increased the level of productivity. This basic notion – of labour productivity and not, it should be noted, MFP, TFP, or KLEMS – is not too difficult to transpose onto the worker's whole factory, or even onto a group of similar factories, classified together in an industry. "Labour power" can be measured in hours no matter the characteristics of the individual worker, and the products are the same, so every number in this productivity formula can be meaningfully added together and compared.[2]

But the moment one tries to "scale up" the assessment of productivity across different industries, especially if the goal is to understand and then trigger productivity change, complications emerge.[3] Specifically, the development of aggregate productivity statistics has been stymied on two fronts: first in the search for a standard measure of *output* – a number that would make sense and be comparable no matter what the actual product under consideration was – and second in the attempt to capture, in statistical, standardized form, all of the *inputs* that might cause output to rise or fall in a given firm, industry, or economy.

The history of the DBS in Canada and the NBER in the United States, detailed in chapters 2 and 3, revealed that the statisticians working therein hit both of these analytical roadblocks. Although the drive to "perfect" productivity statistics – to glean "as much knowledge as possible" – dampened scepticism about the ultimate validity of the indicator, there were signs of doubt even then. Harry Magdoff, who, as the chief statistician in the US Works Progress Administration in the 1940s, was tasked with measuring industrial productivity, warned in 1939 and in 1980 that the pursuit of aggregate productivity indicators was foolhardy because of the fundamental problem of "the comparability of product."[4] Writing with Paul Sweezy, his co-editor at the socialist magazine *Monthly Review,* Magdoff explained:

As originally conceived, labor-productivity measures were confined to the sphere of commodities. Thus, if in 1970 a worker produced on the average, say, 40 pairs of men's shoes an hour and then ten years later 60 pairs of the same type of shoes, it makes sense to say that the productivity of workers in men's shoe factories increased by 50 percent during the decade. What makes this a meaningful statement is that the end product is the same in both years. Clearly, if the product made in these factories had changed substantially – let us say, to producing wading boots instead of dress shoes – an index of change in output per worker would lose meaning. There would be no way to know whether the difference in the number of units produced per man-hour was due to the change in the product or to a change in the amount of labor required to produce a unit of the product. Thus, comparability of product is essential to the rational measurement of productivity.[5]

Comparability was hard enough to ensure within a single firm or industry over time, because changing styles – a relatively new phenomenon in the 1940s but rapid and continuous by the 1980s – made meaningful year-over-year comparisons of physical output nearly impossible. Aggregate, cross-industry productivity measures added an additional layer of complexity, as "numbers of automobiles, yards of fabric, tons of steel, and so on ... can't simply be added together to reach a meaningful total."[6] There was a way around this – translating these physical units of output into dollar values – but as noted in chapter 3, it was initially too difficult because government statisticians lacked a suitable way of dealing with deflation. Eventually, after the NRP folded in 1939, changes to the National Accounts putatively eliminated the problem. Statisticians were bequeathed a method that was, at least, "rational" – there was a logic to the comparison of labour-hours to labour-hours and money to money.[7] But productivity researchers still faced the additional problem of how to measure output in industries and firms – such as the growing "service sector" – that did not produce discrete commodities for sale and consumption. Moreover, the problem of comparability of output would return when new techniques were developed to deal with inflation and intermediate inputs.

The Productivity of "Unproductive" Work

When the DBS's Productivity Research Section was established in 1961, the public service, banks, and other service industries were obviously important to the National Economy. People – including the DBS statisticians – earned their livings in those industries and sectors, and they created things, performed services, and managed or carried out processes that were of value. But their outputs – services and other intangibles – were even more difficult to reconcile with "numbers of automobiles" than "yards of fabric" had been. This is the problem the new Research Section began to tackle as soon as it was created, when it confronted the question of how the contributions of "non-production" workers and non-"goods-producing" industries might fit into a calculation of national productivity.[8] In the postwar Canadian economy, as manufacturing contracted and moved overseas, productivity statistics that only counted physical commodities might be more reliable, but they would not be as relevant. Service sector employment rose dramatically between 1950, when it employed 44 per cent of Canadian workers, and 1979, when it employed 67 per cent. Measures of service sector growth in terms of output (or percentage of GDP) are less reliable, but for what it is worth they showed a slightly less dramatic increase, from about 48 per cent of GDP to 63 per cent over the same period. The most recent figures, from 2014, put the share of employment at 78 per cent and the share of GDP at around 70 per cent.[9]

As Brett Christophers has pointed out in his historical geographical examination of banking, postwar statisticians trying to measure total national economic output (the numerator in a productivity equation) in this "new" service economy faced a two-pronged challenge: where to draw the old line, inherited from Adam Smith, between productive and unproductive work, and how to measure "productiveness" once that line was drawn. This was not the first time in the history of economic thought or economic statistics that "experts" fiddled with that line. The marginalists from chapter 1 – Clark, Bohm-Bawerk, Hawley, and Walker among them – convinced their contemporaries that capital itself was productive and that the "mental labour" of capitalists was too. As I argued there, although this debate took place in scientific economic journals, it was also a moral matter: a battle to "prove" through empiricism and logic who or what *deserved* the spoils of production.

In the period Christophers examines, "finance" (as distinct from capital) was "made productive, not in a literal sense but rather in a perceptual sense," with similarly moral or normative connotations. Banks had "been considered economically unproductive for most of [their] long history," associated with usury and, accordingly, immorality. Interestingly, it was "the new calculative technology of national accounting" that rendered banks "productive."[10]

The techniques enabling this transformation were complex. Among several different ways of calculating GDP, only one – the "gross value added" (GVA) or "product method" – could capture production in a manner that allowed banking's "product" to be extracted for measurement. And as Christophers shows, a disturbing set of data manipulations, including many imputed values and even "dummy" variables representing imaginary industries, underlie the final measurement of banking's output today.[11] The most troubling aspect of banking's boundary crossing, chronicled in Christophers's work, is the role that financial institutions themselves played in wedging their "industry" into place alongside manufacturing and other services. To my knowledge, the induction of other services into the national accounts and productivity indicators was not spurred or overseen by parties in insurance, government, retail, or any other non-goods-producing industry – unless one counts the government statisticians themselves.

The service sector presented, and continues to present, a host of measurement problems for national accounting and productivity research. Statisticians have puzzled over how to account for the "quality" of service outputs, the role and contribution of the service *user* and "service culture," the different contributions of high- and low-skilled workers, and the fact that "a high proportion of certain service outputs are used as intermediate inputs elsewhere."[12] It has proven extremely difficult to reconcile the productivity concept with types of work and commodities that were considered fundamentally *un*productive by the earliest theorizers of productivity, and that were marginal concerns in the industrial moment when productivity statistics were initially conceived of.[13]

The attempt to do so has had interesting ramifications. As early as 1969, researchers with the NBER and the DBS noticed that although employment growth in the service sector was growing much faster than in the goods sector, productivity growth in the service sector was slower.[14] Many different explanations were forwarded and tested – perhaps the quality of "labour inputs" was lower in the service sector, perhaps the higher incidence of part-time hours could explain it, or maybe it was the lower level of capital investment.[15] Concerns that it might be "measurement bias" arose in the late 1960s, but were tested and downplayed.[16]

But by the 1990s, the service sector's "lagging productivity" was back in the spotlight, and several influential studies had convinced the "epistemic community" of government statisticians that problems with the measurement of service sector productivity were to blame.[17] Specifically, researchers started to believe that productivity growth in the service industries might have been underestimated for decades by techniques not properly calibrated for that sector's unique mix of inputs and outputs. Very few, however, were willing to see this as a terminal issue; instead the fixation was on the need to *perfect* the measurement of service sector productivity.

Magdoff and Sweezy were among the minority trying to pump the brakes, and by that time had been warning about the problems with productivity measurement for decades. Repeating Magdoff's line from 1939, they had urged statisticians in 1980 to accept that there was "no such thing as a straightforward or 'true' measure of productivity ... even in the realm of commodities where a reasonable, if limited, meaning can be given to the concept," and *especially* in the realm of services:

> There are of course service jobs that consist of routine, repetitive operations e.g., in typing pools – where productivity measures may have some meaning. But how would one go about measuring the productivity of a fireman, an undertaker, a teacher, a nurse, a cashier in a supermarket, a short-order cook, a waiter, a receptionist in a lawyer's office? It is in the very nature of the case that in most services qualitative changes are intertwined with quantitative changes; hence there is no continuity in the "output" from one period to another with which changes in employment can be compared. Moreover, it is typical of many of the service areas that the "output" cannot be separated from the labor engaged in the performance of the service; for that reason too there is no sensible way of comparing changes in output and labor. In other words, the notion of a productivity measure for most service occupations is nonsensical and self-contradictory. Unfortunately, such considerations of elementary logic have not prevented statisticians and economists from producing a whole array of productivity measures, applicable not only to the private economy (combining commodity-production and services) but in some cases to government as well, useful for ideological and policy-making purposes. And by dint of endless repetition and selective emphasis, these statistical phantoms (to use *Business Week's* apt expression) have attained the status of indisputable facts and have entered into the realm of scientific discourse.[18]

Although other, more mainstream economic statisticians were not willing to abandon the project of measuring service sector productivity, they *did* accept that there were real conceptual and analytical problems with it. For example, in the late 2000s there was a surge of interest in revising the national accounts data to include the "intangibles" that were widely accepted as integral to the "knowledge economy," a concept taken for granted as both new and real by that time. Experimentation with extant data showed that GDP and productivity estimates varied significantly depending on whether things like computer software, "R&D," copyright fees, and advertising were classified in econometric models as "capital assets" or "expenses."[19] Then, in 2013, the US Bureau of Economic Analysis (BEA) revised its GDP estimates all the way back to 1929 to include R&D as a capital investment rather than a firm expense, as it had been before the revision. The result of this arbitrary, albeit rational, decision was a "bump" in the GDP of almost 3 per cent. Statistics Canada made the same shift around the same time, but the revision of GDP estimates in Canada did not get the same media attention as in the United States, nor did it come close to making near the 3 per cent difference it made there. It seems this was rather quietly taken as more shameful evidence of Canada's "lagging" R&D investment relative to its international "competitors."[20]

The reclassification of R&D spending in the national accounts, from expense to capital investment, still stopped short of the larger problem represented by the purported growth of the knowledge economy. Specifically, it was clear to any observer that technical knowledge and information – text, graphics, video, communication, *ideas themselves* – were at the start of the twenty-first century integral to people's jobs, the value and profile of companies, the education and training of workers, and profit-making. But the experts could not get a handle on how to measure those things: Were they inputs or outputs? Were they commodities with a monetary value analytically separate from wages, tuition, and market prices? The US BEA's revisions were interpreted as a move to capture more of the knowledge economy, but they were clearly only a half-measure. After all, it makes sense that the technological skills of employees, "web savvy," and other assets to the knowledge economy worker would be considered "inputs" affecting the quality and quantity of a company's outputs. Yet one can only imagine how Magdoff and Sweezy would react to an attempt to add the value of a new computer programming language, or employees' knowledge thereof, to that of a rubber boot and its components.

Another problem that has arisen frequently in considerations of service sector or knowledge economy productivity is "double-counting." This is a general concern even outside the non-goods-producing sectors. Given that one industry's output often becomes another industry's input (e.g., automotive parts in the production of whole cars), calculations of product and productivity must ensure that outputs are only counted once.[21] The potential for inputs and outputs to be double-counted has been known from some of the earliest attempts to calculate the national income.[22] It represents an ongoing and not insignificant problem: for every new product or service counted in the national accounts (and thus, in aggregate productivity indicators), there is a forensic process to be done of subtracting any inputs that have already been counted as an output somewhere else, so that the final number represents only the "value added" by the industry in question and not the value that came to it in the form of inputs.[23] When the inputs and outputs in question are intangibles, it only gets more difficult to separate them out. On top of that, these "value-added" calculations subsequently run into an additional challenge, whether in the service or the goods-producing sector: inflation.

Right Arithmetic, "Crazy" Units

Inflation – the decrease, over time, in the value of a dollar relative to the cost of particular goods – means that when comparisons are sought between productivity one year and the next, as they usually are, it becomes necessary to deflate the second year's currency in order to make it comparable to the first year.[24] Measuring change in "constant dollars" is another way of putting it, and it is a routine practice in any statistical analysis that involves money. The results of these deflated calculations are usually referred to as "real" (e.g., "an increase of 20 per cent in *real* dollars") because money itself is an abstract concept, and purchasing power (how much we can buy with our dollar) is the only way we experience money as a *real* thing. Accordingly, the standard measure of value added in national statistics – and the figure on which productivity indicators are based – is "real value added."

The international norm, to which Statistics Canada conforms, is to calculate real value added using the "double deflation" method. This method deflates both inputs and outputs by industry to match a chosen "base year," yielding results that can ostensibly be compared year over year because the value of the dollar has been kept "constant" throughout. The assumption is that the results can be summed to obtain real value added for the whole national economy, and interpreted either in dollars *or* in the amount of product those dollars can buy. Thus double-deflated real value added can, in theory, represent both the volume *and* the value of the goods, depending on how one interprets it.[25]

The DBS is actually credited with pioneering double-deflation, beginning with its use of the method "on a trial basis in the late 1950s." The bureau was also responsible for "one of the first studies done by a statistical agency ... highlighting the use of measures of 'real net output' for projecting real GDP by industry of origin."[26] Unfortunately for them, the validity of double-deflated real value added, like that of the other "leading indicators," has been called into question.[27] And every time the "value added" indicator is adjusted to respond to criticisms, it becomes increasingly difficult to explain or to interpret in terms that have any relationship to real life, work, income, and standards of living.

For example, the measure was found to be incredibly sensitive to changes in the chosen "base year." This was not an insurmountable problem; it was recommended that a "chain index" method be used, ensuring that each year in a multi-year analysis was compared to the previous year rather than to a fixed, single base year. Explaining what an increase of X per cent actually means, to a layperson, is thus increasingly difficult even though this approach is presumably more accurate. But never mind that: the chain index method still could not account for improvements in the "terms of trade" anyway (i.e., the value of one country's exports relative to the cost of its imports), nor could it address the fact that prices and quantities of inputs and outputs are not independent of one another, because the cost of a product has an effect on how much of it sells. Like any measure of national production and productivity, the chain index method of double-deflation also confronts the additional problem of whether and how to account for the contributions of low-wage workers in the Global South to products that spent their final moments on the production line in the Global North. Does the labour that created the shoelace in Bangladesh get counted as part of the completed shoe that eventually gets boxed in and shipped from the US Midwest? What about the labour-hours of the Colombian farmhands that supplied the Toronto barista with his medium?

These and other persistent problems have led some outspoken economists to conclude that double-deflation, in its original iteration *and* in the version that results from efforts to address all of these issues, creates "fictitious" indicators.[28] Clopper Almon, Emeritus Professor of Economics at the University of Maryland, has argued repeatedly that one need only display the assumptions and methods of double-deflation in a simple input–output table to see that "the results make as much sense as saying that five squirrels minus three elephants equals two lions. The arithmetic is right but the units are crazy."[29]

But Almon, like Magdoff and Sweezy and every other economist or statistician who has pointed to the absurdity of economic indicators, is outnumbered by experts who have knowingly pressed on, in the face of all of these conceptual problems, believing that they just need better, more robust data and more "sophisticated" techniques to analyse it.

Importantly, this ongoing pursuit of a fuller understanding of production and productivity is, as it has been throughout the history covered here, justified by connecting it to the achievement of greater prosperity. But this justification, like the methodological and epistemological assumptions underpinning aggregate productivity measurement, has attracted increasing criticism the further it drifts from the industrial, welfare capitalist context in which it emerged. Such criticisms have created the second "crack" in the productivity concept's legitimacy.

The Second Crack: Productivity and Prosperity

Productivism's Historical Moment

The persistent, discursive linkages between productivity and prosperity – in a word, productivism – are plainly evident in the history of productivity measurement in the DBS and in the mandates and activities of the NPC and ACOA. The historical context in which productivity became such a critical piece of the national accounting framework in Canada, the United States, and the rest of the world is critical for explaining why this is so, and why productivity continues to have such a hold on economic and political thought, as well as in the everyday lives of ordinary people. But that historical context also serves as a baseline, throwing into sharp relief the political economic *drift* that has occurred over the past five or six decades, illuminating the impetus for many of the burgeoning critiques of productivity and productivism that will be explored in the next chapter.

The chain reaction between a particular understanding of productivity's importance, and its induction into the roster of economic facts that a national government had to study continuously, took off during a period of economic growth and wealth distribution unlike any other before or since. The decades following the Second World War saw an unprecedented rise in median incomes, employment, and the share of the world's production undertaken in North America, Western Europe, and Britain. Western economies were absolutely booming, and it seemed as though everyone was sharing in the gains, in the form of higher incomes, stable jobs, access to affordable consumer goods, and the accumulation of private property by normal working people. Every graph and chart, including the ones Simon Kuznets produced and shared with the world, showed productivity and median incomes rising in tandem. Thus, a discourse that was already persuasive just because it seemed logical – the idea that "a rising tide lifts all boats" – now appeared to be backed up by undeniable empirical proof.

The problem, as perhaps we are only now coming to see, is that the relationship between productivity and prosperity that looked like a universal law to some analysts and officials in the 1960s was anything but universal or law-like. In fact, we know very little for certain about how productivity, on its own, affects the prosperity of nations and the people who live and work in them. We are stymied by the aforementioned problems with the measurement of productivity itself; furthermore, our knowledge about productivity's connection to prosperity depends on how we measure the latter. Research on two of the foremost indicators of prosperity – employment rates and purchasing power – offers few straightforward or unequivocal answers.

Academic theories connecting productivity to real wages and employment rates were (and are still) "ambiguous."[30] One idea that has been around since the postwar era holds that rising productivity will translate into lower unemployment as firms manage to increase their output, and their profits, and hire more workers to keep up with increased demand. Other established theories, in contrast, predict a scenario where productivity-enhancing technology is used to *replace* workers rather than simply increase their output, resulting in higher unemployment. On both sides are more specific theories positing that the effects of increased productivity on employment levels differ in the short and long run – for example, some predict a surge of layoffs immediately following spikes in productivity, with employment slowly recovering and eventually exceeding pre-spike levels.[31] Unfortunately for those who want answers, empirical tests of these and other theoretical models have produced conflicting results, and even anecdotal evidence is mixed. Part of the ambiguity stems from differences in the level of analysis. Is TFP taken as the measure of productivity? Is it at the national, aggregate level or the industry level? Which industries? Are there intervening variables, such as inflation, terms of trade, or welfare state policies? How do we control for those intervening variables at greater and greater levels of aggregation? The answers to these questions are important just for calculating the base production data from which productivity is calculated, and thus they also determine the measured impact of productivity on employment.

Turning to productivity and wages, methodological and data-related idiosyncrasies mean there is more evidence to work with – and clearer answers to the question at hand – but it doesn't paint a pretty picture.[32]

Regarding productivity and real wages, the trend since the end of the Second World War has been characterized best as "growing together then pulling apart." Lawrence Mishel, president of the Economic Policy Institute, a US think tank, writes that

> productivity growth has risen substantially over the last few decades but the hourly compensation of the typical worker has seen much more modest growth, especially in the last 10 years or so. The gap between productivity and the compensation growth for the typical worker has been larger in the "lost decade" since the early 2000s than at any point in the post-World War II period. In contrast, productivity and the compensation of the typical worker grew in tandem over the early postwar period until the 1970s.
>
> Productivity growth, which is the growth of the output of goods and services per hour worked, provides the basis for the growth of living standards. However, the experience of the vast majority of workers in recent decades has been that productivity growth actually provides only the potential for rising living standards: Recent history, especially since 2000, has shown that wages and compensation for the typical worker and income growth for the typical family have lagged tremendously behind the nation's fast productivity growth.[33]

Canadian data yield similar findings. According to a report by the Centre for the Study of Living Standards (CSLS), data from the 2006 census revealed that between 1980 and 2005, median inflation-adjusted annual earnings "increased ... a mere $53," while "over the same time period, labour productivity in Canada rose 37.4 per cent."[34] The CSLS set out to explain the "divergence" and found that much of it depended on how earnings were measured. Specifically, the productivity–income gap narrows considerably when "supplementary labour income" (SLI) – which includes pension and other benefits – is added to hourly wages or annual income. (Whether or not this provides a fair estimate of people's economic security is up for debate.)

But even after accounting for SLI, there is still a wide gulf between productivity and real income. The rest of it, according to the CSLS's elaborate models, can be attributed to three other factors. The first and most significant is rising income inequality, and specifically the documented concentration of income among top-earners. The second is a deterioration in "labour's terms of trade"; what this means is that the prices of goods *produced* by Canadian workers are not rising as fast as the prices of goods they *consume*. The third and final explanatory factor is the fall in "labour's share" of GDP – that is, the portion of national income going to workers compared to the portion (i.e., everything else) going to capital (as profits). On this point, it should be clear that the models do not so much "explain" *why* productivity growth has not translated into rising wages (which is more of a value question) as account for where the money that could have been wages actually went.[35]

In any case, the data have been unequivocal in the United States and Canada: productivity growth has generally outpaced growth in compensation, no matter how either variable is measured. Data from other OECD countries show a varied picture, with productivity growing faster than income in certain periods and certain countries, and reversing at other times and in other places.[36] Yet, somehow, and especially in North America, the discursive relationship between productivity and prosperity has been buttressed since Kuznets's time by an impermeable wall that has shut out not only the centuries-old warnings about productivity from political economists like Marx and Ricardo, but also the counter-evidence that began to mount in the 1970s. Productivity "improvements" have apparently eliminated or deteriorated more jobs than they have created or enhanced, and have been found to be unrelated to any increase in wages for anyone except the top income earners, yet the notion that the quality of life for a country's citizens depends on their ability to continually produce more with less has persisted.[37] Productivity might not yield the same strong incentives to hard, efficient work that it once did, but it has certainly not lost all legitimacy in economic affairs. Such is the power of the productivist ideational regime.

Curiously, Statistics Canada does not monitor on a *routine* basis any part of the relationship between productivity and measures of prosperity, such as cost of living or median incomes, or the internationally recognized indices of well-being and equality (e.g., the GINI coefficient). The connection between productivity and prosperity is, in other words, an assumption rather than an empirical observation, and it has almost *always* been that way (including during the heyday of the DBS). Evidence to the contrary is greeted with shock and treated like a temporary and perplexing reversal of the natural relationship. And there is much bound up in believing in this natural relationship. As chapter 4's exploration of the NPC illustrated, productivity has the curious tendency to straddle the empirical and the normative – to serve, on the one hand, as an indisputable scientific measure of economic performance, and on the other hand, as part of a moral, nationalistic project that hinges prosperity, equality, and progress on the cooperation and *faith* of workers, employers, and government within a capitalist system of production. But lately, as this chapter has shown, productivity's "performance" – this time, a dramaturgical one and not an economic one – in its normative *and* empirical roles, has been less convincing.

"Not wrong as such, but wrongly used"

Productivity is one of a host of concepts in trouble; among them, GDP (from which productivity is calculated) has probably received the most scrutiny over the last decade. As *New York Times* writer Jon Gertner put it in 2010, surveying the mounting academic critiques and the more recent challenges from "a variety of world leaders" and "international groups," "it has been a difficult few years for G.D.P."[38] Indeed, in 2008, French president Nicholas Sarkozy commissioned three leading economists to conduct a study to "identify the limits of GDP as an indicator of economic performance and social progress, including the problems with its measurement; to consider what additional information might be required for the production of more relevant indicators of social progress; to assess the feasibility of alternative measurement tools, and to discuss how to present the statistical information in an appropriate way." Sarkozy was, as the final report put it, "unsatisfied with the present state of statistical information about the economy and the society." He chose Joseph Stiglitz, Amartya Sen, and Jean-Paul Fitoussi to lead the commission – three economists whose previous research and writing converged on issues of social justice, wealth inequality, and redistribution. Aided by twenty-two other academics and practitioners, largely from the United States and Europe, the commission concluded that "the time [was] ripe for our measurement system to shift emphasis from measuring economic production to measuring people's well-being." Although they did not advocate fully "dismissing GDP and production measures," they urged for recognition that such measures "emerged from concerns about market production and employment." In the commission's view, these concerns and the techniques to measure them had drifted too far away from "what counts for common people's well-being."[39]

The commission joined a chorus of academics, writers, politicians, and other public voices calling for a re-evaluation of GDP's importance to government. In Canada and elsewhere, GDP's critics noted what the measure *does not* include – notably, pollution and leisure – and put forward alternative measures – "well-being" indices – that were purported to capture more of what matters to the quality of people's lives.[40] The King of Bhutan had declared "Gross National Happiness" (GNH) to be more important than GDP as early as the 1970s, but it was when the newly democratized Bhutan committed itself to the pursuit of GNH in its first constitution in 2008 that interest in the concept spiked worldwide.[41] Environmentalists like David Suzuki have more recently begun to point out the connections between rising GDP and global warming, sedentary lifestyles, and detachment from nature, thus lending support to alternative indicators.[42]

Often central to these critiques of GDP are more specific critiques of productivity – a logical extension, given that labour productivity is defined (by Statistics Canada, for example) as GDP per hour worked. Mathieu Dufour and Philippe Hurteau, writing for Montreal's Institute de recherché et d'informations socioeconomiques in 2013, pointed out that measuring productivity in GDP's money terms introduced an irrational element to the practice. Workers in finance, for example, could become "immensely productive" in a matter of seconds by doing a single large trade if the measure of productivity is GDP per hour worked. But, they asked, "is this work really productive?" Moreover, the sensitivity of GDP per hour worked to fluctuations in prices means that a worker could "be very 'productive' by efficiently making a car that is very inexpensive but ... will *appear* less economically productive than if [they] produce a car less efficiently that sells at a higher price."[43]

Dufour and Hurteau, like the 2008 French commission, also pointed out that neither GDP nor the productivity measures it enables account for "household production" or any other activity producing outputs that are not commodified, such as unpaid care work, many kinds of volunteer work, and exchanges of services and goods among community members.[44] In addition, as Stiglitz, Sen, and Fitoussi emphasized, publicly provided (i.e., government) services, and services that are paid for by a third party (e.g., medical services by health insurers), posed their own conceptual challenges. Specifically, they argued that the relationship between "government-provided individual services" and people's well-being is qualitatively different from the relationship between privately purchased consumer goods and quality of life. Thus, for the commissioners, "better measurement" of public services should be "central to the assessment of living standards."[45] Their report also explored the possibility of "valuing leisure," viewing education as an "investment" that improves life rather than a purchase that improves productivity, and putting a value on "the long run advantages of a safer climate."[46] Thus, even in the most damning critiques of economic statistics, there is a hope for their improvement rather than a call for their abandonment.

An Empirical and Normative Slide

There are two lines of critique running through the above reflections on GDP, taken as a single yet heterogeneous body of critique. These are relevant to the story of productivity given the relationship between productivity measurement and GDP, and the way critiques of each are intertwined; one can reasonably swap productivity for GDP and find the same critiques applicable. The first line draws attention to the methodological issues, the logical fallacies, and the statistical "fictions" built into the GDP indicator – it casts light on the absurdities of what counts and does not count as productive, and how products are made measurable. It includes as well the debates about validity, such as the one described in chapter 2 between Diewert, Yu, and Statistics Canada in 2013, and the methodological revisions those debates sometimes spur. The second line says that regardless of the statistical validity of GDP – regardless of its ability to capture and represent what it claims to – it is not indicative of our standard of living and quality of life anyway. The challenge this second critique poses to GDP is important, and affects the productivity concept, because it can be a challenge to productivism: it can (but does not always) refuse, on the basis of empirical evidence and a certain kind of logic, to accept the assumption that increasing productivity or GDP is a good thing in itself. The two lines of critique come together to cast doubt, both on the idea that we can fully *know* productivity scientifically, and on the idea that knowing more will better us in the first place.

Increasingly, then, scholars, activists, and politicians are noting a clear disconnect between the *statistical* measurement of an otherwise "useful" term – productivity – and what is *actually* "good" for people.[47] Some, like Robert and Edward Skidelsky, have noted that we do not even *talk about* what constitutes "the good life," let alone have a way of measuring it.[48] When productivity and other economic statistics are afflicted with these doubts and disconnections, we lose faith in their capacity to lead us to the right action. Hence, the quest – exemplified in the French commission's work, the development of indices of well-being, and even the efforts of mainstream statisticians and economists to rescue productivity from its contradictions – to come up with better, more accurate conceptions, first of what is *good* and *valuable,* and second of how to measure and express those values as numerical functions. But the disjuncture between "taken for granted" economic concepts and life as we experience it is not purely or even primarily a concern for statisticians and politicians. As the next chapter will show, the small-p political discourse about productivity, both outside and within economics and statistics, has sustained critiques of productivism and productivity all along. The explicit attention paid to power and ideology in these discourses, and their translation into demands for social and political-economic change rather than methodological revision alone, add to the critique of productivism building in this book. The "cracks" in the productivity concept described in this chapter, triggered largely by revelations about statistical data, were not the first to weaken productivity's ideological force – not by a long shot.

Conclusion: Productivity's Future and the Limits of Growth

Think of what this means to the whole country. Think of the increase, both in the necessities and luxuries of life, which becomes available for the whole country, of the possibility of shortening the hours of labor when this is desirable, and of the increased opportunities for education, culture, and recreation which this implies.[1]

Frederick Winslow Taylor, 1911

Unless people agree on a process that can be continuously, convivially, and effectively used to control society's tools, the inversion of the present institutional structure cannot be either enacted or, what is more important, precariously maintained. Managers will always re-emerge to increase institutional productivity and capture public support for the better service they promise.[2]

Ivan Illich, 1973

How Productivism Makes Itself True

There is a great and long tradition in sociological thought of reflecting on the power of ideas to constrain and enable action. Ideas and action are each conceptualized in a multitude of ways in this broad corpus. Max Weber was interested in how specifically religious beliefs affected people's conduct, especially their conduct at and relating to work.[3] Karl Marx and Friedrich Engels dissected the relationship between ideology, consciousness, and reality (what they *really* said, or meant, about the relative autonomy of these things, is still the subject of rigorous debate).[4] Gramsci's theories of ideology and hegemony sought to explain how ruling classes used ideas to deceive subordinate classes and mystify the source of their subordination.[5] Karl Mannheim in *Ideology and Utopia* tackled the problem of "how men actually think," an investigation he counterposed to the exercise of "philosophers" who were only interested in analysing how they *themselves* thought.[6] Sociologists have, since the interventions of Marx, Weber, Gramsci, and Mannheim, picked up the tools offered by Michel Foucault to analyse discourse, its "formations" and "effects"; they have continued to wrestle with ideology and hegemony.[7] And they have subjected to great scrutiny, under the banner of "reflexivity," the concepts and terms invented by their own discipline.[8]

A key puzzle that all of these varied works confront is how some ideas come to exercise a disproportionate amount of power and influence over social (including political and economic) life. This is the puzzle at the heart of Margaret Somers and Fred Block's aforementioned work. As they put it: "Ideas matter. But equally important is that all ideas are not created equal. Only some ideas can exercise the causal power to undermine, dislodge, and replace a previously dominant ideational regime."[9] For them, "the relative strength" of ideas, vis-à-vis "political outcomes," is "an empirical question," and they offer "the concept of 'epistemic privilege' to describe ideas with … comparative advantage."[10] Taking a line from the late, eminent sociologist Pierre Bourdieu, they argue that this privilege and advantage stems mostly from the fact that "epistemically privileged" ideas have inherent and "internal claims to veracity." As they put it, quoting Bourdieu, "a theory that has 'the means of making itself true' has an obvious advantage over a theory that lacks its own epistemological bootstraps."[11]

What does it mean for a theory or an idea to "make itself true"? For Bourdieu, it meant that certain ideas, because they reflect, protect, and legitimate the interests of powerful people and institutions (e.g., senior government officials, owners of the world's largest corporations), have an easier time accessing the gears that make the world turn. Describing neoliberalism as one such dominant mode of thought, Bourdieu noted that it "has on its side all of the forces of a world of relations of forces, a world that it contributes to making what it is."[12] He explained that neoliberalism has "*the means of making itself true and empirically verifiable*" because the people who believe in it most, and believe they will benefit from it most, also have the power to enact legislation (and, in this case, trigger and uphold financial *de*regulation) supportive of global capital accumulation.[13]

Accepting this rendering of the place of ideas in social life, and reflecting on the story of productivity and productivism told in this book, I wish now to ask: Is the productivist ideational regime – and especially its twin supports, which link productivity with prosperity and growth with "the good" – one of those ideas with the power to make itself true? How did productivism come to frame Canadian governmentality and nearly all political and most academic economics discussions about productivity in Canada, from the interwar years to the present?[14] If I can be so bold as to predict the future, what is the likelihood of some other ideational regime displacing productivism in the decades to come? Bolder still, I want to ask the value-rational, perhaps even utopian question: What *should* we think, say, and do about productivity from this point forward? Answering all of these depends, to some degree, on first going back into the archives of Anglo economic and political thought, and following the roads less travelled.

Alternatives to Productivism

One of the most common mistakes in the sociology of ideas is the assumption, on the part of reader or writer, or both, that the dominance of one idea means the absence of competing ideas. Works that posit the "hegemony" of one way of thinking can erroneously imply that any other way of thinking is or was impossible in the face of such power. It is doubtful that many sociologists of ideas, living or dead, would agree to this implication. *Of course* there are alternative ideas. There are always alternative ideas.[15] In asserting that dominant modes of thought channel and control what can be said, we never mean that they completely silence everything else.

For those of us who adhere to the loose-knit family of explanations offered by Somers and Block, Bourdieu, and Foucault, dominant ideas "win" by either delegitimating or co-opting (i.e., reinterpreting and claiming as their own) competing ideas, so that alternatives never get the traction they need to influence the "mechanisms" by which society's institutions are "shaped, regulated and organized."[16] Because ideational regimes say as much about what *ought* to be as they do about what *is*, when they squeeze out other ideas they also cut off, if only partly or temporarily, the possibility of doing things differently. Thus the genealogy of ideas, the historical sociology of concept formation, or whatever we want to call it, focuses on the ephemeral, condensed, or diffuse moments when a choice between alternative futures arose and "all of the forces of [the] world" went one way, taking the rest of the world with them.[17] The point is not, however, to illuminate the reasons why things will never change; rather, it is to remind us that we get chances sometimes. That is the insight I wish to focus on in the final pages of this book.

What follows is a brief and necessarily *selective* genealogy of *anti*-productivism, from the late 1700s all the way up to the present. Over this period, beginning long before the statistical measurement of productivity ran into empirical and conceptual snags, there are revealing patterns of thought – regularities in argument, in rhetoric, and in statements of problems and solutions proposed – that suggest that as long as there has been productivism, there has been an alternative to it. And what is especially intriguing is the way in which the productivity concept has factored into these alternative discourses. Those who challenge the pursuit of economic growth for growth's sake often do so by challenging the endless pursuit of productivity gains, by calling into question the assumed link between productivity and prosperity, by asking *why* increased productivity has failed to give ordinary people more free time, and by proposing that we redraw, in various ways, the connection between "productive" labour and human well-being. At the end, I will return to the question posed at the beginning of this final chapter: How has productivism made itself true in the face of available alternatives? And what does this insight tell us about the Canadian case studies examined in this book?

Anti-Productivism in the Industrial Age

In the history of the productivist ideational regime, there have been many moments of choice, many "lines of flight" branching off from the dominant regime.[18] One such moment occurred seventy-two years after the publication of Smith's *Wealth of Nations*, when a British political economist and philosopher named John Stuart Mill published *Principles of Political Economy*. In the preface to this 1848 work, Mill described what he had written as "similar in its object and general conception to that of Adam Smith, but adapted to the more extended knowledge and improved ideas of the present age."[19] It departed from Smith's work (and that of Ricardo and Bentham, whose theories Mill also studied) in many ways, but one division is of particular relevance to the history of productivism. Specifically, Mill was one of the first to explicitly dwell on the question of the *point*, and the *limits*, of economic growth. His thoughts on the matter are worth reprinting at length. He wrote:

> The preceding chapters comprise the general theory of the economical progress of society, in the sense in which those terms are commonly understood; the progress of capital, of population, and of the productive arts. But in contemplating any progressive movement, not in its nature unlimited, the mind is not satisfied with merely tracing the laws of the movement; it cannot but ask the further question, to what goal? Towards what ultimate point is society tending by its industrial progress? When the progress ceases, in what condition are we to expect that it will leave mankind? ... It must always have been seen, more or less distinctly, by political economists, that the increase of wealth is not boundless: that at the end of what they term the progressive state lies the stationary state, that all progress in wealth is but a postponement of this, and that each step in advance is an approach to it. We have now been led to recognize that this ultimate goal is at all times near enough to be fully in view; that we are always on the verge of it, and that if we have not reached it long ago, it is because the goal itself flies before us.[20]

Although the notion of a low- or no-growth economy would again be advanced as the pinnacle of progress towards a "social economy" in the post-capitalist thought of the 1940s to 1960s, earlier generations of political economists – those who came between Smith and Mill – found the idea of the "stationary state" "unpleasing and discouraging."[21] Clearly, today's mainstream economists and the political leaders they inform are similarly loathe to consider – incapable of it, even – a future in which the economy stops growing. (Even at the level of institutions – universities, retail stores, product manufacturers, and even cities! – the productivist emphasis on growth is the only imaginable option.) Mill, in contrast, refused to "identify all that is economically desirable" with growth and "that alone." He went on:

> I know not why it should be a matter of congratulation that persons who are already richer than any one needs to be, should have doubled their means of consuming things which give little or no pleasure except as representative of wealth; or that numbers of individuals should pass over, every year, from the middle classes into a richer class, or from the class of the occupied rich to that of the unoccupied.[22]

Mill believed instead that the goal should be, first, "a good distribution of wealth" rather than merely "a rapid increase of it." This concern with distribution led him, like many in his day, to recommend "a stricter restraint on population," but he also proposed other means of redistribution, such as restraints on how much wealth an individual could receive.[23] And, heralding the many critics of productivist thought who would follow him over the next 150 years, he pointed out the paradox of productivity improvement: that contrary to most predictions, the machines and divisions of labour that were supposed to make production more efficient had not led to a reduction in work for human beings:

> Hitherto it is questionable if all the mechanical inventions yet made have lightened the day's toil of any human being. They have enabled a greater population to live the same life of drudgery and imprisonment, and an increased number of manufacturers and others to make fortunes. They have increased the comforts of the middle classes. But they have not yet begun to effect those great changes in human destiny, which it is in their nature and in their futurity to accomplish.[24]

Against nascent productivist ideas, he also pondered the meanings of value and happiness, prosperity and good living. Like the statisticians and economists who would reassess GDP in the twenty-first century, Mill questioned the association most political economists made between happiness and well-being, "progress" and growth. And, finally, he worried about the destruction of the natural world for the sake of that progress:

> If the earth must lose that great portion of its pleasantness which it owes to things that the unlimited increase of wealth and population would extirpate from it, for the mere purpose of enabling it to support a larger, but not a better or a happier population, I sincerely hope, for the sake of posterity, that they will be content to be stationary, long before necessity compels them to it.[25]

Mill's concerns – about the failure of technology to liberate people from "toil," about ecological destruction in the pursuit of profits, and about the equation of money and wealth with happiness and betterment – presage the warnings and critiques that have since coexisted and competed with productivism, and that comprise in a sense the alternative(s) to the productivist ideational regime. They are in all the times and places studied in this book, finding expression and gaining attention at particular junctures through particular works of philosophy and economics, and through social and political movements.

My reading strongly suggests that these alternative discourses tend to be drawn into three powerful currents of critique and related "demands" for change.[26] The first current takes issue with how much and how hard people *work* for productivist reasons, and demands the increase and protection of non-work time. Often, this current points to flourishing technologies that could reduce human work time already. At the dawn of industrialization, heavy machinery in factories promised reduction in work time. In the mid-twentieth century, it was home appliances, early computers, and other gadgets. Today, it is information and digital technologies from the Internet to 3D printers. But while the specific technologies have changed, the basic argument against the counterintuitive tendency for work to intensify rather than ease up has been consistent.

The second current of critique argues that there are ecological limits to economic growth, that exceeding those limits will destroy the environment and degrade human life, and that environmental protection must be prioritized ahead of economic productivity. The last point is sometimes expressed in terms of demands to enact environmental protections in policy. In the 1800s and much of the 1900s, it was resource depletion and the encroachment of human infrastructure on wilderness areas that caused concern for the environment. Since the late 1900s and early 2000s, as readers are no doubt aware, critiques of economic growth have been spurred by carbon emissions and climate change. But the general idea is the same.

The third current of critique targets consumption – and more specifically consumerism – as an intoxicating, deadening, and individualizing feature of capitalist societies. For some, consumerism is problematic because it creates so much waste and destroys the natural world; for others, it is most harmful to the human spirit and to social bonds. (For still others, as we will see, it is not a problem but rather a promising solution.)

These three currents, focused on work, ecology, and consumerism respectively, can each be traced to Mill's *Principles,* if not earlier; since then, they have at times been blended into a single critique, and at other times they have been sharpened to point at the discrete, egregious symptoms of productivism in particular socio-historical contexts.

As a genealogical device, the act of tracing these currents reveals something striking about the productivity concept. Specifically, we find that those who have critiqued or envisioned alternatives to productivism's growth-centric society, from at least the nineteenth century onward, have often done so by troubling the notion of productivity itself, questioning the imputed benefits of its increase, and pressing the arbitrary (and, as seen in the case of finance, moveable) distinction between productive and unproductive labour. What this suggests is that productivism, as an ideational regime, depends to some degree on a particular understanding of productivity, and is thus vulnerable wherever that notion of productivity is weakened. This point can only be made clearer by continuing to trace the three currents of anti-productivist critique – targeting work, ecology, and consumerism.

Nineteenth-Century Anti-Productivism

The work of Karl Marx, emerging around the same time as Mill's *Principles*, is not widely known for its expression of any of these critiques. Yet there are anti-productivist ideas throughout Marx's writing, and even more pronounced anti-productivist arguments in the Marxist scholarship that has grown out of his work. After all, he endorsed struggles for shorter workdays and criticized the intensification of labour in capitalist economies as much as he valorized work, in general, as a fundamental human activity. Still, some of Marx's contemporaries and more of his successors have argued that his theses on capitalism were quite in favour of both productive work and economic growth. He disparaged the idleness of the wealthy and argued that it was only possible because of the labour of the proletariat, but he did not wish to win access to that idleness for the proletariat. Many of Marx's writings suggest that his problem with capitalism, as Kathi Weeks has noted, was not that it was work-centric, but that the work at its centre was alienated and exploited. He imagined a world in which work would be "perfected" rather than diminished in importance. Most of the traditions of thought that have grown out of his writings – that is, most contemporary Marxist theory and analysis – display similarly "productivist tendencies." Thus, while there is an anti-productivism in Marx and Marxism, of which many have made good use, it exists in tension with "an endorsement of economic growth, industrial progress, and the work ethic similar to the ones that can be found in bourgeois political economy."[27] (The exceptions to this are discussed further below.)

Over in the more orthodox marginalist school of economics, there was, in the 1800s, a shred of concern about the scarcity of natural resources, the unsustainability of economic growth, and the risk that humans would fail to see such limits before it was too late. For example, W.S. Jevons's study of the "depletion" of coal reserves, published in 1865, ends on this note of conflict and caution:

> After all commerce is but a means to an end: the diffusion of civilization and wealth. To allow commerce to proceed until the source of civilization is weakened and overturned is like killing the goose to get the golden egg. Is the immediate creation of material wealth to be our only object? Have we not hereditary possessions in our just laws, our free and nobly developed constitution, our rich literature and philosophy, incomparably above material wealth, and which we are beyond all things bound to maintain, improve, and hand down in safety? And do we accomplish this duty in encouraging a growth of industry which must prove unstable, and perhaps involve all things in its fall?[28]

Jevons's convictions about growth, however, were shaken by the possibility that all of the non-material, "free and noble" types of wealth he listed – the literature and philosophy, the laws and constitution – might have depended on his country's industrial progress, and indeed its "expenditure of ... material energy." He was perplexed by the question of whether restricting the latter might mean "strangling" the former. He concluded that the British Empire faced "the momentous choice between brief greatness" – through its cultural and economic expansion at home and in overseas colonies – "and longer continued mediocrity."[29]

By now, it is clear that Jevons's home country chose greatness; the question of its length or brevity depends on perspective, and even more so on what happens in the next fifty years. But that choice – to put the growth of industry ahead of the conservation of resources – represents one of those moments when the road ahead branched into a productivist path on one side and an alternative on the other. The alternative ideas were there. But productivism was stronger, likely because it appealed both to elite interests in profit-making and to the more classless trifecta of imperial pride, belief in progress, and faith that economic expansion would mean prosperity for all. Productivism also meshed up, as I will explore further below, with the evolving work ethic in the West, which, as Weber wrote at the time, equated hard work and productivity with virtue and even religious salvation.[30] To place a limit on economic growth, in this formula, would be to place a limit on virtue.

Still, the alternative ideas expressed by Jevons and Mill continued to smoulder. In 1880, they were stoked by none other than Marx's son-in-law, the French journalist and revolutionary Marxist Paul Lafargue. (Although, Marx disagreed with Lafargue's radical revolutionary beliefs and famously said, to Engels, that if Lafargue and his friends were Marxists, then he – Marx – was not.) While exiled in London, Lafargue wrote and published a seditious manifesto called *The Right to Be Lazy*, a title meant to mock a French revolutionary slogan (indeed, "principle") from 1848: the demand for the "right to work."[31] Lafargue could not accept the idea that work was a right worth fighting for, because "in capitalist society work is the cause of all intellectual degeneracy, of all organic deformity." He was vexed that "the proletariat" had "invited" the miseries of work by claiming it as a right, and especially outraged that they accepted mere reforms to working conditions for children rather than the abolition of child labour. Had he been religious, he said, he would have liked to see such reformers go to hell.[32]

If the "proles" could just escape from the "dogma of work," Lafargue wrote, they could realize a utopia that was closed off to them only by the moral and ideological commitment to toil: a future in which work was "a mere condiment to the pleasures of idleness, a beneficial exercise to the human organism, a passion useful to the social organism only when wisely regulated and limited to a maximum of three hours a day."[33] Looking around himself, it appeared to Lafargue that the consequence of *not* resisting this dogma was the "overproduction" of goods. And that, he argued, "forced" capitalists into idleness, leisure, and frivolous consumption, while the working classes continued to churn out more goods than were socially necessary and to surrender much of the free time they would need to enjoy those goods themselves. Even when workers rose up to condemn the unearned luxury of the wealthy, they fell back on the dogma of work: they asserted that "he who will not work Neither shall he Eat," reinforcing the connection between survival and wage work that bound them to their own miserable employment.[34] Lafargue's manifesto hit two of the anti-productivist notes listed above: it was primarily a critique of work, but his warning about "overproduction" was also critique of growth for growth's sake.

The trope of the idle capitalist class would emerge again in 1899, eight years before the publication of *The Right to Be Lazy* in English, in Thorstein Veblen's *Theory of the Leisure Class*. Veblen's critique of "conspicuous consumption" stopped short of questioning the pursuit of growth *per se*, focusing instead on the more immediate issues of "waste." Veblen insisted that he meant only to *describe*, not critique, the "exemption" of wealthy people from "industrial toil" and their tendency to display their status through material possessions. But in characterizing the "non-productive" use of time as "wasteful," and in asserting that humankind was endowed by nature with a propensity to work, he certainly implied that workers' industriousness was to be praised and wealthy idleness exposed as a continuation of barbaric social norms. In any case, Veblen's work was hardly an explicit critique of productivism.[35]

Twentieth-Century Anti-Productivism

The anti-productivism in Jevons's and Mill's writings was reignited in the early twentieth century by the First World War and the subsequent economic crash and Great Depression. In the middle of that period, in 1924, the Canadian National Museum's head anthropologist, Edward Sapir, wrote a scathing essay about *American* individualism and industrial society. He proposed that "any rapidly complicating civilization" – a description which surely applied to Canada as well – faced the urgent question of "how to reap the undeniable benefits of a great differentiation of functions, without at the same time losing sight of the individual as a nucleus of live cultural values."[36] Channelling the congruence of cultural anthropology and social liberalism that Brick convincingly describes, he despaired that a "genuine" culture could not spring up from an industrial society in which people were "cogs" in industrial production. To Sapir, it seemed that the economic growth so prioritized in the wake of the war threatened to diminish social and cultural life.[37]

In 1931, John Maynard Keynes – the man who introduced the world to The (National) Economy, drew attention to its imperfections and contradictions, and showed statisticians how to measure it – reflected on the point of economic "progress" in an essay titled "Economic Possibilities for Our Grandchildren." The essay, written for a lecture in 1928 and revised over the following three years to address the onset of the Depression, is now widely known for its prediction that in one hundred years, technological improvements would reduce the workday to three hours. But that is only a small piece of a much larger engagement with the limits of economic growth.

For Keynes, the Depression felt especially awful because standards of living had, in the eighteenth and nineteenth centuries, improved more quickly and dramatically than they ever had before. Prior to the eighteenth century, due to "the remarkable absence of important technical improvements and to the failure of capital to accumulate," such "progress" had been slow.[38] Against the "bad attack of economic pessimism" that set in during the Depression, Keynes argued the present downturn was simply a "growing pain" that the world had to endure and was in the process of overcoming.

In the mid-1930s, a movement sprang up in France around the work of Jacques Ellul and Alain Charbonneau, which "criticized modernity," *especially* its central values of "productivity and individualism."[39] They posited "nature" – and getting close to it – as an antidote and a mode of resistance to industrial, modern capitalism. They believed that societies and economies should be scaled down to a size that facilitated personal contact and interdependence. They are widely credited with beginning the movement that would come to be known as political ecology: a body of literature and a community of action concerned with the ecological limits of economic growth.

Ellul and Charbonneau paid attention to work only insofar as its organization, in factories and corporations, was one manifestation of the productivism that was their main interest. Their scaled-down societies would entail a reduction in working hours, but this was not so much about work as it was about the need to ramp down production and, specifically, put an end to "overproduction."[40]

In his 2006 book *Transcending Capitalism*, Howard Brick points out an intriguing ambiguity in social thought around this time, regarding "the corporation" as a newly dominant business entity. Specifically, for many in the "post-capitalist" strain of thought that Brick traces from the eighteenth to the twenty-first century, "corporate organization" in the early part of the twentieth century "signaled capitalist ascent *and* the possible supercession of capitalism itself."[41] This was the basis of a 1932 book, Adolf Berle and Gardiner Means's *The Modern Corporation and Private Property*, which argued that "the corporation [was] a medium of change toward a social economy." The idea had many adherents, and not just those driven by "'corporate liberal' motives." Many quite progressive thinkers believed that "organized capitalism," built around the "falsely privatized" modern corporation, was a step on the way towards a more "social economy."[42] Thus, just as not all critiques of corporatization were anti-productivist, not all endorsements of the corporate structure were endorsements of the contemporary economic order *tout court*.

British philosopher Bertrand Russell, on the other hand, levelled a critique directly at productivism in one of his most famous essays, from 1932: *In Praise of Idleness*. Russell's argument therein was akin to Lafargue's in *The Right to Be Lazy*: that productivity-boosting technology *should* have led to shorter hours of work for all people, but it didn't. Instead, it had created unemployment (and "starvation") for some and "overwork" for the rest. The conditions of the war – the same conditions that spurred the DBS to begin a more centralized, coordinated collection of economic data in Canada – had revealed to Russell that it was "possible to diminish enormously the amount of labor required to secure the necessaries of life for everyone."[43] He thought the wartime production levels could have been "preserved" after the war, giving people of all classes more leisure time. That this didn't happen Russell took as a sign of the morality of work – the elevation of industriousness to the status of virtue – and the resistance on the part of "the rich" to "the idea that the poor should have leisure."[44] In other words, Russell argued, long working hours were maintained in spite of technological advances because people were afraid of what the lower classes would do with time outside work. These concerns about idleness, he noted, did not extend to that of the wealthy; taking up Marx's quarrel with the idle rich, and echoing Veblen, Russell pointed out that their idleness was only "rendered possible by the industry of others." Yet where Marx and even Veblen seemed at times to be disgusted by *anyone* ducking necessary labour, Russell wanted to extend that privilege to everyone.

The generality of Russell's critique does gloss over some interesting particularities of the interwar era. In the 1920s, according to Brick, "liberalism" in America especially "was updated with a substantial admixture of evolutionary socialist principles."[45] As Benjamin Hunnicutt (and others, including David Roediger) have shown, there was actually a "brief interest in shorter hours among welfare capitalists such as Henry Ford after 1914 and within movements such as scientific management (or 'reformed Taylorism') through the 1920s," thanks in part to the budding human relations school's influential "claims ... about the positive relationship between shorter hours and increased efficiency (resulting from reduced fatigue)."[46] During the Great Depression, around the time of Russell's essay, there was "considerable" support for "share-the-work arguments for shorter hours," with US president Herbert Hoover on board and "30-hour workweek legislation ... often near passage" as part of the New Deal.[47] W.K. Kellogg and Henry Ford were among the industrialists who saw a six-hour day as "a new way of life" that "recognized the changed balance between leisure to live and productivity to supply the means of living." Thus, in some quite unexpected places, it was believed that the best and "most logical" way to improve the standard of living was to increase leisure.[48]

But alas, Hunnicutt's research is about the *end* of shorter work hours, and the entrenchment of "work without end." By the mid-1930s, disagreements between labour and employers (and within the two groups) over such matters as whether to legislate reduced work hours (at that point, voluntary), and whether productivity and loyalty should be induced through work reductions or through wage increases, halted the momentum towards shorter workdays. Labour complained that employers were cutting wages wherever they cut hours. In collective bargaining, they began to push for more control over the workplace, and to fight to protect their wages, giving up the shorter hours demand as a concession. Businesses, for their part, embraced the "job creation" efforts of the New Deal government, tacitly agreeing that *more* work, not less, should be the goal. This unravelling of support for shorter hours has had lasting effects. As Hunnicutt wrote, "the idea of 'the more work, the better' has evolved into one of the most widely shared assumptions about modern economies," such that governments are implored to "create jobs" and replace those lost to technology:[49] "Instead of viewing human progress as transcending work, necessity, and economic concerns, and far from believing that increased freedom from toil is a constituent of that progress, much of the industrial world shares the belief that work is an end in itself, the ultimate measure of progress and the definition of prosperity."[50]

In the end, the New Deal, in Hunnicutt's reading, "saw making work and not making leisure as its priority."[51] Businesses, supported by the implicit productivism in government decisions and even in the positions adopted by labour itself, began to pursue "increased efficiency and productivity through the elimination of workers" instead of prioritizing full employment, as the latter was clearly not their responsibility, but government's. All of this, Hunnicutt suggests, pushed "eternal economic growth" and the continual search for "new things for consumers to need, work for, and buy" to the centre of North American, and perhaps global, governmentality.[52]

In 1932, Russell said nothing substantial about the pursuit of economic growth. But over the next three decades, after the "abandonment" of "shorter hours for the right to work," as Hunnicutt puts it, Russell's arguments about reducing work time, along with Marx's underappreciated anti-productivist, "autonomist" ideas, would be joined up with the types of concerns raised by Mill, Jevons, Ellul, and Charbonneau, in political ecology, ecological economics, and the burgeoning "de-growth" movement fuelled by such thought.[53]

Anti-Productivism after the Postwar Boom

In the 1950s and 1960s, there was a "drift" in what Brick calls "liberal social analysis." Once prominent critics of laissez-faire, and thus a source of support for the welfare state and "economic planning," left-liberal intellectuals began "either to displace economics from centrality or to assume that growth itself rendered the economic order malleable."[54] Gunnar Myrdal, C.P. Snow, and Robert Heilbroner and "a number of Keynesians" all believed that growth and "abundance" would inevitably usher in an era in which the economy was subordinate to society and people were more in control of production, consumption, and wealth.[55]

This drift towards complacency might explain the relative shortage of anti-productivist thought during that period, as the usual sources of dissent were quieted, like everyone else, by the improvement in material standards of living in the West. But a current of anti-productivist critique continued. In the 1960s, Charbonneau and Ellul – but mostly Ellul – were still working on the critique of growth-oriented societies they had begun in the 1930s. Like a handful of others – including, according to Brick, J.K. Galbraith – they believed that growth would not automatically lead to the "submission of the [economy] to [society] but the infusion of economic standards of output throughout all of social relations."[56] Ellul and Charbonneau's arguments targeted "gigantism" – the growth of giant factories, corporations, advertising, and so on – and the unrestricted development and use of technology.[57] (These, the reader might recall, were the same sorts of developments the Canadian government sought to measure more precisely in order to govern more completely.) By this time, Charbonneau and Ellul were part of a global movement railing against the spread of industry and the domination of humans by their technologies and tools. This larger movement included German philosopher Herbert Marcuse (who was then living and teaching in the United States), French philosopher Andre Gorz, and the Austrian philosopher Ivan Illich. Connecting these three to Ellul and Charbonneau was a shared, radical critique of societies that hinged income and liberty on productive work, and thus put work (and consumption) at the centre of social and political life.

Marcuse's *One-Dimensional Man*, first published in 1964, argued that technological progress and "free enterprise" had ushered in a kind of totalitarianism – an "economic-technical coordination" – that prevented (insofar as it "contained") social change, made "nonconformity" "socially useless," and curtailed people's "autonomy."[58] Like many in the selective anti-productivist tradition I am outlining here, Marcuse targeted productivity specifically. It is not a coincidence that they did so at the very moment it was becoming possible to measure, in statistical form, national, aggregate productivity on a regular basis. Indeed, one might say that instead of merely becoming possible to do, it was, at this time, becoming *impossible not to do*. The level of this now concrete and precise "productivity" – and the constant increase thereof – in industrial society was, Marcuse argued, "destructive of the free development of human needs and faculties."[59] He saw productivity (and efficiency) as integral to the process by which technological advance, the manufactured "needs" of consumer society, and rising standards of living all frustrated any attempt to imagine, let alone create, a different world.

Especially fascinating is Marcuse's analysis of the role that "technological rationality" played in the destruction of freedom or, as he put it, "domination." He proposed that there was a close relationship "between scientific thought and its application, between the universe of scientific discourse and that of ordinary discourse and behaviour."[60] Making an argument that today looks an awful lot like an explanation of governmentality, Marcuse wrote that the way scientists thought about the world, and the way ordinary people went about living in it, "both move[d] under the same logic and rationality of domination."[61] Although much of his discussion focused on "science" in general, in several passages he made reference to "statistics." He argued that statistics

> become mystifying to the extent to which they are isolated from the truly concrete context which makes the facts and determines their function. This context is larger and other than that of the plants and shops investigated, of the towns and cities studied, of the areas and groups whose public opinion is polled or whose chance of survival is calculated. And it is also more real in the sense that it creates and determines the facts investigated, polled, and calculated.[62]

Marcuse's observation certainly reflects the interplay of statistical abstraction and horizons of thought throughout the history of the productivity concept presented here. The increasingly aggregated, imputed, adjusted, and otherwise manipulated productivity indicators in use today, as described in the last chapter, are indeed "mystifying," as well as "isolated" from any "concrete context." Yet as methods to measure productivity became more refined, thinking about an economy based on anything but ever-increasing levels of productivity became, to use Marcuse's terms, irrational. Importantly, these advances in measuring the world went hand-in-hand, historically, with rising living standards. Here, I have focused on the way that conceptions of productivity's *inherent* relationship to prosperity were informed by measurement of that relationship at one peculiar and perhaps *unique* postwar moment; Marcuse, in contrast, viewed the problem from roughly its other side, concerning himself with the socio-political ramifications of technical rationality and rising standards of living. The result, according to him, was a complacent, conformist society that took science at its word and was too comfortable to complain anyway.

This was the same desensitized society that irked Ivan Illich, who in the 1970s released a series of radical critiques of modern Western education, medicine, industry, and technology. All of Illich's writings, no matter their immediate target, centred on a common thesis: that "growing dependence on mass-produced goods and services gradually erodes the conditions necessary for a convivial life," the latter defined by individual freedom, interdependence, and creativity.[63] Critiquing the economic order as Illich and Marcuse did, at a time when it seemed to be working better than ever before (or had just recently entered a rocky patch) – a time of "capitalist triumphalism," when wages and standards of living had been on the rise, when the glitzy wealth of Wall Street seemed attainable to anyone willing to work for it, when the very existence of society was denied in some quarters – was a difficult task, far more difficult than the task of anti-productivist ideas now that the empirical link between productivity and prosperity has been more fervently called into question.[64] But it struck a chord, with Marcuse's best-seller garnering critics' attention in the *New York Times* and *The Nation*, and Illich's work gaining praise in *The New York Review of Books*.

Two of the most influential works in Illich's oeuvre were critical of the same general phenomenon as addressed by Ellul, Charbonneau, and Marcuse: the increasing sophistication, specialization, and ubiquity of technology since the Industrial Revolution, and its impact on liberty and autonomy. For Illich, the focus was "tools," both in the sense of material implements like syringes, cars, and telephones, and in the governmentality studies sense (although he did not call it that) of institutions and techniques. In his 1971 book *Tools for Conviviality*, he sketched out a "lifestyle" and a "political system" that would give "priority to the protection, the maximum use, and the enjoyment of the one resource that is almost equally distributed among all people: personal energy under personal control." Such a society would establish "procedures to ensure that controls over the tools of society are established and governed by political process rather than by decisions by experts."[65]

At the heart of this society was a quality (an "intrinsic ethical value") that Illich called "conviviality": "autonomous and creative intercourse among persons with their environment," and "individual freedom realized in personal interdependence." Importantly, Illich saw conviviality as "the opposite of industrial productivity."[66] In a follow-up to *Tools*, titled *The Right to Useful Unemployment*, he extended the critique of "disabling" technologies to a critique of "disabling professions": the process by which needs and desires that people had once been permitted to satisfy on their own, for free, for themselves, their families, and their neighbours, became the sole purview of a professional, certified few, who controlled "what ought to be sold and must not be given for free."[67]

The anti-productivism from the later 1970s to the 1980s must not be confused with that of the "post-industrial" analysts that Howard Brick chronicled in his genealogy of post-capitalist thought. Looking back from the 1980s on slow growth in the 1970s, this group "advocated planned investment in education, technology, and human resources" and "insisted that the integration of social and economic concern was the way forward to renewed growth." They saw the "greater measure of equity and social security" for which they called as a *requirement* for economic "expansion." Thus, "the issue for them was not one of surpassing industry per se but moving on to a new formula of industrial growth, and in so doing, they also forcefully reinstated the priority of a competitive search for profits."[68]

In contrast, Illich's work, like that of Marcuse, is primarily a critique of "development." It is also important to note its focus on the detrimental impacts of "technical progress" on humanity rather than on the natural environment (although in both men's thinking, the two issues are no doubt closely related).[69] This is not to say that either ignored questions of ecology; for his part, Illich suggested that societies would need to wake up to the limitations that economic growth and the intensification of industry placed directly on their humanity and liberty – their freedom to do, make, say, and think as they pleased – before they would care about the plight of the environment. "Ecology will provide guidelines for a feasible form of modernity," he explained, but "only when it is recognized that a man-made environment designed for commodities reduces personal aliveness to the point where the commodities themselves lose their value as means for personal satisfaction."[70] In this way, Illich – like Charbonneau and Ellul, and to a lesser extent Marcuse – offered a blend of the three currents of anti-productivism, with a little bit of energy devoted to destabilizing assumptions about work, a little bit directed at the perils of consumerism, and bit more reserved for the need to protect and prioritize the "natural environment" unspoiled by highways, buildings, and trash.

Anti-Productivism and Anti-Work

Despite paying only scant attention to the environment in their critiques of industry and work, Marcuse and Illich are often swept into the tradition of political ecology, a school of thought to which both philosophers were connected by way of a personal friendship with one of the movement's principal thinkers: André Gorz. In 1983's *Farewell to the Working Class*, the second of his books to get significant attention in the English-speaking world (after 1967's *Strategy for Labor*), Gorz predicted that a crisis of mass unemployment was just around the corner, and made the provocative argument – no doubt influenced by Illich and Marcuse – that this could actually be a promising opportunity and not a catastrophe. For Gorz, it had the potential to expand human freedoms, open up more time "for living," and reduce wealth inequalities *if* the transition away from a wage work society was controlled democratically.[71]

Farewell was only one of several books that Gorz would write to critique work and describe a possible future in which everyone did less of it. His *Critique of Economic Reason* (1988) and *Reclaiming Work* (1999) would carry this line of thought nearly to his death in 2007. In focusing on work and the sometimes arbitrary distinction between productive and "non-productive" activity (as found and occasionally critiqued in Marx, Veblen, Smith, and nearly every other economist and social scientist of the previous two hundred years), Gorz took the burgeoning "political ecology" school of thought in a new direction. But he was not alone on this path. The women's liberation movement of the 1960s and 1970s was also there, launching one of the biggest challenges to work-as-we-know-it, and indeed to productivism, that the twentieth century ever saw.

This was, incidentally, the same moment when Canada's NPC launched its series of labour–management seminars. Importantly for my purposes, it was also a moment that saw a swell of anti-productivist thought. Although much attention focuses today on the "success" of the women's movement in getting women into the workforce and the halls of political power, one of the most powerful and controversial critiques that came out of the movement was a proposed *rejection* of both paid work outside the home *and* unpaid work inside the home – and the forms of success and respect that came with each. Granted, many women's liberationists sought to free women from domestic work so that they could take up paid employment. But one influential camp argued, in line with Marcuse, Gorz, and other political ecologists, that paid employment was actually no liberation at all. Selma James and Mariarose Dalla Costa, an American and Italian feminist, respectively, led this camp with their co-authored manifesto *The Power of Women and the Subversion of the Community.*

According to Kathi Weeks's reading, James and Dalla Costa's intervention was to "demand" wages for housework *without* valorizing the family and domesticity, on the one hand, or paid employment on the other. The "Wages for Housework" movement they led had gained traction in Canada by the mid-1970s. They laid some of the groundwork for the development of an impressive tradition of feminist political economy in Canadian universities from the late 1970s onward. Outside academe, their work even inspired the creation of Wages for Housework Committees – the most active of which was established in Toronto – which pushed for the implementation of a "family allowance" to remunerate women for their labour inside the home.[72]

But not all Canadian feminist scholars and activists agreed with James and Dalla Costa's proposals. Far from it. As Ruth Roach Pierson has documented, the federal New Democratic Party (NDP), despite being the mainstream party most sympathetic to social justice and feminist causes, came out *against* the family allowance. They believed it would be too costly and come at the expense of other measures to increase equality; they also posited, in line with many other feminists at the time, that wages for housework would tie women even more tightly to their domestic roles.[73] Meg Luxton's *More Than a Labour of Love* (1980), one of the most widely read contributions to feminist political economy in Canada, rejected wages for housework as a policy solution for some of the same reasons as the NDP. Luxton emphasized instead the need to *reduce* work time, inclusive of the home-based work of "social reproduction." In this way, Luxton's highly influential book mounted an even more expansive challenge to the productivist fetishization of work than the Wages for Housework movement, because it targeted waged *and* unwaged labour and called into question both the necessity and the virtue of doing so much of either.

The innovation in Luxton's work, and in the feminist organizing and advocacy of which it was a part, was to tie the kind of anti-productivist critique of overproduction found in Ellul, Charbonneau, and Illich's work, with its emphasis on human liberty, to a more specific demand for *women's* liberation. The immediate struggle, for anti-productivist feminists, was to free women from domestic duty, but this was explicitly understood as part of a larger struggle to free everyone from the duty to further capital accumulation through economic growth. As Silvia Federici, a key figure in the "autonomist Marxist feminist" tradition, put it, "calling domestic labor 'work' was not meant to elevate it but was imagined rather as 'the first step towards refusing to do it.'"[74] Federici and other autonomist Marxist feminists, picking up the anti-productivist threads in Marx's writings, dared to connect the dots between women's subordination, the wage system, and capitalism. Although the act of "punching in and punching out" at work had been understood to separate "the time we belonged to capital and the time we belonged to ourselves," they argued that "we have never belonged to ourselves, we have always belonged to capital every moment of our lives. And it is time that we made capital pay for every moment of it."[75]

Anti-Productivism, Anti-Work, and Neoliberalism

What these feminists could not have foreseen was that the next decade would usher in the era and the dominant political economic world view we now call neoliberalism. Its influence on economic theory and policy has served to increase and protect global capital accumulation and to increase the amount of time society as a whole spends at work. Neoliberal economics has drawn more people into wage work while at the same time displacing more into the ranks of the unemployed and the precariously employed. Even those who celebrate work in the abstract and who claim it is essential for human existence and happiness cannot find much to rejoice about in the expansion of increasingly insecure, dangerous, or "precarious" jobs.[76]

The fact that there are more women in the workforce; that they now make up the majority of students in most post-secondary institutions in the West; that more households are now headed by women insofar as the woman is the primary breadwinner – all of these have been taken, in some quarters, as signs that feminists won. But when one takes into account the heterogeneity of feminist orientations to work, and especially the critique of work mounted by autonomist Marxist feminists, the Wages for Housework Movement, and related strands, developments after 1970 look like more of a loss than a win. Moreover, for some feminist scholars, even feminism itself – where it is not being rejected as either irrelevant or simply off-putting – has been overtaken by neoliberal thinking.[77] And when feminism and neoliberalism get "married" in this way, the result is a hyper-productivist, wage-work-centric agenda that ties women's rights and their humanity to paid employment.[78] Describing this "disturbing trend," sociologist Christine Williams explains that "unlike liberal feminism, which relies on the state to rectify problems of women's unequal opportunities and underrepresentation, neoliberal feminism promotes individual responsibility, limited government, market-driven solutions to social problems, and what Arlie Hochschild ...has called the commercialization of intimate life."[79]

The evolution of a neoliberal feminism, for Williams and others, is just one more example of "capitalism's ability to appropriate and commodify discontent."[80] However, the popularity of neoliberal feminist ideas – such as those contained in Sheryl Sandberg's bestselling *Lean In* – suggests that contemporary societies are extremely receptive to a brand of feminism (pun intended) that "works" for capitalism – that seeks to intensify and glorify, rather than challenge or critique, the place of waged work, corporate profit, and economic growth in people's lives.[81] Although this is certainly not without precedent, it is nevertheless curious that an argument like Sandberg's, for *more* work for women, finds a more appreciative audience than any book about doing less work could conceivably find today, whether it was written by a feminist or not. It is curious because one must wonder what it is that readers of any gender believe that "leaning in" to work would actually do to better their lives. Aside from the pleasure and feelings of self-worth women are assumed to gain as they ascend the corporate ladder – and maybe, if we are generous, the intangible corporate benefits of having more gender-diverse leadership – the primary beneficiary of women "leaning in" to the workplace is what Weeks calls "the work society." In this society, the question of who benefits, who loses, and how, is complicated by the existence of wages and their role as a mediator between a person and nearly every other "good" in the world. In the work society, "waged work" is "the centerpiece" of life:

> It is, of course, the way most people acquire access to the necessities of food, clothing, and shelter. It is not only the primary mechanism by which income is distributed, it is also the basic means by which status is allocated, and by which most people gain access to healthcare and retirement. After the family, waged work is often the most important, if not sole, source of sociality for millions. Raising children with attributes that will secure them forms of employment that can match if not surpass the class standing of their parents is the gold standard of parenting. In addition, making people capable of working is, as Nona Glazer notes, 'the central goal of schooling' ... Helping to make people "work ready" and moving them into jobs are central objectives of social work ... a common rationale for the prison system, and an important inducement to perform military service. Indeed, enforcing work, as the other side of defending property rights, is a key function of the state.[82]

Weeks's book, which takes on the difficult task of estranging us from our most familiar relationship with work, builds on the tradition of thought, traceable to the political ecologists of the 1960s and 1970s, that critiques work's place in our lives. Her book is unique today in its reliance on autonomist Marxist feminist theory as a foundation, but it is not alone in asking why "we," inhabitants of the late twentieth and early twenty-first centuries, work as long and as hard as we do despite the very real possibility of working less and still living reasonably comfortable, even at times luxurious, lives.

Post-1980, this same line of thinking can be found, for example, in the economist-turned-sociologist Juliet Schor's bestselling 1991 book, *The Overworked American*. Based on an empirical analysis of employment and time-use statistics in the United States, *Overworked* showed that after a small initial reduction in working time post-1970, the time Americans spend at work had gradually and steadily increased. The time they devoted to other pursuits – community participation, sports, politics, hobbies or, God forbid, doing absolutely nothing – had

decreased accordingly. For Schor, the most important victim was quality of life. Her point was to question not only the value assumptions
concealed in orthodox economics (e.g., the equation of material possessions with good living), but also the everyday value assumptions of
ordinary working people. However, subsequent books and editions of
Overworked have made the additional connections between overwork
and consumerism, debt, capitalism, and environmental destruction – a
theme to which I will return below.

I see Schor's book as the most popular edge of a much larger wedge
of contemporary social criticism, spanning the 1990s and 2000s, that
advances a multifaceted critique of a world revolving around economic
production in one way or another. These publications owe an intellectual debt to, and often cite, writers like Gorz and Marcuse – indeed,
Gorz himself continued writing in this vein until 2003 – but they reflect
changes in social theory, political discourse, and economic structures.
They are made sensible, rational, and indeed possible by the cracks,
discussed in the previous chapter, in the validity of productivity as a
statistical indicator and a condition for prosperity. Without those cracks,
there would be little room for a critique of productivism to take hold.
These are not all works of political ecology; although they acknowledge
our responsibility to be stewards of the natural environment, its welfare is not their starting point – work is. I will briefly survey some of the
most prominent books in this broad theme before narrowing my focus
to the ones that challenge rather than accept the productivist ideational
regime.

Soon after Schor's bestseller informed Americans that they were
working too much, three other authors stepped into the spotlight to
remind them that soon there wouldn't be enough work to go around.
Stanley Aronowitz and William DiFazio, in *Jobless Future* (1994), argued
that technological progress had killed more jobs than it created, and
would continue to do so if society continued on its current trajectory.
Jeremy Rifkin's *The End of Work* (1995) presented a similar view, predicting that technological change would all but ensure mass unemployment in the foreseeable future. Aronowitz and DiFazio were careful to
distinguish their position from that of Rifkin and others writing about
disappearing work during this period. "Unlike others," they explained,
"we refrained from accepting the idea that work itself has disappeared.
What is disappearing is not work but real jobs: the assumption of
long-term employment that entailed pension, health insurance, and
other benefits; the concept of 'careers' in which people could expect

progressively greater responsibility on the job and more income as a reward for hard work. According to this definition, jobs are an endangered species."[83] Despite this difference, Aronowitz and DiFazio still arrived at similar conclusions to those who predicted the disappearance of "work itself": like Gorz, Marcuse, and even Rifkin, they proposed an amended "social contract" that would entail shorter working hours and some form of a social wage to redistribute work time and at least partly mitigate the dependence of survival and well-being on paid employment.[84]

In 1999's *Reclaiming Work*, Gorz would jump back into the fray with a more optimistic message: that if society, and "the left" in particular, managed to control the downscaling of "heteronomy" (i.e., wage work, extracted from some individuals by others), they could ensure that it led to a fairer redistribution of socially necessary labour rather than to Bertrand Russell's "overwork for some, starvation for others" scenario. Gorz was not afraid to propose utopian visions of a world with less working and more living. Those visions are always in the background and sometimes in the foreground of *Reclaiming Work* and *Critique of Economic Reason* (1983). Thus while he might have seen the same developments on the horizon as Rifkin, Aronowitz, and DiRazio, he was more hopeful than they were. Where Rifkin imagined a future in which currently unwaged work became waged – in other words, where people were put back to work – Gorz imagined that we might enjoy more free time.

This is what sets Gorz apart from other influential works of the same period: Ulrich Beck's *Brave New World of Work* (2000) and Richard Sennett's *The Corrosion of Character* (1999). These two sociologists lamented the more specific disappearance of fulfilling, permanent, and stable work, and warned of the negative consequences for identity, social cohesion, and, in Sennett's case, character. Their point is not to be dismissed – certainly, there can be rewarding work, and work can be an immensely satisfying activity – not to mention essential for survival! – in a person's life. The loss of opportunities to do expressive or instrumental work that is sustaining, relational, interesting, and validating, is something to be mourned. But the most stringent anti-productivist thought pushes those acknowledgments to the side in order to avoid adding any support to a work ethic that is in need of no more support. Thus, Beck and Sennett exhibit some of the "productivist tendencies" that Weeks finds in much Marxist thought; they lack the stronger anti-productivist thrust of Gorz, and to a slightly lesser extent Aronowitz and DiRazio.[85]

That kind of anti-productivism surfaced again in economic historian James Livingston's even more irreverent take on work, developed over the course of several books and many more blog posts. Livingston's position on work, consumption, and economic growth challenges the work society, but he is somewhat unique in his embrace of – or at least his refusal to completely reproach – consumerism. In 2012's *Against Thrift*, he makes the case for consumerism by making the case *against* productivism. And critiquing productivity – indeed, the *"pathos of productivity"* – is a key argument in this case. "We still suffer from the 'pathos of productivity,'" Livingston writes – "an almost Puritan belief in the redeeming value of producing as against consuming, saving as against spending, working as against whatever comes after."[86] But where Weber, Weeks, and many others have sought to challenge these "almost Puritan" beliefs for what they say about producing, saving, and work, Livingston sets his sights on the convictions about consuming, spending, and leisure. For him, they have outlived their usefulness: being thrifty no longer guarantees people a comfortable retirement – it's not enough; economic growth no longer depends on the savings of individuals or even corporations; and thrift is no longer the route to social mobility, because "career success" in a company doesn't hinge on savings the way entrepreneurialism might have.

Curiously, those who take issue with Livingston's argument tend to be at peace with his rejection of work but at odds with his endorsement of consumerism – especially his dismissal of concerns about consumerism's ecological consequences.[87] (Curious, because all anecdotal and social scientific evidence points to the majority of us in our everyday lives being quite desirous of consumer goods and happy with consumer society, and also quite attached to our jobs and accepting of the necessity of work.) In any case, to my reading it seems that Livingston's objective is not to describe some utopia in which we somehow cease working altogether and spend all our time buying trinkets, but rather to prod us to reflect on how an anti-productivist rejection of consumerism might inadvertently prop up the very puritan work ethic we intend to take out at the knees. Granted, Livingston maintains, against those who (like me) take his argument with a large grain of salt, that he *is*, "in fact, 'defending actually existing capitalist consumerism'" because he doesn't "see capitalism as a closed system, a totality that excludes socialism or any other mode of production."[88]

His point is that a socialist society, too, is a consumer society. And of course it can be – because it can also be a productivist society.

Thus a socialist critique of capitalism grounded in a critique of consumerism is the wrong tool for illustrating why socialism is the better option. Likewise, a socialist critique of capitalism grounded in a critique of productivism cannot prove that socialism is inherently a better system. Both capitalism and socialism have historically been, and thus have the potential to be, consumerist, productivist models. This underscores the need for reflexivity about the productivist assumptions that are contained in – and thus the productivist horizons that delimit – many other arguments for political economic change. And much of what Livingston has written elsewhere suggests that this is his objective.

In fact, he has proposed that "the left" adopt a new "slogan": "FUCK WORK." In an exchange with other left intellectuals who had criticized *Against Thrift* in the magazines *Jacobin* and *Dissent* – a debate that carried over onto his own blog – Livingston expressed bafflement at his interlocutors' desire to "put us back to work." It seemed that to them that "a world without work would ... be a world drained of humanity." In response, he pressed them to explain why they could not "accredit ... consumption" instead of work "as the essence of human existence." His challenge to them is worth reproducing at length because it points to the role that the work ethic plays in upholding the productivist ideational regime, even among people who claim to want to radically transform the economy:

> To be more polemical about it, why not say, Fuck Work? ...Why do we want full employment when more work for all means less income and less enjoyment for everybody? In plain sight of the simple fact that we can increase output without increasing inputs of either capital or labor – when socially necessary labor is disappearing – why do we seek out the deferral of desire that work requires, regardless of how collective and cooperative, or how lonely and artful, it must be? Why are we bound to this slave morality? Because it provides us the grounds for a "left-egalitarian critique of idle rentiers and capitalists, living off the efforts of others" ...? Because we have to work and they won't? The ancient Christian and the modern socialist causes were informed by the criterion of need ("from each according to his abilities, to each according to his needs") – once upon a time, the goal was the detachment of income (thus social standing) from work, not more work. The end of socially necessary labour was a promise to be kept in the future, not a reason to mourn the past.[89]

One of the "anti-consumerist" "leftists" that Livingston identifies in another blog post is the economic anthropologist David Graeber, author of *Debt: The First 5000 Years*. According to Livingston, "like ... almost every other leftist out there," Graeber "see[s] unbridled consumerism as the gravest threat to the environment, and, accordingly, to [our] souls." But the two align on their irreverence towards work, or at least, to borrow from Gorz, Aronowitz and DiFazio, or Weeks, their irreverence toward the "dogma," "ideology," or "ethic" of work as we know it.

In 2013, Graeber wrote an essay titled "On the Phenomenon of Bullshit Jobs" for the independent political magazine *Strike!* The piece subsequently garnered Graeber mention and interviews in more mainstream publications, including *Salon* and even *The Economist* and *The Guardian*.[90] His argument was scathing and simple: that many, if not most, jobs in the twenty-first century would not be missed if they suddenly disappeared. "Huge swathes of people, in Europe and North America in particular, spend their entire working lives performing tasks they secretly believe do not really need to be performed," Graeber wrote. Pointing yet again to the puzzling increase of work despite the availability of so much ostensibly "labour-saving" technology, he remarked:

> Rather than allowing a massive reduction of working hours to free the world's population to pursue their own projects, pleasures, visions, and ideas, we have seen the ballooning not even so much of the "service" sector as of the administrative sector, up to and including the creation of whole new industries like financial services or telemarketing, or the unprecedented expansion of sectors like corporate law, academic and health administration, human resources, and public relations. And these numbers do not even reflect on all those people whose job is to provide administrative, technical, or security support for these industries, or for that matter the whole host of ancillary industries (dog-washers, all-night pizza deliverymen) that only exist because everyone else is spending so much of their time working in all the other ones.[91]

These "bullshit jobs" continued to exist primarily as a means of social control because, as *Guardian* columnist Oliver Burkeman put it, "a population kept busy with bullshit has no time to start a revolution."[92] Graeber concedes that the preponderance of bullshit jobs only emerged through "trial and error" and not conscious design, but concludes that "the only explanation for why, despite our technological capacities, we are not all working 3-4 hour days" is that this system somehow works for "the ruling class." And in his estimation, that elite stratum of people "figured out that a happy and productive population with free time on their hands is a mortal danger (think of what started to happen when this even began to be approximated in the '60s)." Echoing Weeks and Lafargue, he notes that "the feeling that work is a moral value in itself, and that anyone not willing to submit themselves to some kind of intense work discipline for most of their waking hours deserves nothing, is extraordinarily convenient for them."[93]

Graeber's essay, although it might seem frivolous, counts as one more contribution to the pile of modern anti-productivist thoughts, a pile that has, as chronicled here, been growing since at least the nineteenth century. Like many of the others, Graeber's piece is directed at one aspect of productivism: in this case, the stability or increase in heteronomous (i.e., imposed from outside) work, in spite of technological progress that promises to reduce the need for human labour. This is the same paradox noted by most of the writers discussed in this chapter, from Mill to Russell to Gorz: that greater use of labour-saving technologies (inclusive of material technologies like computers and conveyor belts as well as management technologies like the assembly line and scientific management) had failed to deliver on the promise of less work and more leisure for all. As Hunnicutt's examination of shorter workdays at Kellogg's and Ford showed, even the seemingly promising experiments with less work and more leisure failed, despite very promising starts.

Academics and radical activists have never been the only ones scratching their heads about this paradox. Indeed, popular writers and commentators, especially in the post-2000 age of social media, have arguably been more astute than intellectuals in recognizing the creep of productivism into everyday life. Not that it was ever confined to workplaces, as is evident from the early 1900s "efficiency craze"; but it has sprung up in new ideals and tactics, new ethics of work that are uniquely adapted to the so-called Information Age. In *The New Statesman*, Stephen Poole wrote an essay assailing the relentless pursuit of productivity and "hard work," which, to him, appeared limitless. "We are everywhere enjoined to work harder, faster and for longer – not only in our jobs but also in our leisure time," he noted. "The rationale for this frantic grind is one of the great unquestioned virtues of our age: 'productivity.'" For Poole it seemed as if even leisure had been transformed into a space in which people had to *be* productive, or at least be restoring and preparing their bodies and their minds so that they could be productive when they went back to work:

> To the long-evolving demands of productivity at work we must now add the burden of productivity everywhere else. As the Nike T-shirt's slogan implies, even when we're not at work, we must be doing work ... "Exercise," advises one business magazine feature. "It makes you more productive." In a perfect world, you would be getting exercise while you work – standing desks and even treadmill desks are sold as magical productivity enhancers.[94]

Of course, the treatment of leisure time as a support for work time, rather than a time to be enjoyed for what it is, long pre-dated the advent of treadmill desks and Nike T-shirts. As Michael Seidman shows in his history of workers' movements in 1930s France and Barcelona, "leisure" was "defended in productivist terms as restoration after work or as effective employment of the jobless."[95] Indeed, both Weeks and Aronowitz found that the idea of doing absolutely nothing, for no instrumental purpose, has terrified us for centuries.[96] But it would be dangerous to assume that, because we have always had these thoughts, nothing, even with the changing techniques and technologies at our disposal, has truly changed. It has. And one of the more interesting revelations of social media is that even when ordinary people can produce content with the potential to reach every wired corner of the world – even when they can say *anything they want* – they often choose to convey the dogma of work. Whether in motivational memes (handwritten posters with "Just do the work" in curling, pastel font), inspirational "listicles" (e.g., "The 10 Habits of Highly Productive People"), or life-organizing apps, the virtue of productivity is today reinforced from the grassroots, bottom up.

But these online products do more than simply *inspire*. They instruct and they train, and they offer the technologies to aid people's efforts to be more productive. Poole cites some additional examples that reveal this Tayloristic (i.e., systematic, scientific) quality of many Internet productivity boosters:

> In the vanguard of "productivity" literature and apps was David Allen's "Getting Things Done" (GTD) system, according to which you can become "a wizard of productivity" by organising your life into folders and to-do lists. The GTD movement quickly spread outside the confines

of formal work and became a way to navigate the whole of existence: hence the popularity of websites such as Lifehacker that offer nerdy tips on rendering the messy business of everyday life more amenable to algorithmic improvement.[97]

On one level, Allen and other productivity gurus are the "managers" described by Illich in the opening quotation for this chapter – they promise productivity enhancements to help us acquire "better" and "more" of everything we ostensibly want. But their *everywhereness* is remarkably new. And the Internet's enablement of almost any user to be an author and perhaps an influencer means that anyone with an Internet connection has the capacity (if not the inclination) to be that manager, that promiser of productivity gains at home, at work, at the gym, in the kitchen, at the grocery store, at any place and any task we complete for ourselves or others. Moreover, smartphones – not to mention smart glasses and watches – enable we privileged to attach to our bodies the technologies that promise to help us Get Things Done, such that we can monitor our productivity in real time and record every second of it for posterity (and tomorrow's inspiration). Aronowitz and DiFazio's insight – that it was not just giant manufacturing machines but also tiny, wireless, personal digital technologies that had altered our relationship(s) to production and consumption, and changed the context in which both productivism and productivity acquire their social meanings – rings especially true, more than twenty years after they wrote it down.

So much about the social, physical, economic, and political world has changed, but the productivist ideational regime remains more or less intact. Even when it seems to be under assault, today as in the past, it is adapting. Even in anti-productivist critiques, productivism is there, in traces. The result, at times, is mystifying. Poole points out that even in Graeber's "bracingly critical" "Bullshit Jobs,"

the signal virtue of "productivity" is left standing, though it is not completely clear what it means for the people in the "real" jobs that Graeber admires. It is true that service industries are not "productive" in the sense that their labour results in no great amount of physical objects, but then what exactly is it for the "Tube workers" Graeber rightly defends to be "productive," unless that is shorthand for saying, weirdly, that they "produce" physical displacements of people? And to use "productive" as a positive epithet for another class of workers he admires, teachers, risks acquiescing rhetorically in the commercialisation of learning. Teaching as production is, etymologically and otherwise, the opposite of teaching as education.[98]

Poole's analysis of Graeber's logic and language underscores the characteristic hegemony of ideational regimes. Productivism is so pervasive and inclusive that it *nearly* prohibits people from thinking and saying anything that does not adopt at least some of its assumptions.

But since the turn of the twenty-first century, a movement that (in theory anyway) challenges almost every part of the productivist ideational regime has been steadily gaining support. Its key texts, both popular and academic, cite many of the anti-productivist works detailed in this chapter. It combines arguments from political ecology, steady state economics, autonomist Marxists, and radical feminists, merging them into a critique of economic growth and a "demand," as Weeks would see it, for the pursuit of growth's opposite. That movement is called *de-growth*.

Anti-Productivism and De-Growth

The contemporary de-growth movement traces its origins to a Romanian economist – Nicholas Georgescu-Roegen – who in the late 1960s proposed in a theory of "entropy" that the various forms of energy used for economic production were not wholly renewable: that there were, in other words, physical limits on economic growth.[99] This "Limits to Growth" idea surfaced as well in a 1970 think tank report by that name, which used econometric modelling to predict the disastrous potential of pursuing limitless economic growth in a world with finite resources.[100] Apparently "widely ridiculed" at the time, the report was "vindicated" in the first decades of the twenty-first century, when it was updated, re-released, and corroborated by environmental scientists who had come to nearly the same conclusions.[101]

But the first report, along with Georgescu-Roegen's theory, won some adherents at the time. In France, they mobilized under the banner of "décroissance," a name taken from the title of one of Georgescu-Roegen's books.[102] (*Décroissance* is translated, in English, as de-growth.) Given the legacy of political ecology, anti-work, and autonomist Marxism in central and southern Europe, it may not be surprising that many of de-growth's most prominent thinkers reside in France and Spain. In 2008, three Spanish academic proponents of de-growth organized an international conference on the topic in Paris, which was swiftly followed by more de-growth conferences in Europe and Canada. Those organizers – Giacomo D'Alisa, Federico Demaria, and Giorgos Kallis – produced, with contributions from dozens of de-growth researchers, a handbook of sorts for the movement's activists and academics titled *Degrowth: A Vocabulary for a New Paradigm*. Reflecting on the growing momentum of the "new paradigm" in the foreword, the editors asserted that the "question" of "the possibility of continuous material growth, the basis of productivist societies," had "only become more insistent" since the 1970 Club of Rome report. They listed six reasons for this: environmental degradation, resource depletion, "the unsustainable contradictions [of] capitalism," "renewed interest" in non-productivist ways of life, a "growing counter-productivity of institutions" (*à la* Illich), and "the attempt by many to disconnect from mass consumption and give new meaning to their lives."[103]

A surge of publications since 2008 that promote de-growth – some of them quite popular – suggests that the editors of *Degrowth: A Vocabulary* are on to something; the idea that economic growth might be the number one threat to the environment, to human life, and to a *good* life seems to be catching legs. But as they make clear in their edited volume, de-growth is not just one idea; it "defies a single definition," it has multiple "entry points," and it overlaps with other schools of thought. No matter what, it gravitates towards "new responses" to social and economic problems "that are not articulated around the twin imperatives of growth and development."[104] As French economist Serge Latouche put it, "de-growth is … no more than a banner that can rally those who have made a radical critique of development … and who want to outline the contours of an alternative project for a post-development politics. Its goal is to build a society in which we can live better lives whilst working less and consuming less."[105]

In his work, Latouche uses the term "productivism" as a shorthand for the opposite of his alternative – a society that pushes heteronomous production and consumption to the centre of life as if it is the highest moral, political, and social duty. And although there are many dimensions in the de-growth literature, much of the thought that emerges or is marshalled in the name of de-growth, whether it uses the term or not, explicitly critiques productivism.[106] It challenges the way people work, earn and spend income, consume resources, give to and take from institutions, and relate to one another and their natural and spatial environments. It channels the three currents of anti-productivist thought followed in this chapter – challenges to the industrial and post-industrial work ethics, warnings about the ecological limits of economic growth, and critiques of mass, materialistic consumerism – into a more coherent desire for radical change and a body of ideas – indeed a vocabulary – with which to articulate that desire.

After 2008, it has also forged a stronger connection with newer environmentalist discourses that seek to end or radically transform global commodity chains, carbon emissions, and climate change. Using D'Alisa and colleagues' helpful perspective, we can see how the "vocabulary" of climate change has been integrated into that of de-growth (environmentalists might see it as the other way around; it does not matter). This integrated way of thinking and speaking about our world and its alternatives has, in my view, advanced both "social justice" and "climate justice" movements further than they could have gotten on their own. Many environmentalists have pointed out that the ecological crises of climate change, rising sea levels, melting polar icecaps, erratic weather, deforestation, and carbon pollution, are social, political, and economic crises too – that climate justice is inseparable from social justice. But this nuanced perspective has been boiled down into ideas and slogans that, in the popular mind, reference only the "natural" world of trees, oceans, and animals: going "green" is a way to protect them, not us. However, the growing popularity of de-growth, and the growing acceptance of its arguments, appears to be drawing more attention to the important point that concern for the environment is not just the avocation of "tree-huggers" and vegans.

For example, Naomi Klein's 2014 bestseller *This Changes Everything* was lauded in the de-growth movement and promoted many of its ideas and arguments to a wider audience than it had ever reached before. The book was also anxiously anticipated and then enthusiastically embraced by environmentalists and Green political parties. It is partly – and not at all indulgently – Klein's autobiography, chronicling her awakening to climate change and climate justice, issues that she had more or less ignored for most of her life as a writer focused on other dimensions of capitalism and globalization. She tells the story of how she came to believe that the only way to change course and avoid the "grim future" where "our children will spend a great deal of their lives fleeing and recovering from vicious storms and extreme droughts" was to dismantle capitalism – hence the subtitle of her book: *Capitalism vs The Climate*.

This view of the climate problem is what leads Klein to endorse an idea that many "de-growthers" also get behind: the basic, guaranteed annual income. Although there are many different models of basic income that are compatible with de-growth, the fundamental idea is always the same: "a wage given to every person, regardless of income, as a recognition that the system cannot provide jobs for everyone and that it is counterproductive to force people to work in jobs that simply fuel consumption. As Alyssa Battistoni, an editor at the journal *Jacobin*, writes, 'While making people work shitty jobs to "earn" a living has always been spiteful, it's now starting to seem suicidal.'"[107]

Many of the thinkers covered in this chapter have also embraced the idea of a basic income: Gorz was a proponent, as are Aronowitz and Difazio, Latouche, Weeks, and Livingston.[108] Interestingly, so is Fred Block – interesting, because of the likely connection between this stance and his work assailing the productivity concept.[109] For Klein, a basic income makes sense as a policy solution to climate change because it removes the incentive for "desperate people" to do "desperate things" to earn a living. And it is desperation, she argues, that leads so many to accept industrial activity that threatens their health, to work in jobs that are likely to kill them and certain to help destroy the environment. The idea of a "carefully planned economy" that "ensures that everyone has the basics covered," she admits, "clash[es] directly with our reigning economic orthodoxy at every level."[110] And this is what makes tackling climate change – and confronting the ecological limits of economic growth – so monumental a task:

> Such a shift breaks all the ideological rules – it requires visionary long-term planning, tough regulation of business, higher levels of taxation for the affluent, big public sector expenditure, and in many cases reversals of core privatizations in order to give communities the power to make the changes they desire. In short, it means changing everything about how we think about the economy so that our pollution doesn't change everything about our physical world.[111]

This ideological rule-breaking is what makes the "demand" for basic income, according to Weeks, "a utopian demand." It is utopian because it "would be difficult – though not impossible – to realize in the present institutional and ideological context," because its realization hinges on "shifts in the terrain of political discourse." Thus, the demand for basic income, like any "utopian demand," "prefigures ... in fragmentary form ... a different world."[112] As the other chapters in this book have, I hope, made clear, ushering in a different world – one that would accept a basic income – is in large part a matter of ushering in a new ideational regime to replace the dominant, productivist one. On the other hand, this might be putting the cart before the horse: the policy change could come first, by some fortuitous combination of political will and legislative power (and perhaps, as Klein argues, an economic and environmental crisis that compels us to act), and this change in governmentality and everyday life would have the effect of transforming what can be thought, said, and done about making a living.

The reader who has gotten to this point may feel as if she has been led down a rabbit hole. What are the connections between the genealogy of the productivity concept, the case studies of it at work in Canadian government apparatuses, the cracks destabilizing both the science and the morality of the productivity concept, and the anti-productivist idea of a basic income? What is to be made of the fact that those who challenge productivism in the three channels of critique followed here tend to agree not only on (a) the idea that we work too much, (b) the existence of ecological limits to economic growth, and (c) the need to decrease consumption, but also (d) the need for a basic income, and (e) the absurdity of constantly increasing productivity when it doesn't seem to give us any more time or income to do with "what we *will*"?[113]

How Productivism Makes Itself True

I argue that the act of tracing the alternative, anti-productivist thoughts that have dared to exist in the otherwise totalizing ideational regime of productivism is a way of understanding more about how productivism "makes itself true." By looking at what forces and discourses anti-productivist ideas are up against, so to speak, we gain insight into what it is that gives productivism its power and protects its dominance. The genealogical exercise in this chapter reveals that productivism is reinforced by ideas and practices that venerate work – whether we understand these ideas and practices as comprising a "work ethic," a "dogma," or an "ideology" of work. It is sustained by willful blindness towards the mysticism of economic indicators, ecological warning signs, and the common sense that growth cannot go on, unabated, forever. It is fortified by attachment to consumer society, especially when consumption is understood as something to be earned only by working for income, and when consumer goods and services are designed to serve single purposes and become obsolete.

This ideational regime works to the benefit of those who make more money and/or wield more power to do what they want when both productivity and consumption are high and rising. Productivism is especially helpful because it appeals to the morality and the virtue of hard work, and makes it so that anyone who questions the goodness of productivity gains can be dismissed as a loafer attempting to escape his duty. The same applies to the provinces and other polities that fail to keep up with productivity elsewhere and begin to ask if there are other ways to survive. And so the productivist ideational regime gains support, even from those whom it helps least and exploits most, by promising, against the evidence, that increasing productivity and growing the economy is the only way to secure or increase prosperity for the individual. But this final support is also a source of weakness, because it is held up by an increasingly tenuous belief in – not to mention increasingly "flaky" statistics about – the connection between productivity and prosperity, between working harder (or just smarter) and living better.

Of course, it is not just belief that holds productivism together. Productivism makes itself true, indeed it *is* true, because *there are no guarantees of (adequate) income outside the increasing production and consumption of goods and services*. To be without paid work, and therefore without income, is usually to be barely scraping by, if not destitute. And this is true because all financial regulations and regimes of social assistance make it so that to be marginal to the production process is to be devalued and unhappy. Even the productivity bargaining discussed in chapter 4, although it seemed like a "win" for workers at the time, plays a part in reinforcing productivism and is therefore another structure to be dismantled if we are to move in a new direction.

As I see it, the demand for a basic income is the most effective proposal that destabilizes the productivist ideational regime because it kicks out, once and for all, the assumption that, as the genealogy and case studies show, has propped up productivism for centuries: that increasing productivity means (whether *de facto* or through "opportunities") increasing prosperity for all. And it does this not by asking for a bigger piece of the pie, or pointing to labour's importance in production, or examining the "tide" and our "boats" to see where Kuznets went wrong. These tactics have been tried before. Instead, basic income irreverently dismisses the very idea that income and well-being should hinge on productivity at all. As Livingston writes,

> we don't need work to fashion our genuine selves, to produce character and authenticity. There's not enough real work to go around, anyway, so we might as well get on with a discussion of *why the relation between the*

production of value and the receipt of income can never again be understood as a transparently cause–effect relation. We might as well get on with a discussion of how to detach one from the other – income from work – and entertain, accordingly, the practical applications of the criterion of need, "from each according to her abilities, to each according to his needs." We're already involved in this discussion when we debate so-called transfer payments and entitlements. More to the point, we're already involved when we disagree about the meanings of consumer culture.[114]

I believe that Livingston and I are talking about the same thing; he calls it "the relation between the production of value and the receipt of income" and I call it the relation between productivity and prosperity. The demand for a basic income, which today seems to be gaining ground on the momentum of the de-growth movement, *is,* and is an *expression of,* a lost faith in the link between work and income, productivity and prosperity. Not only does it seek to "detach" income from work, as Livingston puts it; it is also meant to be jarring, obnoxious, and irreverent, to awaken people to the fact that their well-being does not have to (because it *does not,* actually, anymore) depend on their own productivity or, for that matter, the productivity of The (National) Economy. It encompasses attempts to expand the definition of socially necessary labour, so that care and civic participation count as contributions to individual and community livelihoods. It encompasses, as well, arguments for work-sharing and reductions in work time. Indeed, there are many small movements capable of chipping away at productivism by redrawing the connection between producing goods or services and making a living. There are even small instances, documented in chapter 6, of economists and statisticians chipping at productivism from the inside out.

But productivism is sturdy. It will not go down easy. If millions of people are downloading apps to make themselves more productive in their exercise routines (so that they can be more productive at work), there are many ideational, not to mention moral, psychic, and emotional, connections to be severed in addition to the theoretical and statistical relationships between work and income. Resistance to changing these connections is what pervades all concern with productivity, throughout the genealogy of economic thought and the case studies of Canadian governmentality: resistance to the realization that as we get better at producing the things we need, unless we come up with more needs (as we have done quite fantastically over the last century and a half), work becomes less and less central to life. There is a deep anxiety about this prospect because, at the societal level, we believe that work is what makes us human. Like the committee members in the NPC, we are still afraid of what we might become – not to mention what we might get up to – if we have more time to do things outside work.

But as this book has shown, the productivity concept is a historical development, not a foundational and timeless fact. The relationship it has to prosperity is, likewise, not a fundamental law but rather a contingency of particular historical, political-economic, and social alignments. Moreover, the relationship we believe in – in which both productivity and prosperity rise together – may be impossible (even suicidal) to re-create. Coming to terms with the history of productivity constructed in this book is one way of preparing ourselves to think and do something different in the future.

Notes

Introduction

1 The reader wishing to know more can visit my earlier work on the discourse/ construct of "generation" and the theories of discourse on which it drew. See Foster, *Generation, Discourse and Social Change*. See also Purvis and Hunt, "Discourse, Ideology."

2 Block and Burns, "Productivity as a Social Problem."

3 Ibid., 778; italics mine.

4 Latouche, *Farewell to Growth*, 7.

5 Foucault, "On the Genealogy of Ethics," 256.

6 Diewert and Yu, "New Estimates."

7 Gu, "Estimating Capital Input."

8 The work covering the historical sociology of concept formation and related concepts includes Somers and Block, "From Poverty to Perversity"; Somers, "What's Political or Cultural"; Somers, "Narrating and Naturalizing"; and Somers, *Genealogies of Citizenship*. In the field of governmentality studies, I draw mainly on Dean, *Governmentality*; and Walters, *Governmentality*.

9 Somers, "What's Political or Cultural," 137.

10 Ibid., 115.

11 Somers, *Genealogies of Citizenship*, 2. The public narratives that make up an ideational regime can be metanarratives – stories that appear capable of explaining nearly everything and that are politically and socially powerful. Somers compares metanarratives to paradigms, both of which "not only [provide] the range of acceptable answers but also [define] both the questions to be asked and the rules of procedure by which they can rationally be answered." See Somers, "Narrating and Naturalizing," 234.

12 Somers and Block, "From Poverty to Perversity," 265. Being taken for granted does not mean that dominant ideational regimes are the same thing as "common sense," insofar as the former are explicitly political and claim legitimacy from the fact that they do not originate with "the masses" but rather with expertise, science, and other kinds of authority.

13 Ibid.

14 See chapter 2 in Foucault, *The Archaeology of Knowledge*.

15 Purvis and Hunt, "Discourse, Ideology," 478.

16 Foucault, *The Foucault Effect*, 2.

17 Walters, *Governmentality*, 1.

18 Ibid., 2.

19 Dean, *Governmentality*, 12.

20 Li, "Governmentality."

21 Ibid., 276.

22 Dean, *Governmentality*, 17–18; emphasis added. This is where studies of governmentality align with the historical sociology of concept formation, and in particular the latter's emphasis on conceptual networks, ideational regimes, and ideational embeddedness. Both approaches are adept at accounting for how new *conceptions* of extant things (spaces, people), often made possible by new *techniques* of measuring, as well as new ways of actually *seeing* such things, make possible new *ideas* about how best to adapt to or govern them. For example, governmentality studies have shown how and where the concept of "the international" emerged, enabling new ways of seeing the whole world as an ordered space – ways of seeing that challenged or at least departed from other lenses for seeing the world, such as empire. Others have used insights from the governmentality perspective to show how constructions of the "deservingness" (or lack thereof) of "the poor," and discursive framings of their "*capacities* and *motivations*," greatly shape "how policy-makers go about fostering desired behavior" among that "target population." See Foster, "Social Science and Liberal Internationalism"; and Guetzkow, "Beyond Deservingness."

23 Somers, *Genealogies of Citizenship*, 2; Dean, *Governmentality*, 21.

24 Dean, *Governmentality*, 45; Somers, *Genealogies of Citizenship*.

25 Somers, *Genealogies of Citizenship*, 9.

26 Foucault, *Politics, Philosophy, Culture*, 36.

27 Furlong, *Foucault*.

28 Walters, *Governmentality*, 17.

29 Mitchell, "Fixing the Economy," 84.

30 Dean, *Governmentality*, 57. There are a great many other concepts, very powerful today, that could be subjected to this kind of analysis: innovation,

competitiveness, entrepreneurialism, or – one of my favourites – "disruptive technology."

31 Walters, *Governmentality*, 18; emphasis added.
32 Ibid., 18.
33 Somers, *Genealogies of Citizenship*, 9.
34 Latouche, *Farewell to Growth*.
35 Somers, *Genealogies of Citizenship*, 2.
36 Somers, "What's Political or Cultural," 115; on symbolic violence, see Bourdieu, *Masculine Domination*. See also Purvis and Hunt, "Discourse, Ideology," for a discussion of the variability of ideology theory as it pertains to hegemony, interests, and consciousness.
37 On the link between the idea of economic growth and the idea of progress, see Victor, *Managing without Growth*.
38 Latouche, *Farewell to Growth*, 9.
39 For published work, see, for example, Latouche, *Farewell to Growth*; Russell, "In Praise of Idleness"; Illich, *The Right To Useful Unemployment*; and Stein, *The Cult of Efficiency*. Social movements have also taken up this line of argument; for example, Argentina's labour activists used the slogan "less work so we can all work" in their campaigns for a (shortened) six-hour workday.
40 Piketty, *Capital in the 21st Century*.
41 Latouche, *Farewell to Growth*, 92.

1 The Discovery of Productivity

1 Mitchell, "Fixing the Economy," 84.
2 Ibid.
3 Mitchell, "Fixing the Economy," 85.
4 Goodwin, *Canadian Economic Thought*, 110–11. The division between protectionists and laissez-faire liberals was mainly around their stance on free trade, with protectionists against and laissez-faire liberals for it. Economics and political economy were considered not as scientific or academic fields, but as normative and political positions synonymous with laissez-faire.
5 Hugo Munsterberg's industrial psychology is full of references to "economy" in this sense. See Munsterberg, *Psychology and Industrial Efficiency*.
6 Mitchell, "Fixing the Economy," 84.
7 Ibid., 85.
8 Ibid., 85; see also Tily, "John Maynard Keynes."
9 Mitchell, "Fixing the Economy," 85.
10 Ibid., 88.

11 Ibid., 89.
12 Ibid., 89.
13 Ibid., 89.
14 Karabell, *The Leading Indicators*, 50.
15 Mitchell, "Fixing the Economy," 90; emphasis added.
16 The standardization of calendars, school curricula and documents, and government structures helped bring about "the nation" as an "imagined community" in Benedict Anderson's terms, but the standardization and centralization of economic and other statistics helped keep it alive. See Anderson, *Imagined Communities*.
17 Karabell, *The Leading Indicators*, 50.
18 Livingston, *Pragmatism and the Political Economy*, 95.
19 Smith, *An Inquiry*.
20 John Stuart Mill, *Principles of Political Economy*.
21 Esch and Roediger, "One Symptom of Originality," 9.
22 Brick, *Transcending Capitalism*, 34–5.
23 Ibid., 35.
24 Böhm-Bawerk, "Capital and Interest Once More"; and "The Positive Theory of Capital." The idea spread beyond the Austrian school. See also Clark, "Natural Divisions"; and "Concerning the Nature of Capital."
25 Marx, *Capital*; and *Foundations*. See also Tucker, *The Marx–Engels Reader*.
26 Blaug, "Was There a Marginal Revolution?," 273.
27 Goodwin, "Marginalism Moves to the New World," 556–7.
28 Ibid.; Neill, "Francis Bacon, John Rae."
29 The emphasis on *necessary* labour time is meant to highlight the point that a less efficient labourer – one who takes more time to produce a commodity, whether because he does it by hand when machines are available, or is simply a slower worker – will not create a commodity more valuable than one created by a more efficient labourer. The labour theory of value holds that value is determined by the labour-time necessary, on average, to produce a given commodity. Value is not, in other words, determined on a case-by-case basis.
30 Gudeman, "Piketty and Anthropology," 8.
31 Livingston, *Pragmatism and the Political Economy*, 60.
32 Livingston convincingly argues that the ideological and empirical thrusts of marginalism cannot be separated from each other; they emerged from the same need. See ibid.; see also Livingston, "The Social Analysis of Economic History."
33 Livingston, *Pragmatism and the Political Economy*, 50.
34 Ibid., 49.

35 Goodwin, "Marginalism Moves to the New World."
36 Clark, "Distribution as Determined by a Law of Rent"; see also Clark, "Natural Divisions in Economic Theory" and "Concerning the Nature of Capital."
37 Livingston, *Pragmatism and the Political Economy*, 54.
38 Ibid., 55.
39 Ibid.
40 Christophers, *Banking across Boundaries*, 50.
41 Cf. Livingston, *Pragmatism and the Political Economy*; Christophers, *Banking across Boundaries*.
42 Neill, "Francis Bacon, John Rae," 391.
43 Hawley, "The Fundamental Error."
44 Walker, "Dr. Boehm-Bawerk's Theory of Interest."
45 Haynes, "Risk as an Economic Factor."
46 Livingston, *Pragmatism and the Political Economy*, 56.
47 Clark was not the only economic mind attributing productivity to capital; Quesnay and other physiocrats viewed land and capital as productive forces. But Clark was arguably the loudest American voice and, by accident of timing, the most influential in shaping the burgeoning discipline.
48 Livingston, *Pragmatism and the Political Economy*, 56.
49 Livingston, "The Social Analysis of Economic History," 72.
50 Jevons, *The Coal Question*.
51 Blaug, "Was There a Marginal Revolution?," 279.
52 Ibid.; Winch, "Marginalism and the Boundaries of Economic Science." For an intriguing discussion of the moral dimensions of economics, political economy, and sociology, see Ward, "Contemporary Sociology."
53 Fisher, "Cournot and Mathematical Economics," 119.
54 Ibid., 120.
55 Ibid., 127.
56 Ibid., 130.
57 Goodwin, "Marginalism in the New World," 557.
58 See, for example, Edgeworth, "The Theory of Distribution," 159–219; and Cannan, "The Division of Income."
59 Johnson, "The Effect of Labor-Saving Devices upon Wages"; Ward, "Contemporary Sociology," 499.
60 Granted, not all economists shy away from moralizing – Edgeworth in "The Theory of Distribution" and Cannan in "The Division of Income" are just two examples from the period under investigation here – but the tendency is toward logic and empiricism and away from moral argumentation.
61 Latouche, *Farewell to Growth*, 32.

62 Block and Burns, "Productivity as a Social Problem," 769.
63 Cummings, "Levasseur's 'L'Ouvrier Américain,'" 85.
64 Ibid., 89.
65 Ibid., 93.
66 Ibid., 93.
67 Polanyi, *The Great Transformation*, 85, 93.
68 North, "Levasseur's American Workingman," 324.
69 North, "Levasseur's American Workingman," 324.
70 Cummings, "Levasseur's 'L'Ouvrier Américain,'" 86.
71 Ibid., 99–100.
72 Anderson, *Imagined Communities*.
73 Curtis, "The Missing Memory", n.p.
74 Marshal (pt 1), "Outline."
75 Flux, "Industrial Productivity."
76 See, for example, Foster, "Social Science and Liberal Internationalism"; and Greenhill, "Recognition and Collective Identity Formation."
77 Mitchell, "Fixing the Economy."

2   Managing and Measuring Productivity

1 Owram, *The Government Generation*, 13.
2 Nyland, "Scientific Management and Planning," 56; Nerbas, *Dominion of Capital*, 9.
3 *Report of the Royal Commission on the Relations of Labor and Capital in Canada* (Ottawa: Dominion of Canada, 1889), 3.
4 Craven and Traves, "Class-Politics of the National Policy."
5 Ibid.
6 Chandler, *The Visible Hand*, 6–7.
7 Ibid., 56.
8 Esch and Roediger, "One Symptom of Originality."
9 Nerbas, *Dominion of Capital*, 8.
10 Inwood and Chamard, "Regional Industrial Growth During the 1890s," 101. There were important regional variations, not only in the 1890s but before and after, and these are described well in Inwood and Irwin, "Land, Income and Regional Inequality." See Livingston, "The Social Analysis of Economic History," for US data.
11 Livingston, "The Social Analysis of Economic History."
12 Another reason given was overcompetition – something business supported government in addressing through regulation. See Kolko, *The Triumph of Conservatism*.

13 Livingston, "The Social Analysis of Economic History," 75.

14 Slichter, "The Current Labor Policies of American Industries."

15 Esch and Roediger, "One Symptom of Originality," 32–4.

16 Livingston, "The Social Analysis of Economic History," 79; emphasis added.

17 Taylor, *The Principles of Scientific Management*, 5–6.

18 Ibid., 6, emphasis added.

19 Ibid., 6–7. According to McKinlay and Wilson, the whole engineering profession was fixated on changing mentalities as the first step toward greater efficiency. McKinlay and Wilson, "'All they lose is the scream.'"

20 See Esch and Roediger, "One Symptom of Originality," for a discussion of the "scientific" (albeit devoid of empirical evidence) foundations of race management.

21 A. O'Connor, *Poverty Knowledge*, 3, 27.

22 B. Foster, *Social Science and Liberal Internationalism*.

23 Thomas C. Leonard, "Retrospectives," 208. See also Bryson, *One Summer*.

24 Ross, *The Origins of American Social Science*; B. Foster, *Social Science and Liberal Internationalism*.

25 Esch and Roediger, "One Symptom of Originality," 10, 13, 19–20.

26 Ross, *The Origins of American Social Science*.

27 Casey, "Efficiency, Taylorism, and Libraries." On the "productivity movement" in government, see Bouckaert, "The History of the Productivity Movement."

28 Stein, *The Cult of Efficiency*; McKinlay and Wilson, "All they lose," 47.

29 Taylor, *The Principles of Scientific Management*, 11. Taylor's thinking is (not coincidentally) reminiscent of Adam Smith's view of efficiency: that an efficient division of labour would propagate a system in which the pursuit of self-interest would control excess, waste, and prices. See Stein, *The Cult of Efficiency*, 16.

30 Ibid., 10.

31 Ibid., 83.

32 In the piece rates approach, workers would earn a set amount per unit produced, up to a certain point – for example, 70 units of output – but then each unit produced in excess of the base 70 units would earn them a higher piece rate. In the former approach, workers who exceeded their scientifically determined targets were to be paid "a large daily bonus." See Taylor, *The Principles of Scientific Management*, 85.

33 Ibid., 74.

34 Ibid., 136.

35 Somers, "What's Political or Cultural"; "Narrating and Naturalizing Civil Society"; *Genealogies of Citizenship*.

36 Livingston, "The Social Analysis of Economic History," 94.
37 J. Burnham, *The Managerial Revolution*; Chandler, *The Visible Hand*.
38 Jenks, "Early Phases of the Management Movement," 432.
39 Ibid., 428.
40 Ibid., 425.
41 Ibid., 426.
42 Ibid., 433.
43 C.D. Howe, the Canadian government's "minister of everything" from the 1930s to the 1950s, was prodded to leave his work as an engineering consultant and general contractor to run for office as early as 1921. And before taking office as the President of the United States in 1929, Herbert Hoover was an engineer and a leader in the efficiency movement. Bothwell and Kilbourn, *C.D. Howe*, 45.
44 McKinlay and Wilson, "All they lose," 51; see also Grandin, *Fordlandia*.
45 McKinlay and Wilson, "All they lose," 52.
46 Jenks, "Early Phases of the Management Movement," 433.
47 Ibid., 435.
48 Livingston, "The Social Analysis of Economic History," 94–5; See also Jenks, "Early Phases of the Management Movement," 438.
49 Livingston, "The Social Analysis of Economic History," 79.
50 Crain, "There Was Blood." http://www.newyorker.com/magazine/2009/01/19/there-was-blood
51 Braverman, *Labor and Monopoly Capital*, 86.
52 For more, read Crain, "There Was Blood."
53 Ibid.
54 Hallahan, "W.L. Mackenzie King," 411.
55 King, *Industry and Humanity*. https://archive.org/details/industryhumanit00king. It should be noted that Rockefeller did not expound too extensively on management, at least not in the sense of scientific management and managerialism. Likewise, the industrial representation plan that Mackenzie King designed for him focused more on establishing non-union mechanisms ("special officers" to liaise between workers and stockholders) whereby workers could air grievances than on establishing a managerial structure. But both Rockefeller and Mackenzie King did concentrate on interactions between foremen – who could tend toward arrogance and abuse of power – and the pool of labour from which they were often pulled. Also, Mackenzie King in his later work would write more extensively about the importance of good management (and its "guiding genius"). Moreover, the basic idea behind the IRP was the same one used to support the expansion of a new kind of management: that companies had to

restore the "personal relation" in order to solve the "labour problem." For Rockefeller, the IRP seemed to have done just that. After establishing it at the Colorado Fuel and Iron Company, he reported that the mine was "working quite to the limit of its capacity in the production of coal" and had no trouble attracting labourers to its camps despite the bloody, brutal events that had taken place there just three years earlier.

56 Kaufman, Beaumont, and Helfgott, eds., *Industrial Relations to Human Resources and Beyond*, 307.
57 Livingston, "The Social Analysis of Economic History," 94.
58 Ibid., 94.
59 On the birth of industrial psychology, see E. O'Connor, "The Politics of Management Thought," 123.
60 Munsterberg, *Psychology and Industrial Efficiency*.
61 Rockefeller, "The Personal Relation in Industry."
62 Craven and Traves, "Class-Politics of the National Policy," 32.
63 In Canada, the CMA and the CRA also believed that employers and employees would both benefit from protectionism – higher tariffs on foreign manufactures – and sought to gain labour's support for that position. Ibid.
64 Taylor, *The Principles of Scientific Management*, 16–17.
65 Bothwell and Kilbourn, *C.D. Howe*, 160. On O.D. Skelton's advocacy, see Owram, *The Government Generation*.
66 Casey, "Efficiency, Taylorism, and Libraries."
67 Bouckaert, "The History of the Productivity Movement," 55.
68 Shore, *The Science of Social Redemption*, xiii.
69 Ibid., 55–6.
70 Ibid., 55–6.
71 Ibid., xii.
72 E. O'Connor, "The Politics of Management Thought," 120.
73 Mayo, *The Human Problems of an Industrial Civilization*, 2.
74 Ibid., 2.
75 E. O'Connor, "The Politics of Management Thought," 124.
76 Landsberger, *Hawthorne Revisited*.
77 E. O'Connor, "The Politics of Management Thought," 129.
78 Foster, Mills, and Weatherbee, "History, Field Definition and Management Studies."
79 Ibid.
80 Taylor, *The Principles of Scientific Management*, 16.
81 Ibid., 94.
82 Ibid., 96.
83 Jenks, "Early Phases of the Management Movement," 436.

84 Ibid., 440.

85 Braverman, *Labor and Monopoly Capital*, 86–7.

86 Ibid., 87. See also M. Schumann, "New Concepts of Production and Productivity."

87 Poole, *Human Resource Management*, 517.

88 Fishbein, *The Censuses of Manufactures*, 8.

89 Ibid., 19.

90 Ibid., 20.

91 Ibid., 27.

92 Ibid., 31.

93 Owram, *The Government Generation*, 144–6.

94 Taussig, "Labor Costs in the United States," 96.

95 Ibid., 99.

96 Mason, "The Doctrine of Comparative Cost."

97 Cole, "Comparative Costs in the Worsted-Cloth Manufacture."

98 Douglas, "The Cost of Living for Working Women."

99 Persons, "Labor Problems as Treated by American Economists"; Walling, *American Labor and American Democracy*.

100 More on resistance to economic planning appears in chapter 3, but see Coates, "The National Productivity Council of Canada."

101 Foenander, "The Forty-Four Hours Case in Australia." It is worth noting that Foenander argues here that the work week and similar cases should be left to economists' commissions, not judges, because in them "economic and social and not legal principles are supreme" (324).

102 So, for example, Cole, "Comparative Costs in the Worsted-Cloth Manufacture"; and "The American Rice-Growing Industry."

103 Mitchell, "Fixing the Economy," 88.

104 This general use of the word "economy" appears, for instance, in letters written by Keynes and Hayek (with several colleagues) to the *New York Times* in 1932. See Gregory et al., "Letters," 17 October 1932.

105 Consult Google's *nGram* tool.

106 But see Slichter's "The Current Labor Policies of American Industries" for one attempt at assessing productivity per worker across industries; Levasseur's *Oeuvre* is similar in scale and generality. See Cummings, "Levasseur's *Ouevre*."

107 Mitchell, "Fixing the Economy."

108 Nerbas, *Dominion of Capital*, 15. On a certain level, the national economy is simply the imaginary but consequential terrain occupied by regional business elites who all share the goal of capital accumulation and benefit from the national structure (tariffs, railways).

109 Apart from trade, no other statistics-generating concept seems to have been deemed important enough to warrant an agency devoted entirely to its measurement and conceptualization.

110 Polanyi, *The Great Transformation*.

111 Burns, "The Measurement of the Physical Volume of Production," 243.

112 Flux, "Industrial Productivity in Great Britain and the United States."

113 Nerbas, *Dominion of Capital*, 16.

114 Sub-Committee of the Interdepartmental Advisory Committee [IAC], *The Measurement and Analysis of Productivity*.

115 Nerbas, *Dominion of Capital*, 24–5.

116 Owram, *The Government Generation*.

117 Block and Burns, "Productivity as a Social Problem," 769.

118 Ibid.

119 Ibid., 770.

120 Ibid., 771.

121 Ibid., 769.

122 Jorgenson and Griliches, "The Explanation of Productivity Change," 249.

123 Cf. ibid.; Baldwin and Gu, "Multifactor Productivity in Canada."

124 Block and Burns, "Productivity as a Social Problem," 773.

125 Ibid.

126 Ibid., 777.

127 Ibid.

128 Ibid.

129 Marshal (pt 6), *History of the Dominion Bureau of Statistics*, 3.

130 Sub-Committee of the IAC, *The Measurement and Analysis of Productivity*.

131 Sub-Committee on National Income Statistics. *Measurement of National Income*.

132 For more on the history of the GDP and GNP constructs, see Karabell, *The Leading Indicators*.

133 Maul, *Human Rights, Development, and Decolonization*, 135.

134 Brick, *Transcending Capitalism*, 150.

135 On the productivity crisis, see Block and Burns, "Productivity as a Social Problem." See also Krugman, "Where The Productivity Went". Victor, *Managing without Growth*, 154–69, provides an excellent laundry list of economic growth's "disappointments" in Canada.

136 Stanford, "Canada's Transformation under Neoliberalism."

137 Harvey, *A Brief History of Neoliberalism*.

138 Latouche, *Farewell to Growth*, 32. Brick's research has shown that observers during the Cold War recognized that "market and command societies" had something in common: they were "devoted to mass production."

But instead of calling the two "productivist," these "observers and social critics" concluded "that a generic 'industrial society,' rather than capitalism in particular, had become the most salient object for analysis in the modern era." Brick, *Transcending Capitalism*, 6.

139 Stanford, "Canada's Transformation under Neoliberalism."
140 Coates, "The National Productivity Council of Canada," 11.
141 Drummond, "Confessions of a Serial Productivity Researcher," 6.
142 Neill, "Francis Bacon, John Rae."
143 Krugman, "Competitiveness," 30.
144 Ibid., 39.
145 Ardinat, "Competitiveness as Political Policy."
146 Gilson, "Overworked America"; Bauerlein and Jeffery, "All Work and No Pay."
147 Bloom and Van Reenen, *Human Resource Management And Productivity*, 757.
148 See, for example, Beaudry, Collard, and Green, "Demographics and Recent Productivity Performance"; A. Lileeva, "Trade Liberalization and Productivity Dynamics"; and Tang and MacLeod, "Labour Force Ageing and Productivity Performance."
149 "The Onrushing Wave," *The Economist*.
150 Drummond, "Confessions of a Serial Productivity Researcher," 5–6.
151 Diewert and Yu, "New Estimates of Real Income."
152 Arcand, "Has Productivity Growth in Canada Been Stronger?"
153 Gu, "Estimating Capital Input."

3   The Dominion Bureau of Statistics

1 Statistics Canada, *The Canadian Productivity Review*.
2 The *New York Herald*'s "Money Page," first published in 1835, is generally considered the first Business Section to appear in a newspaper. The business sections that followed in other US and international papers have always been more concerned about stock markets than national production statistics.
3 Rehel, "Six-hour workday in Sweden."
4 Hodgson, "Canadian Productivity."
5 Blackwell, "Why Canada's Tech Companies Fail."
6 Hodgson, "Canadian Productivity."
7 Simpson, "Innovation Key to Close Canada's Productivity Gap."
8 Worton, *Dominion Bureau of Statistics*, 59.
9 Crum, "Review of Report," 406.
10 Worton, *Dominion Bureau of Statistics*, 65.

11 Ibid., 59–60; Marshal, *History*.

12 McDowall, *The Sum of the Satisfactions*, 6; emphasis in original.

13 Marshal, *History*. In his work on the creation of the public service in Canada, Hodgetts makes the centralization of statistics the *first* act of centralization: "throughout the years, one can see the administrative response of the federal public service gathering momentum in distinct stages. First, it began to act as a centralized data collecting source; from statistics it went on to research; research results required dissemination and so we move to extensive publication (and some would say public relations); next came conditional grants that required 'policing' by federal officials; ultimately certain programs came to be operated by the federal government." Hodgetts, "Challenge and Response."

14 Ibid., 21.

15 Ibid., 10.

16 Marshal, *Outline*, 5

17 Kuznets, "National Income, 1929–1932."

18 Marshal, "History – Manuscript," 1.

19 Dimand, "Review of Barnett," 83.

20 Kuznets, "National Income, 1929-1932," 1.

21 Dimand, "Review of Barnett," 83; Marshal, "History – Manuscript," 1.

22 Marshal, "History – Manuscript," 2.

23 McDowall, *The Sum of the Satisfactions*, 44.

24 Dimand, "Review of Barnett"; Marshal, "History – Manuscript," 5.

25 McDowall, *The Sum of the Satisfactions*, 79.

26 Marshal, *Outline*, 5.

27 McDowall, *The Sum of the Satisfactions*, 80–1.

28 Ibid., 93.

29 Ibid., 94.

30 Marshal, "History – Manuscript," 12.

31 Ibid., 5.

32 Benedict Anderson, *Imagined Communities*.

33 McDowall, *The Sum of the Satisfactions*, 7; but see, on the (dubious) connection between Keynes and macroeconomics, Tily, "John Maynard Keynes."

34 Marshall, "History – Manuscript," 38; emphasis added.

35 Ibid., 15.

36 McDowall, *The Sum of the Satisfactions*, 8.

37 Marshal, "History – Manuscript," 17.

38 Ibid.

39 Sub-Committee of the IAC, *The Measurement and Analysis of Productivity*.

40 Marshall, "History – Manuscript," 17.

41　Piketty, *Capital in the 21st Century*, 11.

42　Sub-Committee of the IAC, *The Measurement and Analysis of Productivity*, 3.

43　Ibid., 4.

44　Ibid., 5.

45　Marshall, *History*, 17.

46　Ibid., 4.

47　Ibid., 11.

48　Ibid., 4.

49　Taylor, *The Principles of Scientific Management*, 6.

50　Sub-Committee of the IAC, *The Measurement and Analysis of Productivity*, 7–8.

51　Ibid., 8.

52　Ibid., 3.

53　Ibid., 3.

54　Ibid., 4.

55　Compare this with the emergence of national and international labour markets and the impact of the movement (or confinement) of labour, in Polanyi, *The Great Transformation*.

56　Bernolak, "Productivity Research."

57　Ibid., 2.

58　Ibid.

59　In 1938, Dominion Statistician R.H. Coats received a request from the Rowell–Sirois Commission for a study that extrapolated from past population trends to predict possible demographic pressures various regions would likely face. In response to the request, Coats wrote that the bureau thought "it unwise to issue any statement regarding the future population of Canada." Yet in 1946, the DBS published *The Future Population of Canada* (in the 1941 census monograph series), the introduction of which made it quite clear that there were no longer any concerns on the bureau's part about the validity or propriety of such an undertaking: "The value of population projections lies, not in their prophetic qualities, for it cannot be too strongly emphasised that no attempt is made to predict what the total population of a community will be at some future date, but in the examination of what consequences must ensue if no unforeseen agencies intervene to affect drastically past trends." However, the Department of Trade and Commerce was unconvinced. On 6 March 1946, the deputy minister, M.W. Mackenzie, wrote to the assistant deputy minister Oliver Master about *The Future Population*. "The Minister is concerned," he said, "and I think rightly, as to the propriety of … engaging in this field of crystal gazing. I was under the impression that the Bureau restricted its releases to factual material, from which others are quite at liberty to draw predictions or conclusions." Herbert Marshall, who had by that time succeeded Coats as Dominion Statistician, wrote a long memorandum defending the practice, stressing that "in many countries population trends are giving great concern to statesmen, economists, sociologists" and noting that the projections "were prepared initially because information was required by the Dominion–Provincial Committee on Reconstruction to assist them in their deliberations on old age pensions and on provincial subsidies." Marshall argued that "the contents of our bulletins are purely statistical. Naturally it suggests nothing as to policy concerning population ... There have been many estimates of Canada's future population, many based on wishful thinking. It seems desirable that there should be an official estimate based on carefully stated unbiased assumptions." Worton, *Dominion Bureau of Statistics*, 243; M. V. George, "Population Forecasting in Canada," 117–18.

60 Bernolak, "Productivity Research."
61 Ibid., 1–2.
62 Ibid., 5.
63 Ibid.
64 Ibid., 7.
65 Marshal, *History*, 18.
66 Bernolak, "Productivity Research," 6.
67 For an excellent historical examination of banking's representational evolution from unproductive to productive, see Christophers, *Banking Across Boundaries*. In Christophers's view, the national accounts are central to this shift.
68 Ibid., 4–5.
69 Ibid., 5.
70 Solow, "Thomas Piketty Is Right."
71 Katz and Grimm, "In Appreciation."
72 Livingston, "The Social Analysis of Economic History," 83.
73 Jorgenson and Griliches, "The Explanation of Productivity Change," 249–80.
74 Gordon, *Productivity Growth, Inflation, and Unemployment*, 90–3.
75 Baldwin and Gu, "Multifactor Productivity Measurement at Statistics Canada," 9.
76 Ibid., 6; on Statistics Canada's new service-oriented language or "business-speak," see Prévost and Beaud, "On the Genesis of a New Statistical Regime."
77 OECD, *Measuring Productivity*, 7. It is worth noting that Dale Jorgenson's influence is visible throughout the manual, which not only proposes the KLEMS growth accounting framework but also emphasizes the value of constant quality indexes and other ideas from Jorgenson's work.
78 Baldwin and Gu, "Multifactor Productivity Measurement," 19.

79 OECD, *Measuring Productivity*.
80 Jorgenson, "The World KLEMS Initiative," 6.
81 Ibid.
82 Block and Burns, "Productivity as a Social Problem," 774.

4   The National Productivity Council

1 "A Year of Challenge," *Globe and Mail*.
2 Owram, *The Government Generation*, 32–3.
3 Ibid., 30–3.
4 B. Anderson, "Soft Spots Slow Growth of Economy"; R. Anderson, "Foreign Investment in Canada"; Cote, "Aims at Unemployment Heart"; List, "Launch Drive for Training Unemployed"; "The Impossible Happens," *Globe and Mail*; "U.S. Interest In Economy Here Termed Logical," *Globe and Mail*.
5 Coates, "The National Productivity Council of Canada," 11–12.
6 MacDonald, "Hees Takes the Pollyanna View"; Blackmore, "PM Holds Little Fear for Economy"; "Is 'Good' Good Enough?," *Globe and Mail*.
7 Coates, "The National Productivity Council of Canada," 12–13. For more on the Royal Commission on Canada's Economic Prospects, see Azzi, *Walter Gordon*.
8 Ibid., 14.
9 See Scott, *Seeing Like a State*, 97.
10 Carew, "The Anglo-American Council on Productivity."
11 Coates, "The National Productivity Council of Canada," 11–12.
12 Cote, "Aims at Unemployment Heart."
13 Bill C-52, 4th Session, 24th parliament (Canada, 1960).
14 Ibid., 1.
15 Hees, "Statement to the House of Commons," 1–2.
16 Ibid., 6.
17 Ibid., 8.
18 Ibid., 9.
19 Ibid., 9.
20 Coates, "The National Productivity Council of Canada," 20.
21 Ibid., 22–3.
22 Hees, "Statement to the House of Commons," 10.
23 Block and Burns, "Productivity as a Social Problem," 772.
24 Carew, "The Anglo-American Council on Productivity," 52.
25 In Canada, an Industrial Production Co-operation Board was struck in 1944 "to increase production during the war years by encouraging the cooperation of all parties." But after the war ended, "the work of this

committee was transferred to the Department of Labour and the Labour Management Co-operation Service was formed. Coates, "The National Productivity Council of Canada," 2036.

26 Carew, *Labour Under the Marshall Plan*, 227.
27 Carew, *Labour under the Marshall Plan*, 161.
28 Carew, "The Anglo-American Council on Productivity (1948-52)," 53,
29 USAID, "Inspiring Success."
30 Carew, *Labour Under the Marshall Plan*.
31 Ibid., 161.
32 Ibid., 161–3.
33 Ibid., 55.
34 Ibid., 46.
35 Ibid., 58.
36 Ibid., 55.
37 Block and Burns, "Productivity as a Social Problem," 773.
38 Ibid., 773.
39 Ibid., 772.
40 Carew, *Labour Under the Marshall Plan*, 55.
41 Block and Burns, "Productivity as a Social Problem," 772.
42 Ibid., 777.
43 Livingston, *Pragmatism and the Political Economy*, 92–3.
44 Veal, "The Elusive Leisure Society."
45 Livingston, *Pragmatism and the Political Economy*, 93.
46 Carew, "The Anglo-American Council on Productivity," 44.
47 Ibid., 57.
48 Ibid. This, despite the fact that relations deteriorated at the firms the Marshall Plan used as shining examples of productivity-driven industrial peace, as did the UAW-GM agreement.
49 Latouche, *Farewell to Growth*, 42.
50 Haythorne, Letter to George Hees.
51 Ibid., 2.
52 Ibid., 3.
53 Haythorne, Letter to J.A. Roberts.
54 Nerbas has also noted the curious tendency for business elites to prefer "misleading euphemisms such as 'representative citizen'" to describe themselves in such settings during this period. See *Dominion of Capital*, 11.
55 Terminology comes from Bill C-52, 4th Session, 24th parliament (1960); and Phillips, "Too Many Tycoons?," 24. See also Canada, Parliament, House of Commons, Debates, 24th Parliament, 4th session, vol. 3, (1960–62), 2483–2484.
56 Phillips, "Too Many Tycoons?"

57 The *Ottawa Citizen* was more concerned that DeYoung was "American-Born." Ibid.
58 Hees, "Statement to the House of Commons."
59 Coates, "The National Productivity Council of Canada."
60 Lynch, "Productivity Council Holds Jousting Match with Press," 18; Bird, "Jodoin Quits"; *Toronto Star*, "Forgive, Forget".
61 Haythorne, "Remarks."
62 Harrington, "Remarks."
63 McKinnon, "Seeking a Formula for Industrial Peace and Collaboration."
64 Harrington, "Remarks."
65 Lank, "A Positive Look."
66 Papers Given at Dalhousie Seminar, 18 and 19 September 1962. MG28 I103, vol. 529, file 11.
67 Interestingly, Labour's first contribution to the Marshall Plan's Economic Recovery Program was to urge for its "complete reorganization ... so as to gear it entirely to the problem of productivity." See Carew, "The Anglo-American Council on Productivity," 159.
68 Coates, "The National Productivity Council of Canada," 50.
69 Ibid., 51.
70 See note 66.
71 NPC, Proceedings.
72 Ibid.
73 Proceedings of the Montreal Meetings.
74 Coates, "The National Productivity Council of Canada."
75 Koerner, "Background of the Seminar."
76 Ibid., 5.
77 Li, "Governmentality," 276.
78 NPC, "Minutes."
79 Ibid.
80 Coates, "The National Productivity Council of Canada," 39; Hees, "Statement to the House of Commons," 3.
81 Lank, "A Positive Look."
82 Reynauld, "For a Rational Economic Policy."
83 Proceedings of the Montreal Meetings.
84 DeYoung, "Remarks."
85 Haythorne, Letter to J.A. Roberts.
86 NPC, "Minutes."
87 Dymond, "Appendix."
88 Dymond's numbers also highlighted the importance of data to the project of boosting productivity. Dymond noted that government and industry efforts

to predict and prepare for "future requirements of manpower" were stymied by a lack of adequate data. Without knowledge of and access to the right mix of workers with the necessary skills, employers would have difficulty attaining higher productivity. He was optimistic, however, that the DBS's new productivity statistics would prevent such an outcome.

89 NPC, "Minutes." Dymond's presentation triggered all sorts of additional concerns, with council members spinning out, as they often did, in multiple directions: the necessity of (and stigma around) vocational schools, credential inflation, and high school drop-outs.

90 Proceedings of the Montreal Meetings.

91 Hebert, "Remarks."

92 Victor, *Managing without Growth*, 155.

93 Hebert, "Remarks," 10.

94 Paré, "Remarks."

95 Safarian, "The Economic Facts in Canada Today."

96 Lank, "A Positive Look."

97 DeYoung, "Remarks"; Benson, "Remarks," 3; Goldenberg, "Remarks," 7.

98 Safarian, "The Economic Facts in Canada Today," 8.

99 For example, DBS assistant Dominion statistician Simon A. Goldberg, in an address to the Dalhousie Seminar, quoted from President Kennedy to describe productivity as the most important factor in incomes, balance of payments, standard of living, and so on. See, Goldberg, "Measurement of Productivity."

100 NPC, "Minutes."

101 Ibid.

102 Hees, "Statement to the House of Commons," 6.

103 Carew, "The Anglo-American Council on Productivity," 3.

104 Canadian Advertising Advisory Board, "Appendix."

105 NPC, "Minutes."

106 Ibid.

107 Ibid.

108 The *Globe and Mail*, for example, proclaimed that the council would "strike through increased productivity at the heart of Canada's unemployment problem by strengthening Canada's competitive trade position … and by increasing real income" (Cote, "Aims at Unemployment Heart"). The papers also amplified the council's finding that "bad relations" between employers and workers "hampered" productivity more than any other factor (R. Anderson, "Productivity Council Cites"). The *Toronto Star* even pointed out that the main objective of the council was "conditioning … minds" to embrace productivity (*Toronto Daily Star*, "It's a Local Effort").

109 Benson, "Remarks."
110 ECC, "Productivity through New Technology"; *Prices, Productivity, and Employment*; and *A General Incentive Programme*. See also West, "Canada–United States"; and Postner, "Statistical Problems."
111 ECC, *Economic Goals*, 1.
112 Ibid., 42.
113 Ibid., 43–4.
114 Ibid., 187.
115 On union membership, see Statistics Canada, "Table E175-177." On labour unrest, see Palmer, *Canada's 1960s*.
116 ECC, *Towards Better Communications*; Cardin, "Canadian Labour Relations."
117 "Government Proposes Planning Council." .
118 Goldberg, "Measurement of Productivity," 2.
119 L. Auer, *Regional Disparities*.

5   The Atlantic Canada Opportunities Agency

1 Starr, *Equal as Citizens*.
2 Somers, *Genealogies of Citizenship*.
3 Really, the emergence of productivity as a chief governmental concern was more a case of discourse catching up with techniques than a sudden change in objectives, but as is always the case with discourse and governmentality, the practices are only analytically separable from the thoughts.
4 "Atlantic Provinces" refers to the four easternmost provinces in Canada: Nova Scotia, New Brunswick, Prince Edward Island, and Newfoundland and Labrador. However, they joined Canada at different times (NS and NB in 1867, PEI in 1873, and NL in 1949), meaning that "Atlantic" in the past connoted a different geography than it does today. The term "Maritime provinces," on the other hand, refers to the three provinces without Newfoundland. Thus, when describing the period before 1949, I use "Maritime."
5 Summary of The Government Organization Act, Atlantic Canada. Senator Alistair Graham Fonds, LAC, R14032, vol. 1 file 1 (Establishment of ACOA).
6 Starr, *Equal as Citizens*, 18.
7 Inwood and Irwin, "Land, Income and Regional Inequality," 162.
8 Starr, *Equal as Citizens*.
9 Ibid., 29.
10 Thornton, "The Problem of Out-Migration," 28. As Thornton notes, contrary to some interpretations, the uptick in out-migration preceded or "anticipated" the economic downturn. In her view, out-migration was driven by the "pull" of wealth and opportunity down the US eastern

seaboard rather than the "push" of unemployment in Nova Scotia's rural or underdeveloped areas. This is a point worth bearing in mind, as it highlights the systemic character of out-migration and economic development – that is, it suggests there is no simple unidirectional relationship between the movement of working people and the availability of jobs and income. However, this does not negate the fact that inequality between provinces – wage and income differentials, as well as differences in unemployment rates, cost of living, and land availability – is correlated with out-migration from peripheral and especially rural areas toward central and urban ones. In plain, people do follow the money, but money also follows the people. By the 1890s, the drain of the Maritimes' working-age population and the slowdown of its economies was impossible to deny.

11 Starr, *Equal as Citizens*, 8–9.
12 Ibid., 9.
13 Canada, *Report of the Royal Commission on Dominion–Provincial Relations*, 9.
14 Starr, *Equal as Citizens*, 13.
15 Ibid., 9.
16 Ibid., 10.
17 Ibid., 13.
18 Canada, House of Commons Debates, 22nd Parliament, 5986.
19 Starr, *Equal as Citizens*, 11.
20 Canada, House of Commons Debates. 27 April 1988.
21 See, for example, Harvey, *A Brief History of Neoliberalism*; Somers, *Genealogies of Citizenship*; Stanford, "Canada's Transformation under Neoliberalism"; Duggan, *The Twilight of Equality?*; and Giroux, *The Terror of Neoliberalism*.
22 Flyvbjerg, "Five Misunderstandings."
23 Drummond, "Confessions of a Serial Productivity Researcher."
24 Savoie, *Reviewing Canada's Regional Development Efforts*. See also Bickerton, *Nova Scotia, Ottawa*.
25 Savoie, *Reviewing Canada's Regional Development Efforts*, 153.
26 Ibid., 173; see also Starr, *Equal as Citizens*, 119, who notes that DREE spending almost reversed between Nova Scotia and Quebec during the high point of separatism during the Trudeau era.
27 Savoie, *Reviewing Canada's Regional Development Efforts*, 157.
28 It is worth noting that by 2015, even Nova Scotia's Department of Economic and Rural Development had been disbanded, replaced by the farcical-sounding "Department of Business."
29 Savoie, *Reviewing Canada's Regional Development Efforts*.
30 Harvey, *A Brief History of Neoliberalism*.
31 Financial Times, news clipping.

32 Canada, PMO, "News Release."
33 *Chronicle Herald*, news clipping.
34 Canada, House of Commons Debates, 33rd Parliament, 14878.
35 See note 5.
36 Canada, House of Commons Debates. 27 April 1988.
37 Canada, House of Commons Debates, 33rd Parliament, 14883.
38 Ibid., 14885.
39 Ibid., 14886.
40 ACOA, "Profiles of Young Atlantic Canadians."
41 Savoie, *Establishing the Atlantic Canada Opportunities Agency*.
42 Ibid., 6.
43 Ibid., 38–9.
44 See note 5.
45 There is one other exception: a short discussion of productivity in the
    fisheries, and ACOA's role in helping that industry. However, the
    discussion does not in any way imply that it is part of ACOA's mandate to
    improve productivity there or in any other field. See Canada, Parliament.
    House of Commons. Debates, 34th Parliament, 2nd session, vol.4, 1989,
    p. 4890.
46 Canada, House of Commons Debates, 34th Parliament, 4672.
47 ACOA, *Annual Report 1989–1990*, 3.
48 Ibid., 2.
49 Ibid., 13.
50 Thiessen, "Canada's Economic Future."
51 ACOA, "Correspondence," June 1991.
52 Donald Savoie, "ACOA: Transition to Maturity."
53 Ibid., 33.
54 Ibid., 59.
55 Ibid.
56 In 1991, there were scattered and superficial mentions of productivity in
    relation to ACOA-funded projects in Parliament. See, for example, Canada,
    House of Commons Debates, Official Report, 34th Parliament, 3rd Session.
57 ACOA, *Five Year Report 1993* , 1, 7.
58 Ibid., 8.
59 ACOA, "Profiles of young Atlantic Canadians," ii.
60 Ibid., 60.
61 Ibid., 12, 29.
62 ACOA, *Five Year Report 2003*, n.p.
63 Ibid., n.p.
64 Ibid., i.

65 Auditor General, "Chapter 6," 6. Interestingly, this audit mentions productivity twice, but it flips economic development and productivity such that economic development becomes one of the factors affecting productivity and not the reverse.

66 O'Neill, "The Case for Economic Cooperation."

67 Manley, "Putting People First."

68 ACOA, *Annual Report*, 2008.

69 Ibid., 5.

70 Ibid., 6.

71 Ibid., v.

72 Ibid., 75

73 ACOA, *Five-Year Report*.

74 Latouche, *Farewell to Growth*.

75 Canada, House of Commons Debates, 5 May 1988 and 18 January.

76 Harvey, *A Brief History of Neoliberalism*.

77 ACOA, Fact Sheet.

78 Baldwin and MacDonald, "The Canadian Manufacturing Sector," 57.

79 Jackson, "Canadian Deindustrialization."

80 This is a reference to 2013 reforms made to Canada's Employment Insurance (EI) program, which require applicants to seek and accept any job that is in a "similar occupation" to their previous job, pays at least 70 per cent of the previous wage, and is within a one-hour commute. Canada, "Changes to Employment Insurance."

81 NPC records do include several mentions of "skill," but by and large the committee, the seminar discussions, and the research they consulted were more likely to focus on formal "education."

82 One need look no further than the oneNS (aka Ivany) Commission's report and recommendations for evidence of the hopes pinned on the small business or entrepreneur. See oneNS Commission, *Now or Never*.

83 For an example of make-work projects in Canada, see the "Opportunities for Youth" program ca 1970. The hand-wringing about reintegration is visible, for example, in the report of the DBS subcommittee on productivity measurement, discussed in chapter 2, where it was proposed that the government find ways of enticing unemployed workers to move to "actually or potentially" more prosperous regions. Relatedly, it appears that the conception of the worker at the heart of this revised discourse is less like the static "economic man" of times past, and more like the "entrepreneur of self" described by philosophers of modernity – the "flexible" agent who is always potentially able to adapt to new economic demands. See du Gay, *Production of Culture*, 301.

6 The Decline of Productivity

1 Clark and Avery, "The Effects of Data Aggregation," 428.
2 Magdoff and Sweezy, "The Uses and Abuses."
3 Notably, economist Clopper Almon argues the opposite: that calculations of productivity on an *industry* basis are fundamentally flawed, while analyses of national productivity make conceptual sense. See Almon, *The Craft*.
4 Magdoff, "The Purpose and Method"; Magdoff and Sweezy, "The Uses and Abuses," 5.
5 Magdoff and Sweezy, "The Uses and Abuses," 4–5.
6 Ibid., 5.
7 Ibid.
8 Bernolak, "Productivity Research," 6.
9 Statistics Canada, Employment by industry and sex, 2014, CANSIM, table 282–0008. Accessed 18 June 2015 at http://www.statcan.gc.ca/tables-tableaux/sum-som/l01/cst01/labor10a-eng.htm; Statistics Statistics Canada, Gross domestic product at basic prices, by industry, 2014, CANSIM, table 379–0031. Accessed 18 June 2015 at http://www.statcan.gc.ca/tables-tableaux/sum-som/l01/cst01/econ41-eng.htm.
10 Christophers, *Banking across Boundaries*, 1–2.
11 Ibid., 174.
12 Li and Prescott, "Measuring Productivity," 6.
13 Ibid.
14 Worton, "The Service Industries in Canada."
15 Ibid.
16 Ibid., 258.
17 MacLean, "Lagging Productivity Growth"; on "epistemic communities," see Ruggie, "International Responses to Technology."
18 Magdoff and Sweezy, "The Uses and Abuses," 6–7.
19 Van Ark and Hulten. "Innovation, Intangibles, and Economic Growth."
20 Gu, Terefe, and Wang, *The Impact of R&D Capitalization*; Belhocine, "Treating Intangible Inputs"; Baldwin, Gu, and MacDonald, "Intangible Capital and Productivity Growth."
21 Christophers, *Banking across Boundaries*, 116–17.
22 For example, King, *The Wealth and Income*; Mitchell, King, and Macaulay, "The Size of the National Income"; and Burns, "The Measurement."
23 Bernolak, "Productivity Research," 2.
24 Inflation is another economic term with an interesting history. See, for example, Selgin, "The 'Productivity Norm.'"
25 Meade, "Why Real Value Added."

26 Ibid., 3.
27 Karabell, "The Leading Indicators."
28 Ibid.; Almon, "Double Trouble."
29 Clopper Almon, *The Craft.*
30 Pissarides and Vallanti, "The Impact of TFP Growth."
31 Postel-Vinay, "The Dynamics of Technological Unemployment."
32 One theory that should be noted here concerns not wages but purchasing power. The "productivity norm," prominent at the end of the nineteenth century, held that productivity changes would affect the prices of goods – that increasing productivity would lower prices and vice versa – in a more neutral way than inflation, spreading out the gains and losses in purchasing power evenly. See Selgin, "The Productivity Norm."
33 Mishel, "The Wedges."
34 Sharpe, Arsenault, and Harrison, *The Relationship*, 2.
35 Ibid.
36 Ibid., 56.
37 On productivity and wage gains, all of the following studies have found that productivity and real wage growth, which at one time were positively correlated, began to separate around the 1970s in the United States and/or Canada. In other words, rising productivity does *not* mean rising standard of living. Dew-Becker and Gordon, "Where Did the Productivity Growth Go?"; Dufour and Haiven, *Hard Working Province*; Krugman, "Where the Productivity Went"; Russell and Dufour, *Rising Profit Shares*. On productivity and job quality/unemployment, see Braverman, *Labor and Monopoly Capital.*
38 Gertner, "The Rise and Fall."
39 Stiglitz, Sen, and Fitoussi, "Report," 12.
40 See Skidelsky and Skidelsky, *How Much Is Enough?* The Canadian Index of Well-Being, hosted at the University of Waterloo, can be found at https://uwaterloo.ca/canadian-index-wellbeing.
41 Bates, "Gross National Happiness."
42 Suzuki, "Measuring Progress with GDP."
43 Dufour and Hurteau, "Est-ce que les Québécois," emphasis added.
44 Ibid.; Stiglitz, Sen, and Fitoussi, *Report*, 36.
45 Stiglitz, Sen, and Fitoussi, "Report," 101.
46 Ibid., 46, 101, 286.
47 Ibid., 12–13.
48 Skidelsky and Skidelsky, *How Much Is Enough?*

Conclusion

1 Taylor, *The Principles*, 142.
2 Illich, *Tools for Conviviality*, 93.
3 Weber, *The Protestant Ethic*.
4 Purvis and Hunt, "Discourse, Ideology."
5 See Part II in Gramsci and Hobsbawm, *The Antonio Gramsci Reader*.
6 Mannheim, *Ideology and Utopia*, 1.
7 Laclau and Mouffe, *Phronesis Series Hegemony*.
8 Bourdieu and Wacquant, *An Invitation*.
9 Somers and Block, "From Poverty to Perversity," 265.
10 Ibid., 264–5.
11 Ibid., 265.
12 Bourdieu, "Utopia of Endless Exploitation."
13 Thus, although Somers maintains that her approach "does not seek the deep social interests from which theories are derived," it is evident that this is an epistemological decision rather than a strict ontological position; in other words, her uptake of Bourdieu's proposition suggests she accepts that interests are, in the socio-historical context she studies, integral to the process by which some ideas squeeze out all the others. It is merely that her research does not presuppose what those interests are or who has them, nor does it seek to extract and describe them in any detail. See Somers, "What's Political or Cultural," 115. Bourdieu's notion of ideas making themselves true is also relevant to Brett Christophers's work on the transformation of banking into a productive industry, referenced throughout chapter 6.
14 I owe the form of this question – "How is it that …?" – to Pierre Bourdieu's definition of sociology, given in a radio interview recorded for the 2001 documentary *Sociology est un sport du combat* (RDC 95.5, Radio Droit de Cité [RDC], La Val Fourre, France).
15 Swift, *SOS*.
16 Somers and Block, "From Poverty to Perversity," 263–4.
17 Bourdieu, "Utopia of Endless Exploitation."
18 Weeks, *The Problem with Work*, 81.
19 Mill, *Principles of Political Economy*, 5.
20 Ibid., IV, chapter 6, para. 2.
21 Ibid.; Brick, *Transcending Capitalism*.
22 Mill, *Principles of Political Economy*, IV, ch. 6, para. 6.
23 Ibid.
24 Ibid., para. 9.
25 Ibid., para. 8.

26 On "demands" as counterposed to "ideals" or "proposals," see Weeks, *The Problem with Work.*

27 Weeks, *The Problem with Work*, 84.

28 Jevons, *The Coal Question.* Jevons's work is the course of "the Jevons Paradox," a theoretical principle still studied in environmental economics.

29 Mill, *Principles of Political Economy*, IV, ch. 6, para. 9.

30 Weber, *The Protestant Ethic.*

31 Lafargue's influence on French politics may well be a reason why anti-productivism appears to have always had a stronger hold in France than it has in North America and elsewhere in Europe. For a biography of Lafargue, consult the following two volumes by Derfler: *Paul Lafargue and the Founding of French Marxism, 1842–1882*; and *Paul Lafargue and the Flowering of French Socialism, 1882–1911.*

32 Lafargue, chapter 2 in *The Right to Be Lazy.*

33 Ibid.

34 Ibid., chapter 3.

35 Veblen, *The Theory of the Leisure Class.* For a reading that describes this work as "productivist," see Rojek, "Veblen, Leisure, and Human Need."

36 Brick, *Transcending Capitalism*, 87–8.

37 Sapir, "Culture, Genuine and Spurious."

38 Keynes, "Economic Possibilities," 359.

39 Martínez-Alier et al., "Sustainable De-Growth," 1742.

40 Troude-Chastenet, "La décroissance."

41 Brick, *Transcending Capitalism*, 25.

42 Ibid., 56, 84.

43 Russell, "In Praise of Idleness," 554.

44 Ibid., 555.

45 Brick, *Transcending Capitalism*, 10.

46 Hunnicutt, "Kellogg's Six-Hour Day," 476. See also Hunnicutt, *Work without End.*

47 Roediger, Review: "*Work without End.*"

48 Hunnicutt, "Kellogg's Six-Hour Day," 487.

49 Ibid., 519.

50 Ibid.

51 Roediger, Review: "Work without End."

52 Hunnicutt, "Kellogg's Six-Hour Day," 519.

53 Hunnicutt, *Work without End.*

54 Brick, *Transcending Capitalism*, 180.

55 Ibid., 184.

56 Ibid., 218.

57 For example, Ellul, *The Technological Society*.

58 Marcuse, *One-Dimensional Man*, 13–14. Many others drew connections between mass production, industrial (and even post-industrial) society, and conformism. See the discussion of Riesman and Crosland in Brick, *Transcending Capitalism*, 177–80.

59 Ibid., 7.

60 Ibid., 114.

61 Ibid.

62 Ibid., 138.

63 Illich, *The Right to Useful Unemployment*, 7–8; Illich, *Tools for Conviviality*, 11.

64 Brick, *Transcending Capitalism*, 221.

65 Illich, *Tools for Conviviality*, 11–12.

66 Ibid., 11.

67 Illich, *The Right to Useful Unemployment*, 50.

68 Brick, *Transcending Capitalism*, 258.

69 See Katz and Light, *Environmental Pragmatism*, 168; and Abromeit and Cobb, eds., *Herbert Marcuse*, chapter 12, for discussions of Marcuse in/and political ecology.

70 Illich, *The Right to Useful Unemployment*, 72.

71 Gorz, *Farewell to the Working Class*.

72 McKeen, "The Shaping of Political Agency."

73 Pierson, "The Politics of the Domestic Sphere," 11.

74 Federici, quoted in Weeks, *The Problem With Work*, 125.

75 Cox and Federici, quoted in ibid., 131.

76 Standing, *The Precariat*.

77 The dismissal of feminism, at the time of writing, was a hot topic in mainstream media, with celebrities squaring off around who was and wasn't a feminist and what it meant to be or not be a feminist. T-shirts were sold with the bold-print slogan "THIS IS WHAT A FEMINIST LOOKS LIKE," and actress Emma Watson endured both adulation and rape and murder threats after she "came out" as a feminist in 2014.

78 C. Williams, "The Happy Marriage."

79 Ibid.

80 Ibid., 61.

81 Sandberg's thesis is that women "hold themselves back" from greatness at work because they want to be liked (by colleagues, bosses, and friends and family), and because they either anticipate in advance or experience in the moment a tug toward childrearing and the home. She urges them to "lean in" to work. Sandberg, *Lean In*.

82 Weeks, *The Problem with Work*, 7.

83 DiFazio and Aronowitz, *The Jobless Future*.

84 See Rifkin, *The End of Work*, 236–48; and DiFazio and Aronowitz, *The Jobless Future*, chs. 10 and 11.

85 Another sociologist of work, Tim Strangleman, has lumped Rifkin, Beck, and Sennett together as examples of the "end of work thesis" (or as participants in an "end of work debate"), arguing that they all display a kind of nostalgia for work of the past – a nostalgia that in many respects is unfounded. But I believe Gorz, Aronowitz, and DiRazio should be separated out of this tradition because they actually do not long for a return to the permanent and stable work of the past. They advocate instead, as Strangleman even notes, that we challenge the "dogma" and the "ideology" of work itself in a way that Beck, Sennett, and Rifkin simply do not. See T. Strangleman, "The Nostalgia for Permanence at Work?"

86 Livingston, *Against Thrift*, 166.

87 Fisher, "Review of James Livingston's *Against Thrift*."

88 Livingston, "More Work for Father."

89 Ibid. Cf. *Dissent Magazine*, "Has the Left Won?"; Livingston, "Throw the Book at Me."

90 Burkeman, "This Column Will Change Your Life"; Frank, "Graeber: 'Spotlight on the Financial Sector'"; Graeber, "On the Phenomenon"; *The Economist*, "On 'Bullshit Jobs'" and "The Onrushing Wave."

91 Graeber, "On the Phenomenon."

92 Burkeman, "This Column Will Change Your Life."

93 Graeber, "On the Phenomenon."

94 Poole, "Why the Cult of Hard Work Is Counter-Productive."

95 Seidman, *Workers against Work*, 226.

96 Weeks, *The Problem with Work*, 70.

97 Poole, "Why the Cult of Hard Work Is Counter-Productive."

98 Ibid.

99 Georgescu-Roegen, *The Entropy Law*.

100 Meadows, Meadows, and Randers, *The Limits to Growth*; D'Alisa, Demaria, and Kallis, eds., *Degrowth*, xxiii.

101 Meadows, Randers, and Meadows, *Limits to Growth: The 30-Year Update*; Ahmed, "Scientists Vindicate 1972 'Limits to Growth.'"

102 Georgescu-Roegen, *La décroissance*.

103 D'Alisa, Demaria, and Kallis, *Degrowth*, xxiii.

104 Ibid.

105 Latouche, *Farewell to Growth*, 9.

106 Latouche, *Farewell to Growth*; Victor, *Managing Without Growth*, is an example of an excellent book that uses degrowth ideas and, without *naming* productivism as the enemy, critiques it handily.

107 Klein, *This Changes Everything*, 94.

108 The idea of a basic income has a very long history, predating any of the degrowth thinkers listed as supporters. Walter Von Trier's 1995 PhD dissertation traces the basic income debate and "movement" to as far back as 1918. Van Trier, "Everyone a King."

109 Brick, *Transcending Capitalism*.

110 Klein, *This Changes Everything*, 94.

111 Ibid., 95.

112 Weeks, *The Problem with Work*, 176.

113 Kathi Weeks, "'Hours for What We Will.'"

114 Livingston, "Throw the Book at Me."

Bibliography

Abromeit, John, and W. Mark Cobb, eds. *Herbert Marcuse: A Critical Reader*. New York and London: Routledge, 2014.

ACOA (Atlantic Canada Opportunities Agency). *Five-Year Report to Parliament 2003–2008*. 23 September 2011. http://www.acoa-apeca.gc.ca/eng/publications/ParliamentaryReports/Pages/5YearReport_Page8.aspx

– *Annual Report*. Ottawa: Government of Canada, 2008.

– *Annual Report 1989–1990*. Ottawa: Government of Canada, 1990.

– "Correspondence." June 1991. R14032, vol. 1, file 3 (Statistical).

– Fact Sheet: "ACOA's Enhanced Innovation Programming." Last modified 16 July 2014. http://www.acoa-apeca.gc.ca/eng/ImLookingFor/ProgramInformation/Pages/Innovation_FactSheet.aspx

– *Five Year Report to Parliament*. Ottawa: Government of Canada, 1993.

– *Five Year Report to Parliament*. Ottawa: Government of Canada, 2003.

– "Profiles of Young Atlantic Canadians Who Dared to Try." Moncton: 1998.

Ahmed, Nafeez. "Scientists Vindicate 1972 'Limits to Growth' – Urge Investment in 'Circular Economy.'" *The Guardian*, 4 June 2014. http://www.theguardian.com/environment/earth-insight/2014/jun/04/scientists-limits-to-growth-vindicated-investment-transition-circular-economy

Almon, Clopper. *The Craft of Economic Modeling, Part III: Multisectoral Models* (2012). http://www.inforum.umd.edu/papers/publishedwork/books/craft3.pdf

– "Double Trouble: The Problem with Double Deflation of Value Added, and an Input–Output Alternative with an Application to Russia." Paper presented at the Sixteenth Inforum World Conference, Cyprus, 2008, 9. http://sartoris.umd.edu/papers/conferences/2008/Almon.pdf

Anderson, Benedict. *Imagined Communities: Reflections on the Origin and Spread of Nationalism*. London: Verso, 1982.

– "Soft Spots Slow Growth of Economy." *Globe and Mail*, 15 June 1957.
Anderson, R. "Foreign Investment in Canada: Nation's Sovereignty Menaced." *Globe and Mail*, 29 December 1960.
– "Productivity Council Cites Management–Labor Strife as Efficiency Bar." *Globe and Mail*, 1 October 1963.
Arcand, Alan. "Has Productivity Growth in Canada Been Stronger Than Originally Thought?" *Conference Board of Canada*, 24 December 2012. http://www.conferenceboard.ca/economics/hot_eco_topics/default/12-12-24/has_productivity_growth_in_canada_been_stronger_than_originally_thought.aspx
Ardinat, G. "Competitiveness as Political Policy: Staying Ahead." *Le Monde Diplomatique*, October 2012. http://mondediplo.com/2012/10/07competitiveness
Auditor General. "Chapter 6. Atlantic Canada Opportunities Agency: Economic Development." *Report of the Auditor General of Canada*. 2001. http://www.oag-bvg.gc.ca/internet/English/parl_oag_200112_06_e_11827.html
Auer, L. *Regional Disparities of Productivity and Growth in Canada*. Ottawa: Economic Council of Canada, 1979.
Azzi, Stephen. *Walter Gordon and the Rise of Canadian Nationalism*. Montreal and Kingston: McGill–Queen's University Press, 1999.
Baldwin, John R., and Ryan MacDonald. "The Canadian Manufacturing Sector: Adapting to Challenges." Statistics Canada Economic Analysis (EA) Research Paper Series No. 57, 2009.
Baldwin, John R., and Wulong Gu. "Multifactor Productivity in Canada: An Evaluation of Alternative Methods of Estimating Capital Services." *Canadian Productivity Review* 15–206-X, no. 9 (April 2007).
– "Multifactor Productivity Measurement at Statistics Canada." *Canadian Productivity Review* 15–206-X, no. 31 (May 2013).
Baldwin, John R., Wulong Gu, and Ryan MacDonald. "Intangible Capital and Productivity Growth in Canada." *Canadian Productivity Review* 15–206-X, no. 29 (June 2012).
Bates, Winton. "Gross National Happiness." *Asian-Pacific Economic Literature* 23, no. 2 (2009): 1–16.
Bauerlein, M., and C. Jeffery. "All Work and No Pay: The Great Speedup." *Mother Jones*, June 2013. http://www.motherjones.com/politics/2011/06/speed-up-american-workers-long-hours
Beaudry, P., F. Collard, and D.A. Green. "Demographics and Recent Productivity Performance: Insights from Cross-Country Comparisons." *Canadian Journal of Economics / Revue canadienne d'Economique* 38, no. 2 (2005): 309–44. doi:10.2307/3696036

Belhocine, Nazim. "Treating Intangible Inputs as Investment Goods: The Impact on Canadian GDP." *IMF Working Papers* (2009): 1–21.

Benson, E. "Remarks." Fifth National Labour–Management Seminar, Vancouver, 23 October 1963. MG 28, I103, vol. 529, file 11.

Bernolak, I. "Productivity Research." Report by chief of the Productivity Research Section, Industry and Merchandizing Division, Dominion Bureau of Statistics. Sent 21 February 1961 from T.E. Bocking to J.A. Roberts, DM Trade and Commerce. Dominion Bureau of Statistics. RG 20, vol. 859, file 40–2.

Bickerton, James. *Nova Scotia, Ottawa, and the Politics of Regional Development.* Toronto: University of Toronto Press, 1990.

Bill C-52, 4th Session, 24th Parliament. Canada, 1960. RG 20, vol. 2889, file no. 211–0-8 1.1.

Bird, J. "Jodoin Quit over Dief's Inaction on Unemployment." *Toronto Daily Star,* 14 September 1962.

Blackmore, R. "PM Holds Little Fear for Economy." *Globe and Mail,* 6 June 1958.

Blackwell, Richard. "Why Canada's Tech Companies Fail." *Globe and Mail,* 10 April 2014. http://www.theglobeandmail.com/technology/ottawa-needs-tighter-controls-on-resource-wealth-stiglitz-says/article17917310/

Blaug, M. "Was There a Marginal Revolution?" *History of Political Economy* 4, no. 2 (1972): 269–280. doi:10.1215/00182702-4-2-26.

Block, F., and G.A. Burns. "Productivity as a Social Problem: The Uses and Misuses of Social Indicators." *American Sociological Review* 51, no. 6 (1986): 767–80.

Bloom, Nicholas, and John Van Reenen. *Human Resource Management and Productivity.* NBER Working Paper Series. National Bureau of Economic Research, 2010. http://www.nber.org/papers/w16019

Böhm-Bawerk, E. "Capital and Interest Once More: II. A Relapse to the Productivity Theory." *Quarterly Journal of Economics* 21, no. 2 (1907): 247–82.

– "The Positive Theory of Capital and Its Critics." *Quarterly Journal of Economics* 9, no. 3 (1895): 235–56.

Bothwell, Robert, and William Kilbourn. *C.D. Howe: A Biography.* Toronto: McClelland and Stewart, 1979.

Bouckaert, Geert. "The History of the Productivity Movement." *Public Productivity and Management Review* 14, no. 1 (1990): 53. doi:10.2307/3380523

Bourdieu, Pierre. *Masculine Domination.* Stanford: Stanford University Press, 2001.

– "Utopia of Endless Exploitation: The Essence of Neoliberalism." *Le Monde Diplomatique,* December 1998.

Bourdieu, Pierre, and L. Wacquant. *An Invitation to a Reflexive Sociology.* Chicago: University of Chicago Press, 1992.

Braverman, Harry. *Labor and Monopoly Capital: The Degradation of Work in the Twentieth Century*. New York: NYU Press, 1979.

Brick, Howard. *Transcending Capitalism: Visions of a New Society in Modern American Thought*. Ithaca: Cornell University Press, 2006.

Bryson, Bill. *One Summer: 1927*. New York: Anchor, 2014.

Burkeman, O. "This Column Will Change Your Life: How to Tell Whether You Have a Bullshit Job." *The Guardian*, 7 September 2013. http://www.theguardian.com/lifeandstyle/2013/sep/07/column-change-life-bullshit-job

Burnham, James. *The Managerial Revolution: What Is Happening in the World*. New York: John Day Company, 1941.

Burns, A.F. "The Measurement of the Physical Volume of Production." *Quarterly Journal of Economics* 44, no. 2 (1930): 242–62.

Canada. "Changes to Employment Insurance." Government of Canada, 2012. http://www.servicecanada.gc.ca/eng/sc/ei/ccaj/vignettes.shtml

– House of Commons Debates, 22nd Parliament, 3rd Session, vol. 6. Ottawa: Library of Parliament, 1956.

– House of Commons Debates, 24th Parliament, 4th session, vol. 3. Ottawa: Library of Parliament, 196062.

– House of Commons Debates, 33rd Parliament, 2nd session, vol. 2. Ottawa: Library of Parliament, 1988.

– House of Commons Debates, 34th Parliament, 2nd session, vol. 4. Ottawa: Library of Parliament, 1989.

– House of Commons Debates. 17 May. Official Report. 34th Parliament, 3rd Session, vol. 1. Ottawa: Library of Parliament, 1991.

– House of Commons Debates. 27 April. R14032, vol. 1, file 1 (Establishment of ACOA). Ottawa: Library of Parliament, 1988.

– House of Commons Debates. 18 January and 5 May, R14032, vol. 1, file 1 (Establishment of ACOA). Ottawa: Library of Parliament, 1988.

– PMO (Prime Minister's Office). "News Release." 6 June, R14032, vol. 1, file 1 (Establishment of ACOA). Ottawa: 1987.

– *Report of the Royal Commission on Dominion–Provincial Relations*. Ottawa: Queen's Printer, 1954.

– *Report of the Royal Commission on the Relations of Labor and Capital in Canada*. Ottawa: Queen's Printer, 1889.

Canadian Advertising Advisory Board. "Appendix: Letter from the Canadian Advertising Advisory Board (Toronto) to the Canadian Association of Advertising Agencies." 14 December 1961. From "Minutes of NPC Council Meeting," Ottawa, 29 and 30 January 1962. RG 20, vol. 859, file 40–2.

Cannan, E. "The Division of Income." *The Quarterly Journal of Economics* 19, no. 3 (1905): 341–69. doi:10.2307/1882657

Cardin, J.R. "Canadian Labour Relations in an Era of Technological Change."
    Ottawa: Queen's Printer. 1967.
Carew, A. "The Anglo-American Council on Productivity (1948–52):
    The Ideological Roots of the Post-War Debate on Productivity in
    Britain." *Journal of Contemporary History* 26, no. 1 (1991): 49–69.
    doi:10.1177/002200949102600103
– . *Labour under the Marshall Plan: The Politics of Productivity and the Marketing of
    Management Science.* Detroit: Wayne State University Press, 1987.
Casey, Marion. "Efficiency, Taylorism, and Libraries in Progressive America."
    Journal of Library History 16, no. 2 (1 April 1981): 265–79.
Chandler, Alfred. *The Visible Hand: The Managerial Revolution in American
    Business.* Cambridge, MA: Harvard University Press, 1977.
Christophers, Brett. *Banking across Boundaries: Placing Finance in Capitalism.*
    New York: John Wiley and Sons, 2013.
Chronicle Herald (Halifax). News clipping. 17 February 1988. R14032, vol. 1, file
    1 (Establishment of ACOA).
Clark, John B. "Concerning the Nature of Capital: A Reply." *Quarterly Journal
    of Economics* 21, no. 3 (1907): 351–70.
– "Distribution as Determined by a Law of Rent." *Quarterly Journal of
    Economics* 5, no. 3 (1891): 308.
– "Natural Divisions in Economic Theory." *Quarterly Journal of Economics* 13,
    no. 2 (1899): 187–203.
Clark, W.A.V., and Karen L. Avery. "The Effects of Data Aggregation in
    Statistical Analysis." *Geographical Analysis* 3 (1976): 428–38.
Coates, D. "The National Productivity Council of Canada." MA thesis, Cornell
    University, 1964.
Cole, A.H. "The American Rice-Growing Industry: A Study of Comparative
    Advantage." *Quarterly Journal of Economics* 41, no. 4 (1927): 595–643.
– "Comparative Costs in the Worsted-Cloth Manufacture, American and
    Foreign." *Quarterly Journal of Economics* 43, no. 3 (1929): 550–61.
Cote, L. "Aims at Unemployment Heart: Ottawa Productivity Plan
    Supported." *Globe and Mail*, 26 October 1960.
Crain, Caleb. "There Was Blood: The Ludlow Massacre Revisited."
    The New Yorker, 19 January 2009. http://www.newyorker.com/
    magazine/2009/01/19/there-was-blood
Craven, Paul, and Tom Traves. "Class-Politics of the National Policy, 1872–1933."
    Journal of Canadian Studies / Revue d'études canadiennes 14, no. 3 (1979): 14–38.
Crum, F.S. "Review of Report of Departmental Commission on the Official
    Statistics of Canada with Appendix Consisting of Notes of Evidence. Ottawa,
    1913." *Publications of the American Statistical Association* 13, no. 101 (1913).

Cummings, J. "Levasseur's 'L'Ouvrier Américain.'" *Quarterly Journal of Economics* 13, no. 1 (1898): 85–100. doi:10.2307/1882984

Curtis, B. "The Missing Memory of Canadian Sociology: Reflexive Government and 'the Social Science.'" *Canadian Review of Sociology* (forthcoming, February 2016)

D'Alisa, G., F. Demaria, and G. Kallis, eds. *Degrowth: A Vocabulary for a New Era*. New York: Routledge, 2014.

Dean, M. *Governmentality: Power and Rule in Modern Society*, vol. 3. Thousand Oaks: Sage, 1999.

Derfler, L. *Paul Lafargue and the Flowering of French Socialism, 1882–1911*. Cambridge, MA: Harvard University Press, 2009.

– *Paul Lafargue and the Founding of French Marxism, 1842–1882*. Cambridge, MA: Harvard University Press, 1991.

Dew-Becker, I., and R.J. Gordon. "Where Did the Productivity Growth Go? Inflation Dynamics and the Distribution of Income." NBER Working Paper No. 11842, 2005.

DeYoung, George. "Remarks." From the Fifth National Labour–Management Seminar, Vancouver, 23 October 1963. MG 28 I103m vol. 529, file 11.

Diewert, Erwin and Emily Yu. "New Estimates of Real Income and Multifactor Productivity Growth for the Canadian Business Sector, 1961–2011." *International Productivity Monitor* 24 (2012): 27–48.

DiFazio, William, and Stanley Aronowitz. *The Jobless Future*. Minneapolis: University of Minnesota Press, 2010.

Dimand, R. "Review of Barnett, E. (2000). The Keynesian Arithmetic in War-Time Canada: Development of the National Accounts 1939–1945. (Kingston, On.: Harbinger House Press, 2nd ed.)." *Scientia Canadensis* 25 (2001): 82–5.

Dissent Magazine. "Has the Left Won? An Exchange between Tim Barker and James Livingston." 11 September 2012. https://www.dissentmagazine.org/online_articles/has-the-left-won-an-exchange-between-tim-barker-and-james-livingston

Douglas, D.W. "The Cost of Living for Working Women: A Criticism of Current Theories." *Quarterly Journal of Economics* 34, no. 2 (1920): 225–59.

Drummond, D. "Confessions of a Serial Productivity Researcher." *International Productivity Monitor* 22 (Fall 2011): 3–10.

du Gay, P. *Production of Culture / Cultures of Production*. London: Sage, 1997.

Dufour, Mathieu, and L. Haiven. *Hard Working Province: Is It Enough? Rising Profits and Falling Labour Shares in Nova Scotia*. Toronto and Halifax: Growing Gap and Canadian Centre for Policy Alternatives–NS, 2008.

Dufour, Mathieu, and Philippe Hurteau. "Est-ce que les Québécois et Québécoises profitent de l'augmentation de la productivité?" IRIS: 2013.

http://iris-recherche.s3.amazonaws.com/uploads/publication/file/Note-productivite-IRIS.pdf

Duggan, L. *The Twilight of Equality?: Neoliberalism, Cultural Politics, and the Attack on Democracy.* Boston: Beacon Press, 2012.

Dymond, W.R. "Appendix." W.R. Dymon's (from Dept. of Labour) talk to NPC at 30 January 1962 meeting. RG 20, vol. 859, file 40–2.

ECC (Economic Council of Canada). *Economic Goals for Canada to 1970.* Ottawa: Queen's Printer, 1964.

– *A General Incentive Programme to Encourage Research and Development in Canadian Industry: Report to the Economic Council of Canada.* Ottawa: Queen's Printer, 1965.

– *Prices, Productivity, and Employment.* Ottawa: Queen's Printer, 1966.

– "Productivity through New Technology: [Papers] Prepared for the Conference." Conference on Productivity through New Technology. Sponsored by Economic Council of Canada and Ontario Economic Council, Toronto, May 1965. Ottawa: Queen's Printer.

– *Towards Better Communications between Labour and Management.* Ottawa: Queen's Printer, 1967.

Economist. "On 'Bullshit Jobs.'" 21 August 2013. http://www.economist.com/blogs/freeexchange/2013/08/labour-markets-0

– "The Onrushing Wave." 18 January 2014. http://www.economist.com/news/briefing/21594264-previous-technological-innovation-has-always-delivered-more-long-run-employment-not-less

Edgeworth, F.Y. "The Theory of Distribution." *Quarterly Journal of Economics* 18, no. 2 (1904): 159–219. doi:10.2307/1882785

Ellul, Jacques. *The Technological Society.* New York: Vintage, 1967.

Esch, Elizabeth, and David Roediger. "One Symptom of Originality: Race and the Management of Labour in the History of the United States." *Historical Materialism* 17, no. 4 (2009): 3–43.

Financial Times. News clipping, 15 June 1987. R14032, vol. 1, file 1 (Establishment of ACOA).

Fishbein, Meyer H. *The Censuses of Manufactures: 1810–1890.* US National Archives and Records Service Reference Information Paper No. 50, 1973.

Fisher, I. "Cournot and Mathematical Economics." *Quarterly Journal of Economics* 12, no. 2 (1898): 119–38. doi: 10.2307/1882115

Fisher, Michael. "Review of James Livingston's *Against Thrift*: Why Consumer Culture Is Good for the Economy, the Environment, and Your Soul." *Society for US Intellectual History*, 22 March 2012. http://s-usih.org/2012/03/goods-aplenty-against-thrift-and.html

Flux, A.W. "Industrial Productivity in Great Britain and the United States." *Quarterly Journal of Economics* 48, no. 1 (1933): 1–38. doi:10.2307/1884795

Flyvbjerg, Bent. "Five Misunderstandings about Case Study Research."
    Qualitative Inquiry 12, no. 2 (2006): 219–45.
Foenander, O. de R. "The Forty-Four Hours Case in Australia, 1926–1927."
    Quarterly Journal of Economics 42, no. 2 (1928): 320–21.
Foster, Brian. "Social Science and Liberal Internationalism." PhD diss., Carleton
    University, 2012.
Foster, Jason, Albert J. Mills, and Terrance Weatherbee. "History, Field Definition,
    and Management Studies: The Case of the New Deal." *Journal of Management
    History* 20, no. 2 (2014): 179–99.
Foster, Karen. *Generation, Discourse and Social Change*. New York: Routledge,
    2013.
Foucault, Michel. *The Archaeology of Knowledge*. New York: A.A. Knopf, 2012.
– *The Foucault Effect: Studies in Governmentality*, edited by Graham Burchell,
    Colin Gordon, and Peter Miller. Chicago: University of Chicago Press, 1991.
– "On the Genealogy of Ethics: An Overview of Work in Progress." In *Ethics:
    Subjectivity and Truth*, edited by Paul Rabinow, 253–80. New York: New Press,
    1997.
– *Politics, Philosophy, Culture: Interviews and Other Writings, 1977–1984*. New
    York: Routledge, 2013.
Frank, T. "David Graeber: 'Spotlight on the financial sector did make apparent
    just how bizarrely skewed our economy is in terms of who gets rewarded.'"
    Salon.com, 1 June 2014. http://www.salon.com/2014/06/01/help_us_
    thomas_piketty_the_1s_sick_and_twisted_new_scheme
Furlong, M. *Foucault: The Logic of Freedom*. PhD diss., University of Guelph, 2011.
Georgescu-Roegen, N. *La décroissance: Entropie–Ecologie–Economie*, translated
    by J. Grinewald and I. Rens. 3e édition revue et augmentée. Paris: Le Sang
    de la Terre, 2006.
– *The Entropy Law and the Economic Process*. Cambridge, MA: Harvard University
    Press, 1971.
Gertner, Jon. "The Rise and Fall of the G.D.P." *New York Times*, 13 May 2010.
    http://www.nytimes.com/2010/05/16/magazine/16GDP-t.html?_r=0
Gilson, D. "Overworked America: 12 Charts That Will Make Your Blood Boil."
    Mother Jones, June 2011. http://www.motherjones.com/politics/2011/06/
    speedup-americans-working-harder-charts
Giroux, H.A. *The Terror of Neoliberalism: Authoritarianism and the Eclipse of
    Democracy*. St Paul: Paradigm, 2004.
Globe and Mail. "Government Proposes Planning Council." 17 May 1963.
– "Is 'Good' Good Enough?" 28 December 1960.
– "U.S. Interest in Economy Here Termed Logical." 11 October 1956.
– "A Year of Challenge." 31 December 1960.

Goldberg, Simon A. "Measurement of Productivity." Papers given at Dalhousie Seminar, 18 and 19 September 1962. MG 28 I103, vol. 529, file 11.

Goldenberg, H. Carl. "Remarks." Fifth National Labour–Management Seminar, Vancouver, 23 October 1963. MG 28 I103, vol. 529, file 11.

Goodwin, Crauford D.W. *Canadian Economic Thought: The Political Economy of a Developing Nation 1814–1914*. Durham: Duke University Press, 1961.

– "Marginalism Moves to the New World." *History of Political Economy* 4, no. 2 (1972): 551–70.

Gorz, André. *Farewell to the Working Class*. London: Pluto Press, 1982.

Graeber, David. "On the Phenomenon of Bullshit Jobs" *STRIKE!*, 17 August 2013. http://strikemag.org/bullshit-jobs

Gramsci, A., and E.J. Hobsbawm. *The Antonio Gramsci Reader: Selected Writings 1916–1935*, edited by D. Forgacs. New York: NYU Press, 2000.

Grandin, Greg. *Fordlandia: The Rise and Fall of Henry Ford's Forgotten Jungle City*. London: Macmillan, 2010.

Greenhill, B. "Recognition and Collective Identity Formation in International Politics." *European Journal of International Relations* 14, no. 2 (2008): 343–68. doi:10.1177/1354066108089246

Gregory, T.E., F.A. Hayek, Arnold Plant, and Lionel Robbins. Letters written to the *New York Times*, 19 October 1932. https://thinkmarkets.files.wordpress.com/2010/06/keynes-hayek-1932-cambridgelse.pdf

Gu, Wulong. "Estimating Capital Input for Measuring Business Sector Multifactor Productivity Growth in Canada: Response to Diewert and Yu." *International Productivity Monitor* 24 (2012): 49–62.

Gu, Wulong, Berouk Terefe, and Weimin Wang. *The Impact of R&D Capitalization on GDP and Productivity Growth in Canada*. Ottawa: Statistics Canada, 2012.

Gudeman, Stephen. "Piketty and Anthropology." *Anthropological Forum: A Journal of Social Anthropology and Comparative Sociology* 25, no.1 (2015): 66–83. doi:10.1080/00664677.2014.972339

Guetzkow, J. "Beyond Deservingness: Congressional Discourse on Poverty, 1964–1996." *Annals of the American Academy of Political and Social Science* 629, no. 1 (2010): 177.

Hallahan, Kirk. "W.L. Mackenzie King: Rockefeller's 'Other' Public Relations Counselor in Colorado." *Public Relations Review* 29 (2003): 411.

Harrington, A.R. "Remarks." Proceedings of the Montreal Meetings – 4th National Labour–Management Seminar, University of Montreal, 15–16 May 1963. MG 28 I103, vol. 529, file 12.

Harvey, D. *A Brief History of Neoliberalism*. Oxford: Oxford University Press, 2005.

Hawley, F.B. "The Fundamental Error of 'Kapital und Kapitalzins.'" *Quarterly Journal of Economics* 6, no. 3 (1892): 280–307. doi:10.2307/1882460

Haynes, J. "Risk as an Economic Factor." *Quarterly Journal of Economics* 9, no. 4 (1895): 409–49. doi:10.2307/1886012

Haythorne, George. Letter to George Hees, 30 September 1960. RG 20, vol. 2889, file 211–0–8 1.1.

– Letter to J.A. Roberts, 21 September 1960. RG 20, vol. 2889, file no. 211–0–8 1.1.

– "Remarks." Papers given at Dalhousie Seminar, 18 and 19 September 1962. MG 28 I103, vol. 529, file 11.

Hebert, J. Claude. "Remarks." Proceedings of the Montreal Meetings – 4th National Labour–Management Seminar, University of Montreal, 15–16 May 1963. MG 28 I103, vol. 529, file 12.

Hees, George. Statement by the Minister of Trade and Commerce to the House of Commons, Canada, 1960. RG 20, vol. 859, file 40–2.

Hodgetts, J.E. "Challenge and Response: A Retrospective View of the Public Service of Canada." *Canadian Public Administration* 7, no. 4 (1964): 409–21.

Hodgson, G. "Canadian Productivity: Even Worse Than Previously Thought." *Globe and Mail*, 28 August 2013. http://www.theglobeandmail.com/report-on-business/economy/economy-lab/canadian-productivity-even-worse-than-previously-thought/article13988435

Hunnicutt, Benjamin Kline. "Kellogg's Six-Hour Day: A Capitalist Vision of Liberation through Managed Work Reduction." *Business History Review* 66, no. 3 (1992): 475–522.

– *Work without End: Abandoning Shorter Hours for the Right to Work.* Philadelphia: Temple University Press, 2010.

Illich, Ivan. *The Right to Useful Unemployment.* London: Marion Boyars, 1978.

– *The Right to Useful Unemployment and Its Professional Enemies.* Marion Boyars, 2000.

– *Tools for Conviviality.* New York: Harper and Row, 1973.

Inwood, Kris, and John Chamard. "Regional Industrial Growth During the 1890s: The Case of the Missing Artisans." *Acadiensis* 16, no. 1 (1986): 101–17.

Inwood, Kris, and J. Irwin. "Land, Income, and Regional Inequality: New Estimates of Provincial Incomes and Growth in Canada, 1871–1891." *Acadiensis* 31, no. 2 (2002): 157–84.

Jackson, A. "Canadian Deindustrialization." In *Behind The Numbers.* Canadian Centre for Policy Alternatives (CCPA) blog, 15 March 2012. http://behindthenumbers.ca/2012/03/15/canadian-deindustrialization

Jenks, L. "Early Phases of the Management Movement." *Administrative Science Quarterly* 5, no. 3 (1960): 421–47.

Jevons, William Stanley. *The Coal Question: An Inquiry Concerning the Progress of the Nation, and the Probable Exhaustion of Our Coal-Mines.* London:

Macmillan & Co., 1865. Library of Economics and Liberty, http://www.
econlib.org/library/YPDBooks/Jevons/jvnCQ.html

Johnson, A.S. "The Effect of Labor-Saving Devices upon Wages." *Quarterly Journal of Economics* 20, no. 1 (1905): 86–109.

Jorgenson, D. "The World KLEMS Initiative." *International Productivity Monitor* 24 (2012): 5–19.

Jorgenson, D.W., and Z. Griliches. "The Explanation of Productivity Change." *Review of Economic Studies* 34, no. 3 (1967): 249–83.

Karabell, Z. *The Leading Indicators.* New York: Simon and Schuster, 2014.

Katz, A.J., and B.T. Grimm. "In Appreciation: John W. Kendrick (1917–2009)." *Bureau of Economic Analysis Survey of Current Business* 90, no. 2 (2009): 53.

Katz, E., and A. Light. *Environmental Pragmatism.* New York: Routledge, 2013.

Kaufman, Bruce E., Richard A. Beaumont, and Roy B. Helfgott, eds. *Industrial Relations to Human Resources and Beyond: The Evolving Process of Employee Relations Management.* Armonk: M.E. Sharpe, 2003.

Keynes, John Maynard. "Economic Possibilities for Our Grandchildren," In *Essays in Persuasion*, 358–73. New York: W.W. Norton, 1963.

King, Willford Isbell. *The Wealth and Income of the People of the United States.* Boston: Macmillan, 1915.

King, William Lyon Mackenzie. *Industry and Humanity: A Study in the Principles Underlying Industrial Reconstruction.* Boston: Houghton Mifflin, 1918. https://archive.org/details/industryhumanit00king

Klein, Naomi. *This Changes Everything: Capitalism vs the Climate.* Toronto: Knopf Canada, 2014.

Koerner, Walter C. "Background of the Seminar." From the Fifth National Labour–Management Seminar, Vancouver, 23 October 1963. MG 28 I103, vol. 529, file 11.

Kolko, Gabriel. *The Triumph of Conservatism: A Reinterpretation of American History, 1900–1916.* New York: Free Press of Glencoe, 1963.

Krugman, P. "Competitiveness: A Dangerous Obsession." *Foreign Affairs* 73, no. 2 (1994): 28–44.

– "Where the Productivity Went." *New York Times Blog*, 2012. http://krugman.blogs.nytimes.com/2012/04/28/where-the-productivity-went/?_r=0

Kuznets, S. "National Income, 1929–1932." *National Bureau of Economic Research Bulletin* 49 (7 June 1934): 1–12.

Laclau, Ernesto, and Chantal Mouffe. *Phronesis Series Hegemony and Socialist Strategy: New Edition.* London and New York: Verso, 2001.

Lafargue, P. *The Right to Be Lazy: And Other Studies*, translated by Charles H Kerr. Charles Kerr and Co., Co-operative, 1883. https://www.marxists.org/archive/lafargue/1883/lazy/index.htm

Landsberger, H.A. *Hawthorne Revisited: Management and the Worker, Its Critics, and Developments in Human Relations in Industry*. Ithaca: Cornell University Press, 1958.

Lank, Hebert. "A Positive Look at the Problems of Economic Growth and Productivity from Management's Viewpoint." Papers Given at Dalhousie Seminar, 18 and 19 September 1962. MG 28 I103, vol. 529, file 11.

Latouche, S. *Farewell to Growth*. London: Polity Press, 2014.

Leonard, Thomas C. "Retrospectives: Eugenics and Economics in the Progressive Era." *Journal of Economic Perspectives* 19, no. 4 (1 October 2005): 207–24.

Li, T.M. "Governmentality." *Anthropologica* 49, no. 2 (2007): 275–81.

Li, Xiaofeng, and David Prescott. "Measuring Productivity in the Service Sector." Ottawa: Canadian Tourism Human Resource Centre, 2009.

Lileeva, A. "Trade Liberalization and Productivity Dynamics: Evidence from Canada." *Canadian Journal of Economics / Revue canadienne d'Economique* 41, no. 2 (2008): 360–90. doi:10.2307/25478282

List, W. "Launch Drive for Training Unemployed." *Globe and Mail*, 31 December 1960.

Livingston, James. *Against Thrift*. New York: Basic Books, 2011.

– "More Work for Father: Rejoinder to Alex Gourevitch." *Politics and Letters*, 2013. http://politicsandletters.wordpress.com/2013/03/23/more-work-for-father-rejoinder-to-alex-gourevitch

– *Pragmatism and the Political Economy of Cultural Revolution*. Chapel Hill: University of North Carolina Press, 1997.

– "The Social Analysis of Economic History and Theory: Conjectures on Late Nineteenth-Century American Development." *American Historical Review* 92, no. 1 (1987): 69–95.

– "Throw the Book at Me: A Reply to Tim Barker." *Jacobin*, May 2013. https://www.jacobinmag.com/2012/05/throw-the-book-at-me-a-reply-to-tim-barker

Lynch, C. "Productivity Council Holds Jousting Match with Press." *Ottawa Citizen*, 27 September 1961.

MacDonald, B., "Hees Takes the Pollyanna View." *Globe and Mail* 28 December 1960.

MacLean, Dinah. "Lagging Productivity Growth in the Service Sector: Mismeasurement, Mismanagement, or Misinformation?" Working Paper No. 97–6. Ottawa: Bank of Canada, 1997.

Magdoff, Harry. "The Purpose and Method of Measuring Productivity." *Journal of the American Statistical Association* 34, no. 206 (1939): 309–18.

Magdoff, Harry, and Paul Sweezy, "The Uses and Abuses of Measuring Productivity." *Monthly Review* 32, vol. 2 (1980): 19.

Manley, John. "Putting People First: Productivity, Growth, and Living Standards: The Empire Club Addresses (Toronto, Canada)." Speech at the Empire Club of Canada, 18 February 1999. http://speeches.empireclub. org/60377/data?n=34

Mannheim, Karl. *Ideology and Utopia*. New York: Harcourt and Brace, 1954.

Marcuse, Herbert. 1964. *One-Dimensional Man: Studies in the Ideology of Advanced Industrial Society*. Boston: Beacon Press.

Marshal, Herbert. *History of the Dominion Bureau of Statistics*. RG 31, vol 1434, History – Manuscript (pt 1).

– *National Accounts, Standard Classification Systems, and Research and Development*. RG 31, vol. 1434, History – Manuscript (pt 3).

– *Outline*. RG 31, vol. 1434, History – Manuscript (pt. 6).

Martínez-Alier, J., et al. "Sustainable De-Growth: Mapping the Context, Criticisms, and Future Prospects of an Emergent Paradigm." *Ecological Economics* 69 (2010): 1741–47.

Marx, Karl. *Capital (Das Kapital)*, edited by Frederick Engels, translated by Samuel Moore and Edward Aveling. Moscow: Progress Publishers, 1887.

– *Foundations (Grundrisse) of the Critique of Political Economy*. Moscow: Institute of Marx-Engels-Lenin, 1939.

Mason, E.S. "The Doctrine of Comparative Cost." *Quarterly Journal of Economics* 41, no. 1 (1926): 63–93.

Maul, D. *Human Rights, Development, and Decolonization: The International Labour Organization, 1940–70*. London: Palgrave Macmillan, 2012.

Mayo, E. *The Human Problems of an Industrial Civilization: Early Sociology of Management and Organizations*. Hove: Psychology Press, 2003.

McDowall, Duncan. *The Sum of the Satisfactions: Canada in the Age of National Accounting*. Montreal and Kingston: McGill–Queen's University Press, 2008.

McKeen, W. "The Shaping of Political Agency: Feminism and the National Social Policy Debate, the 1970s and Early 1980s." *Studies in Political Economy* 66 (Autumn 2001): 37–58. http://spe.library.utoronto.ca/index.php/spe/article/view/6703

McKinlay, Alan, and James Wilson. "'All they lose is the scream': Foucault, Ford and Mass Production." *Management and Organizational History* 7, no. 1 (2012): 45–60.

McKinnon, A.R. "Seeking a Formula for Industrial Peace and Collaboration." Papers Given at Dalhousie Seminar, 18 and 19 September 1962. MG 28 I103, vol. 529, file 11.

Meade, Douglas S. "Why Real Value Added Is Not My Favorite Concept." Paper presented at the Fourteenth Inforum World Conference,

Traunkirchen, Austria, 2006. http://inforumweb.umd.edu/papers/
conferences/2006/RealValueAdded.pdf

Meadows, Donella, Dennis Meadows, and Jorgen Randers. *The Limits To Growth*. New York: Universe Books, 1972.

Meadows, Donella, Jorgen Randers, and Dennis Meadows. *Limits to Growth: The 30-Year Update*. White River Junction: Chelsea Green Publishing, 2004.

Mill, John Stuart. *Principles of Political Economy with Some of Their Applications to Social Philosophy* (Books II and III). London: Longmans, Green, 1848.

Mishel, Laurence. "The Wedges between Productivity and Median Compensation Growth." *Economic Policy Institute*, 2012. http://www.epi.org/publication/ib330-productivity-vs-compensation

Mitchell, Timothy. "Fixing the Economy." *Cultural Studies* 12, no. 1 (1998): 82–101.

Mitchell, Wesley Clair, Wilford Isbell King, and Frederick R. Macaulay. "The Size of the National Income." In *Income in the United States: Its Amount and Distribution, 1909–1919*, vol. 1: *Summary*, 12–88. Cambridge, MA: NBER, 1921.

Munsterberg, Hugo. *Psychology and Industrial Efficiency*. Boston: Houghton Mifflin, 1913.

Neill, Robin. "Francis Bacon, John Rae, and the Economics of Competitiveness." *American Journal of Economics and Sociology* 58, no. 3 (1999): 385–98.

Nerbas, Don. *Dominion of Capital: The Politics of Big Business and the Crisis of the Canadian Bourgeoisie, 1914–1947*. Toronto: University of Toronto Press, 2013.

North, S.N.D. "Levasseur's American Workingman." *Political Science Quarterly* 13, no. 2 (1898): 321–33. doi:10.2307/2140172

NPC (National Productivity Council). "Minutes of NPC Council Meeting." Ottawa, 29 and 30 January 1962. RG 20, vol. 859, file 40–2.

– Proceedings of 3rd National Productivity Council Labour–Management Seminar, University of Saskatchewan, 23–24 January 1963. MG 28 I103, vol. 529, file 13.

Nyland, Chris. "Scientific Management and Planning." *Capital and Class* 11, no. 3 (1 October 1987): 55–83.

O'Connor, Alice. *Poverty Knowledge: Social Science, Social Policy, and the Poor in Twentieth-Century US History*. Princeton: Princeton University Press, 2002.

O'Connor, Ellen S. "The Politics of Management Thought: A Case Study of the Harvard Business School and the Human Relations School." *Academy of Management Review* 24, no. 1 (1999): 117–31. doi:10.2307/259040

OECD (Organisation for Economic Co-operation and Development). *Measuring Productivity: Measurement of Aggregate and Industry-Level Productivity Growth*. Paris: 2001.

O'Neill, Tim. "The Case for Economic Cooperation in Atlantic Canada." R14032, vol. 1, file 7 (Various Presentations/Papers on ACOA), 1991.

oneNS Commission [aka Ivany Commission]. *Now or Never: An Urgent Call to Action for Nova Scotians. The Report of the Nova Scotia Commission on Building Our New Economy*. Halifax: oneNS Commission, 2014. http://onens.ca/commission-report/

Owram, Doug. *The Government Generation: Canadian Intellectuals and the State, 1900–1945*. Toronto: University of Toronto Press, 1986.

Palmer, B. *Canada's 1960s: The Ironies of Identity in a Rebellious Era*. Toronto: University of Toronto Press, 2009.

Paré, René. "Remarks." Proceedings of the Montreal Meetings – 4th National Labour–Management Seminar, University of Montreal, 15–16 May 1963. MG 28 I103, vol. 529, file 12.

Persons, C.E. "Labor Problems as Treated by American Economists." *Quarterly Journal of Economics* 41, no. 3 (1927): 487–519.

Phillips, B. "Too Many Tycoons? Productivity Council Angers Labor." *Ottawa Citizen*, 1 March 1961.

Pierson, Ruth Roach. "The Politics of the Domestic Sphere." In *Canadian Women's Issues*, vol. 2: *Bold Visions*, edited by R.R. Pierson and Marjorie Griffin Cohen, 1–82. Toronto: James Lorimer, 1995.

Piketty, T. *Capital in the 21st Century*. Cambridge, MA: Harvard University Press, 2014.

Pissarides, C.A., and G. Vallanti. "The Impact of TFP Growth on Steady-State Unemployment." *International Economic Review* 48, no. 2 (2007): 607–40.

Polanyi, Karl. *The Great Transformation*. Boston: Beacon Press, 1965.

Poole, M. *Human Resource Management: Critical Perspectives on Business and Management*, vol. 2. New York: Taylor and Francis, 1999.

Poole, Steven. "Why the Cult of Hard Work Is Counter-Productive." *The New Statesman*, 11 December 2013. http://www.newstatesman.com/2013/12/right-be-lazy

Postel-Vinay, F. "The Dynamics of Technological Unemployment." *International Economic Review* 43, no. 3 (2002): 737–60.

Postner, H.H. "Statistical Problems of Relating Research and Development Data to Productivity Data." Ottawa: Economic Council of Canada, 1983.

Prévost, Jean-Guy, and Jean-Pierre Beaud. "On the Genesis of a New Statistical Regime: The Case of Canada, 1800–2011." *Estatística e Sociedade*, no. 1 (2011). http://seer.ufrgs.br/index.php/estatisticaesociedade/article/view/24547

Proceedings of the Montreal Meetings – 4th National Labour–Management Seminar, University of Montreal, 15–16 May 1963. MG 28 I103, vol. 529, file 12.

Purvis, T., and A. Hunt. "Discourse, Ideology, Discourse, Ideology, Discourse, Ideology ..." *British Journal of Sociology* 44, no. 3 (September 1993): 473–99.

Rehel, J. "Six-Hour Workday in Sweden, e-mail Ban after 6 p.m. in France Signal Shifting Workplace Dynamics." *National Post*, 11 April 2014.

Reynauld, Andre. "For a Rational Economic Policy." Proceedings of the Montreal Meetings – 4th National Labour–Management Seminar, University of Montreal, 15–16 May 1963. MG 28 I103, vol. 529, file 12.

Rifkin, Jeremy. *The End of Work: The Decline of the Global Labor Force and the Dawn of the Post-Market Era.* New York: G.P. Putnam's Sons, 1995.

Rockefeller, John D. "The Personal Relation in Industry." Founder's Day Address at Cornell University, 11 January 1917.

Roediger, David. Review: *"Work without End: Abandoning Shorter Hours for the Right to Work.* By Benjamin Kline Hunnicutt." *Journal of American History* 76, no. 1 (1989): 290–91.

Rojek, C. "Veblen, Leisure, and Human Need." *Leisure Studies* 14, no. 2 (1995): 73–86.

Ross, Dorothy. *The Origins of American Social Science.* Cambridge: Cambridge University Press, 1992.

Ruggie, John Gerard. "International Responses to Technology: Concepts and Trends." *International Organization* 29, no. 3 (1975): 557–83.

Russell, Bertrand. "In Praise of Idleness." *Harpers*, October 1932, 552–9. http://harpers.org/archive/1932/10/in-praise-of-idleness

Russell, Ellen, and Mathieu Dufour. *Rising Profit Shares, Falling Wage Shares.* Ottawa: Canadian Centre for Policy Alternatives, 2007.

Safarian, A.E. "The Economic Facts in Canada Today." Proceedings of 3rd National Productivity Council Labour–Management Seminar, University of Saskatchewan, 23–24 January 1963. MG 28 I103, vol. 529, file 13.

Sandberg, Sheryl. *Lean In: Women, Work, and the Will to Lead.* New York: A.A. Knopf, 2013.

Sapir, Edward. "Culture, Genuine and Spurious." *American Journal of Sociology* (1924): 401–29.

Savoie, Donald. "ACOA: Transition to Maturity," R14032, vol. 1, file 7. Various Presentations/Papers on ACOA, 1991.

– *Establishing the Atlantic Canada Opportunities Agency.* Ottawa: Government of Canada, 1987.

– *Reviewing Canada's Regional Development Efforts.* Report commissioned for the Government of Newfoundland and Labrador Royal Commission on Renewing and Strengthening Our Place in Canada. St John's: 2003. http://www.gov.nf.ca/publicat/royalcomm/research/Savoie.pdf

Schumann, M. "New Concepts of Production and Productivity." *Economic and Industrial Democracy* 19, no. 1 (1998): 17–32. doi:10.1177/0143831X98191002

Scott, J.C. *Seeing Like a State: How Certain Schemes to Improve the Human Condition Have Failed*. New Haven: Yale University Press, 1998.

Seidman, Michael. *Workers against Work: Labor in Paris and Barcelona during the Popular Fronts*. Berkeley: University of California Press, 1991.

Selgin, George. "The 'Productivity Norm' versus Zero Inflation in the History of Economic Thought." *History of Political Economy* 27, no. 4 (1995): 705–35.

Sharpe, A., J.-F. Arsenault, and P. Harrison. *The Relationship between Labour Productivity and Real Wage Growth in Canada and OECD Countries*. Centre for the Study of Living Standards Research Report No. 2008–8. Ottawa: 2008.

Shore, M.G. *The Science of Social Redemption: McGill, the Chicago School, and the Origins of Social Research in Canada*. Toronto: University of Toronto Press, 1987.

Simpson, Scott. "Innovation Key to Close Canada's Productivity Gap." *Vancouver Sun*, 19 February 2013. http://www.vancouversun.com/business/bc2035/Innovation+close+Canada+productivity/7985818/story.html

Skidelsky, Robert, and Edward Skidelsky. *How Much Is Enough? Money and the Good Life*. New York: Other Press, 2012.

Slichter, S.H. "The Current Labor Policies of American Industries." *Quarterly Journal of Economics* 43, no. 3 (1929): 393–435.

Smith, Adam. *An Inquiry into the Nature and Causes of the Wealth of Nations*. London: Methuen & Co., 1776.

Solow, Robert M. "Thomas Piketty Is Right." *New Republic*, 22 April 2014. https://newrepublic.com/article/117429/capital-twenty-first-century-thomas-piketty-reviewed

Somers, M.R. *Genealogies of Citizenship: Markets, Statelessness, and the Right to Have Rights*. Cambridge: Cambridge University Press, 2008.

– "Narrating and Naturalizing Civil Society and Citizenship Theory: The Place of Political Culture and the Public Sphere." *Sociological Theory* 13, no. 3 (1995): 229–274. doi:10.2307/223298

– "What's Political or Cultural about Political Culture and the Public Sphere? Toward an Historical Sociology of Concept Formation." *Sociological Theory* 13, no. 2 (1995): 113–44. doi:10.2307/202157

Somers, M.R., and F. Block. "From Poverty to Perversity: Ideas, Markets, and Institutions over 200 Years of Welfare Debate." *American Sociological Review* 70, no. 2 (2005): 260–87.

Standing, G. *The Precariat: The New Dangerous Class*. London: Bloomsbury, 2011.

Stanford, J. "Canada's Transformation under Neoliberalism." *Canadian Dimension* 48, no. 2 (2014). https://canadiandimension.com/articles/view/canadas

Starr, R. *Equal as Citizens: The Tumultuous and Troubled History of a Great Canadian Idea*. Halifax: Formac, 2014.

Statistics Canada. Employment by industry and sex, 2014, CANSIM, table
    282–0008. Accessed 18 June 2015 at http://www.statcan.gc.ca/tables-
    tableaux/sum-som/l01/cst01/labor10a-eng.htm
– Gross domestic product at basic prices, by industry, 2014, CANSIM, table
    379–0031. Accessed 18 June 2015 at http://www.statcan.gc.ca/tables-
    tableaux/sum-som/l01/cst01/econ41-eng.htm
– *The Canadian Productivity Review.* 15–206-X, no. 017. Statistics Canada, 2008.
– "Table E175-177: Union membership in Canada, in total and as a percentage
    of non-agricultural paid workers and union members with international
    affiliation, 1911 to 1975 (1983). http://www.statcan.gc.ca/pub/11-516-x/
    sectione/4147438-eng.htm#6
Stein, Janice Gross. *The Cult of Efficiency.* Toronto: House of Anansi, 2002.
Stiglitz, Joseph E., Amartya Sen, and Jean-Paul Fitoussi. Report by the
    Commission on the Measurement of Economic Performance and Social
    Progress. Paris: 2010.
Strangleman, T. "The Nostalgia for Permanence at Work? The End of
    Work and Its Commentators." *Sociological Review* 55, no. 1 (2007): 81–103.
    doi:10.1111/j.1467-954X.2007.00683.x
Sub-Committee of the Interdepartmental Advisory Committee on Labour
    Statistics. *The Measurement and Analysis of Productivity.* Report to the Dominion
    Bureau of Statistics. Ottawa, September 1951. RG 17, vol. 3131, file 66–10.
Sub-Committee on National Income Statistics. *Measurement of National
    Income and the Construction of Social Accounts.* Geneva: League of Nations
    Committee of Statistical Experts, 1947. http://unstats.un.org/unsd/
    nationalaccount/docs/1947NAreport.pdf
Summary of the Government Organization Act, Atlantic Canada. Senator
    Alistair Graham Fonds, LAC, R14032, vol. 1, file 1 (Establishment of ACOA).
Suzuki, David. "Measuring Progress with GDP Is a Gross Mistake." David
    Suzuki Foundation (2014). http://www.davidsuzuki.org/blogs/science-
    matters/2014/02/measuring-progress-with-gdp-is-a-gross-mistake
Swift, Richard. *SOS: Alternatives to Capitalism.* Toronto: Between the Lines,
    2014.
Tang, J., and C. MacLeod. "Labour Force Ageing and Productivity
    Performance in Canada." *Canadian Journal of Economics / Revue canadienne
    d'Economique* 39, no. 2 (2006): 582–603. doi:10.2307/3696170
Taussig, F.W. "Labor Costs in the United States Compared with Costs
    Elsewhere." *Quarterly Journal of Economics* 39, no. 1 (1924): 96–114. doi:
    10.2307/1883955
Taylor, Frederick Winslow. *The Principles of Scientific Management.* New York:
    W.W. Norton, [1911]1967.

Thiessen, G. "Canada's Economic Future: What Have We Learned from the 1990s?" Remarks to the Canadian Club of Toronto, 2001. http://www.bankofcanada.ca/2001/01/canada-economic-future-what-have-we-learned

Thornton, P. "The Problem of Out-Migration from Atlantic Canada, 1871–1921: A New Look." *Acadiensis* 15, no. 1 (1985): 4–34.

Tily, G. "John Maynard Keynes and the Development of National Accounts in Britain, 1895–1941." *Review of Income and Wealth* 55, no. 2 (2009): 331–59. doi:10.1111/j.1471-8847.2009.00322.x

Toronto Daily Star. "Forgive, Forget: Council Wants Jodoin Back." 5 December 1962.

– "It's a Local Effort." 7 November 1960.

Troude-Chastenet, Patrick. "La décroissance selon Jacques Ellul et Alain Charbonneau." Cooperative de la Nouvelle Education Populaire (La CEN), 2006. http://archives.la-cen.org/spip.php?article197

Tucker, Robert C. *The Marx–Engels Reader*. New York: W.W. Norton, 1978.

USAID (US Agency for International Development). "Inspiring Success, Part 1: Rediscovering The Marshall Plan Productivity Program." Video, 2010. https://www.youtube.com/watch?v=yWB8U1Mpgqw&feature=youtube_gdata_player

Van Ark, Bart, and Charles Hulten. "Innovation, Intangibles, and Economic Growth: Towards a Comprehensive Accounting of the Knowledge Economy." *Yearbook on Productivity 2007* (2007), 127–46.

Van Trier, Walter. "Everyone a King: An Investigation into the Meaning and Significance of the Debate on Basic Incomes with Special Reference to Three Episodes from the British Inter-War Experience." PhD diss., Katholieke Universiteit Leuven, 1995.

Veal, A.J. "The Elusive Leisure Society, 4th Edition." School of Leisure, Sport and Tourism Working Paper No. 9. Sydney: University of Technology, 2009. http://datasearch.uts.edu.au/business/publications/lst/index.cfm and www.leisuresource.net

Veblen, Thorstein. *The Theory of the Leisure Class: An Economic Study of Institutions*. New York: Dover Thrift Editions, 1994.

Victor, Peter. *Managing without Growth: Slower by Design, Not Disaster*. Northampton: Edward Elgar Press, 2008.

Walker, F.A. "Dr. Boehm-Bawerk's Theory of Interest." *Quarterly Journal of Economics* 6, no. 4 (1892): 399–416. doi: 10.2307/1882511

Walling, W. *American Labor and American Democracy*. Piscataway: Transaction Publishers, 1926.

Walters, W. *Governmentality: Critical Encounters*. New York: Routledge, 2012.

Ward, L.F. "Contemporary Sociology." *American Journal of Sociology* 7, no. 4 (1902): 475–500.

Weber, M. *The Protestant Ethic and the Spirit of Capitalism*. London: Routledge and Sons, 1920.

Weeks, Kathi. "'Hours for What We Will': Work, Family, and the Movement for Shorter Hours." *Feminist Studies* 35 (2009): 101–27.

– *The Problem with Work*. Durham: Duke University Press, 2011.

West, E.C. "Canada–United States Price and Productivity Differences in Manufacturing Industries, 1963." Ottawa: Economic Council of Canada, 1971.

Williams, C. "The Happy Marriage of Capitalism and Feminism." *Contemporary Sociology: A Journal of Reviews* 43, no. 1 (January 2014): 58–61.

Winch, D. "Marginalism and the Boundaries of Economic Science." *History of Political Economy* 4, no. 2 (1972): 325–43. doi:10.1215/00182702-4-2-325

Worton, D.A. *Dominion Bureau of Statistics: A History of Canada's Central Statistical Office and Its Antecedents, 1841–1972*. Montreal and Kingston: McGill–Queen's University Press, 1998.

– "The Service Industries in Canada, 1946–66." In *Production and Productivity in the Service Industries*, edited by Victor Fuchs, 237–86. Washington, DC: NBER, 1969.

Index